Steamboat Treasures

The Inadvertent Autobiography of a Steamboatman

BY

DOROTHY HECKMANN SHRADER

Introduction by
JOHN HARTFORD

Cover art by
GARY R. LUCY

Published by
THE WEIN PRESS
HERMANN, MISSOURI

© 1997 by Dorothy Heckmann Shrader

All rights reserved
including the right of reproduction
in whole or in part in any form

FIRST EDITION, 1997

Published by
THE WEIN PRESS
514 Wein Street
Hermann, Missouri 65041

Telephone 573-486-5522

Manufactured in the United States of America

Library of Congress Catalog Card Number: 93-061111

ISBN 0-9638589-2-0
ISBN 00-9638589-3-9 pbk.

ACKNOWLEDGMENTS

Without the cooperation of a vast number of people, this book would have been impossible. This collection of short stories has been compiled with the intention to make a flowing historical narrative, using the life of William L. Heckmann, "Steamboat Bill," as the glue to hold the stories in an even flow. These stories tell the tale of the passing of steamboats on the Missouri and the struggle it took to keep them running as long as they did. It tells of the lure of the river, its hold on the men who followed the river as a career.

This story collection, peripherally, also tells the story of a river family, a father and seven sons, who devoted their lives to the boats. All eight were licensed as pilots or engineers—one held both licenses. This book records the second generation of this family—the first was well-documented in *Steamboat Legacy*.

The first credit should go to my parents, Ed and Alice Heckmann, who for nine years took me along on a steamboat every summer and gave me a taste of life on the river and a ringside-seat view of the impossible struggle to keep a steamboat going against insurmountable odds.

My uncle, my father's oldest brother, "Steamboat Bill," combined his love of work on the river with a remarkable determination to write about it. He recorded a wonderful bit of history, particularly Missouri River history, and left a full picture of the life and times of the smaller steamers on this river. It was never his intention to write an autobiography, but write one he did. In his stories he brings in the personal narrative to such an extent that he did succeed in recording almost all of the important events in his life. My deepest gratitude to him for these stories and to Nelson Spencer, publisher of the weekly *Waterways Journal* for giving permission to use any material from that publication; to Richard F. McGonegal, editor of the *Jefferson City News Tribune* for reprint permission for stories published both by and about Steamboat Bill. Also to the *Hermanner Volksblatt* and the *Advertiser Courier* for news stories and corroboration of the facts as they occurred. Steamboat Bill wrote more than 2,000 stories, the major portion for *The Waterways Journal*, but a considerable quantity for the Hermann and Jefferson City papers, as well. These papers also often wrote about him.

MY APPRECIATION ... To James Swift of *The Waterways Journal* for his assistance, and to *The Waterways Journal* for granting me reprint privileges. To Ralph Dupae, in collaboration with the Murphy Library at LaCrosse, Wisconsin, for help with both photos and written material.

MY APPRECIATION ... To the Mercantile Library Inland River's Library and Mark Cedeck, Transportation Curator, for use of some of *The Waterways Journal* files; to the Missouri State Historical Society archives and the Western Manuscript Division for research assistance and for photocopies of the printed stories in their files and for access to Steamboat Bill's scrapbooks. To the countless people who sent me material and photos, including Louis Reitz, George Kishmar, Mary Ann Fitchett and Mark Baecker.

IN APPRECIATION... To the family of Capt. Frederick Way Jr. for permission to quote from his stories and for use of his picture.

MY APPRECIATION ... To Gary R. Lucy, Missouri river artist, for use of his painting, "The DeSmet Overnight at the Hermann Landing, 1873," on the cover of this book.

MY APPRECIATION ... To John Hartford for his introduction, encouragement and excellent advice. To Sandy Watts, editor extraordinaire, and to Lucinda Huskey for clerical assistance.

MY APPRECIATION ... To Nan Sellenschutter, Sallie Hancox, James Goodrich and John Hartford for critical first readings.

MY APPRECIATION ... To my husband Bill for extreme endurance, love and support.

TO ALL OTHERS too numerous to mention, my eternal gratitude.
I thank you all.

To Captain William L. Heckmann Jr.
"Steamboat Bill"
1869-1957

INTRODUCTION

Mystery

BY JOHN HARTFORD

I say look my love, back in the trees,
Little shanty boat tied up in a slough.
Ripple of breeze on the river face,
Makes us feel like an Indian canoe.
Out here the water's deep and swift,
We're paddlin' in the flow.
Headin' down out of the mystery above,
Headin' down into the mystery below.

When the sun burns the fog, the hills come out,
Like a slowly developing photograph.
That streak in the water could be a buoy,
Or the ghost of a lumber raft.
The windows jiggle on the Texas deck,
Past tree limbs hangin' low.
Headin' down out of the mystery above,
Headin' down into the mystery below.

I've tried to understand why I love the river,
I've tried to understand why I love to sing.
Seems like if I could understand the river,
Maybe I could understand most anything.
I wonder why the time goes by so fast,

When the trip is slow.
Headin' down way out of the mystery above,
Headin' down into the mystery below.

Lookin' down into the bosom of the deep,
Endless names, faces, and the souls of men,
Who worked on the river for an ancient dream,
That the steamboat's comin' back again.
My love sits smilin', I know she likes to go,
Headin' down way out of the mystery above,
Headin' down into the mystery below.

A couple of logs and an orange peel,
Empty milk jug floatin' past.
The hills and the sky repeat themselves,
In a six o'clock river of glass.
My love she lets her hands fall down,
She's about to let me flow.
Headin' down way out of the mystery above,
Headin' down into the mystery below.

CAPT. JOHN HARTFORD wears many hats—singer, entertainer, writer and, last but not least, pilot. Best known for his hit song, "Gentle on My Mind," Hartford is beloved among river buffs the world over for his songs about life on the river. Less well known is his skill as a pilot. In "Mystery," he captures the feel of the river and how it ensnares men. He knows whereof he speaks.

PREFACE

Mark Twain left a written record of some aspects of the early life of steamboating on the Mississippi River. A generation later, another steamboat writer surfaced, this time on the Missouri River. In time, Capt. J. S. Hacker would dub him "the Mark Twain of the Missouri." My uncle, Capt. William L. Heckmann, known to one and all as Steamboat Bill, was that writer.

The book *Steamboat Legacy* was about my grandparent's generation. It told the story of a Missouri River steamboat family. This sequel—the second book of a steamboat trilogy—is the story of my parent's generation, as told through the writings of Steamboat Bill.

Lack of education did not deter William Heckmann one iota from recording more that 2,000 stories about the river and his life—truly an inadvertent autobiography of a steamboatman. He wrote regularly for *The Waterways Journal*, a weekly publication for the river industry, and for many newspapers. He was widely quoted throughout the Midwest, especially in Missouri. He was a prodigious writer throughout his 65-year career on the river.

Steamboat Bill went to school at Bluffton, a simple country school with a four-month term until he was 10. Then for two years he attended school at Hermann. After that he was on a steamboat, learning the river. Sometimes his thoughts were a bit scrambled, and sometimes his syntax was garbled. But his writing is a rare record of a period of history no one else thought to record. Hansen, Chapell and Chittenden wrote about the upper Missouri and the mountain boats, but Steamboat Bill wrote the only firsthand accounts we have of steamboating on the lower Missouri.

The Mississippi River had been a pathway of civilization, a road leading into a continent's heartland. The Missouri River was the pioneers' road to the West, to wealth and adventure, to furs and gold and the mountains. In his introduction to Steamboat Bill's book, "Steamboating Sixty-five Years on Missouri Rivers," Dan Saults explained that, statistically, the upper Mississippi should be considered a tributary of the Missouri. The Missouri drains 530,000 square miles, while the Mississippi to its juncture with the Missouri drains only 171,000 square miles.

If the Mississippi had been designated the tributary river, the Missouri would be the longest river in the world. It twists and tumbles down from the continental divide to the Gulf of Mexico, there disgorging waters gathered from half the area of these United States, along with 550 million tons of silt, sand and soil annually. The Missouri falls from an elevation of more than a mile, while the Mississippi falls only 1,200 feet from its source.

The Missouri River, which begins at the junction of three small mountain streams high up on the Montana Rockies, drains all or part of 10 states and flows through seven. It forms the northwest boundary of the commonwealth that bears its name, before cutting its way across the center of the state to join the Mississippi just below St. Charles, Missouri, the oldest permanent white settlement on the river.

Erratic and still untamed, the Missouri surprises men and inspires them to conquer. One of Steamboat Bill's better known quotes has been bouncing around for years: "They separated the men from the boys at the mouth of the Missouri river. The boys went up the Mississippi, and the men went up the Missouri." The Heckmanns, father and seven sons, went up the Missouri. Except for brief forays into other waters, they steamboated between Jefferson City and St. Louis.

In 1934 Steamboat Bill piloted the M.V. Patrick Gass on a famous trip to Fort Peck, Montana. Unfortunately, he had to return to his job before the long trip ended, so he never really made it to "the mountains." He wrote, "It may be that I will have a title to scrap when back from this trip. One man has already addressed me as Diesel Boat Bill; and one lady called me Christopher Columbus. Whether this meant we were explorers or that I was old-fashioned enough to believe there is no economy over straight, high-pressure engines up to 600 hp, we will leave for our marine engineers and time to figure out. To me this has never been proven."

The Heckmanns were all steam men, but eventually even they had to convert to running diesel boats—the age of steam was passing. But in earlier times, steamboats had been seen as the answer to the challenge of the wild Missouri. When the steamer Zebulon M. Pike came into St. Louis from New Orleans in 1817, the wonder of travel by water began. Two years later, the steamer Independence went up the Missouri as far as Franklin, and the race to the mountains was on.

The real heyday of steamboating on the Missouri was the decade before the Civil War. The Heckmann family took to the river at the end of the crest, when river traffic was on a downhill slide. Nevertheless, the river provided lifetime work for most of them and the backbone of a flourishing industry for the little community of Hermann. The written records left by the Heckmann family are an invaluable historic legacy. They tell us how a pilot came to be a pilot, pay tribute to the rousters who packed freight on and off the steamers on their backs, and preserve the stories that were told along and on the river.

Note: The original spelling of the Heckmann family name—with a final double "n"—is used throughout this book. In later life, Steamboat Bill changed the spelling of his name to Heckman. To present a proliferation of quotation marks, the writer's words are in italic and Steamboat Bill's are in plain type. The one exception is the chapter on the U.S. Army Corps of Engineers.

TABLE OF CONTENTS

1. Wee Willie's Bluffton Boyhood 1
2. The Parting 29
   Farewell to Childhood
3. Cub Pilot 36
4. Return to Childhood Haunts 61
5. Romance 66
6. The Contest 83
7. Whoppers 106
   Spontaneous Combustion
8. U.S. Army Corps of Engineers 126
   The Story He Forget to Tell
9. Missouri River Pilot 135
10. Adventures in Piloting 162
    Old Pilots Never Quit, They Just Go Fishing
11. Eulogies 200
    Appendix 222
    Mile by Mile on the Missouri River

CHAPTER 1

Wee Willie's Bluffton Boyhood

Come back again, Oh time in thy flight,
And make me a boy again, just for tonight.

William L. Heckmann Sr. and his wife, Mary Miller Heckmann, courted in Bluffton, Missouri, where the Miller family lived, then moved to Hermann after their marriage in 1868. There is no record of exactly when the family returned to Bluffton, but it is known that the steamer Clara sank in 1870 and that William bought the wreck for $50. A carpenter by trade, he towed the remains to Bluffton and built a two-story home for his growing family. It is safe to assume the house was completed sometime in 1871. When the MK&T Railroad came through, the house was moved 300 yards to the east, where it stands today.

By that time the couple's first-born son, William L. Heckmann Jr., had arrived on the scene, as well as a second son, Samuel, known to the family as Greeley. Young Will always said the Bluffton house with its fancy gingerbread in the dining room and bells hooked up to call the children to dinner gave the Heckmann boys an early start in steamboating.

During the last years of his life, Steamboat Bill wrote several detailed manuscripts, never published, filled with happy memories of an idyllic boyhood along the banks of the Missouri River. It is through these accounts that the Miller family—Steamboat Bill's grandparents and aunts and uncles—becomes a very real part of the life of that little settlement.

Out near Lebanon, Pennsylvania, a family by the name of Miller decided to move to Missouri. The father, Samuel Miller, was already a famous horticulturist, and he had been recruited by George Hussmann

Martha Isabella Miller   *Judge Samuel Miller*

to come and supervise the grape vineyards for the new Bluffton Winery. Before leaving Pennsylvania, Grandpa Miller had propagated the famous white grape and named it Martha, in honor of his wife, Martha Isabella Evans.

In the spring of 1867, the Miller family journeyed to Pittsburgh by railroad and loaded their belongings on the Steamer Ezra Porter. The three girls and four boys evidently enjoyed the trip, and Mary, the oldest, recorded the trip in her diary. At Cincinnati, Ohio, they transferred again to the railroad and then in St. Louis, Missouri, again loaded all of their household belongings on the steamer Post Boy. From St. Louis, in less than two days, they were on the banks of the Missouri at what was soon to be the town of Bluffton.

What these good people saw among the hills and mountains was hard to tell, but things began to pop among the spring flowers and desperadoes around these diggings. First they built a large two-story log house, a double house with a big open recess between. While this old house lasted, in summer times in the recess, and winter in the west parlor, one could safely say that more hospitality was shown here then in any other home in this part of Missouri.

•

Dad Miller was a staunch Republican and did not hesitate in saying so. His four big sons were full of devilment that always bordered on honest entertainment. His three girls were beautiful and smart. Martha Miller, their mother, was a large, dark Welsh woman who backed up and praised everything these characters undertook. Two more girls were to be born in Bluffton, Alice and Gertrude.

•

The local doctor, a Dr. Campbell, was a staunch Democrat. On a trip to see the Millers, Dr. Campbell got into a political argument with the two younger sisters, Alice and Gertrude. On the way back home, he said to their brother George that there was no sense arguing with "them two brats; they know more than I ever will, if I live to be 100 years old." At the time Alice was 11 and Gertrude was 9.

•

The Miller and Heckmann children attended the crude one-room Bluffton school for four months of the year, from September to January. Eight years was the end of school for the Millers. After moving to Hermann, the Heckmann children went to a nine-month school. Will Heckmann Sr. did not believe in higher education, so none of his children was encouraged to go to school beyond eighth grade. One son who chose not to follow the river as a career did graduate from high school, as did the youngest daughter.

Before going further with our story, let's say something about the children of this wonderful couple. David Miller was the oldest boy, a giant of a man, 6'4" in his stocking feet. He fell in love with a native girl and went off to make a fortune so he could come back to the flower bedecked and mossy banks of Lora Dora Creek to live with his people. He contracted typhoid and died of "brain fever" at Lexington, Missouri, and lies buried in the hilltop cemetery at Bluffton.

Bob Miller, the next oldest son, was a noted character who will be mentioned time and time again in these pages. He married Justina Heckmann, my half-sister, and spent most of his life on top of a small mountain, Montgomery Hill, and there he raised 10 children. (Not many doctor bills to pay, a few country midwives, a Bible and my sister's prayers seemed sufficient.)

Many have wondered how this couple, with only the income from an occasional stint with the Barnum and Bailey Circus and a few hitches as a steamboat roustabout, ever produced enough income to raise a family of 10 on the bare top of Montgomery Hill. Uncle Bob always had a Country Band and entertained the natives with his own unique form of music and original compositions, but income from this source would only have been minimal.

Roy, the most noted son of the Bob Miller family, is perhaps the most successful pilot on the Illinois and lower Mississippi Rivers today.

Of the Sam Miller sons, John was a homemade philosopher; Sam was a writer of humorous stories and prose. George (always called Pete for some reason) was a noted river character and, in childhood, my almost constant companion. Pete was three years older than I was and capable of thinking up most of our projects.

Grandpop Miller cleared and planted hills and dales with every kind of fruit and berry and anything that bordered on horticulture. He named each section, such as Montgomery Hill, Hussmann's Hill and Miller's Home Grounds and spent a small fortune to show his judgment was right.

•

When the Millers came to Bluffton things were moving along smoothly. Steamboats were numerous and on time—one could ship, almost daily, east or west. Harvests were plentiful, grape cuttings were selling well, and the Miller family was prosperous and happy. But a change was coming.

The Bluffton Wine Company had lured Sam Miller to the area, and for a while things looked wonderful. The hills west of Bluffton were cleared and planted in vineyards. The company spent $150,000 and made a lot of fine wine. Then came a Depression in the early '70s, just when railroads were slowly running the steamboats off the river. Even the Missouri River was changing—Bluffton no longer had a steamboat landing. Since the Katy Railroad had not yet arrived on the north shore of the Missouri River, the Wine Company could not ship its wine and it failed.

Sam Miller was to have other disappointments in his life. Not one of his big sons would take to horticulture. His grapes and all kinds of fruit fell to the ground and wasted away, and it began to look like the Garden after Eve had tasted the forbidden fruit. Local sales were almost nonexistent. However, a Mr. Metzler had a distillery near Rhineland, Missouri, and often his wagons would come to Bluffton to buy peaches, pears and apples at 8 to 10 cents a bushel.

While Grandpop Miller lived at Bluffton he brought out and perfected the Captain Jack strawberry, the largest berry of its kind ever put on the market in America. Fourteen of these strawberries would fill a quart jar; some were so large that they had to be cut in two before they would go through the mouth of the jar. He also brought out a very

CHAPTER 1 ≈ WEE WILLIE'S BLUFFTON BOYHOOD

Built from the wreck of the Steamer Clara, Steamboat Bill's boyhood home still stands today at Bluffton.

large, tame, seedless persimmon, and he had one big pippen apple tree that he practiced grafting other fruit on. At one time, he had seven different kinds of fruit growing on the same tree. He also had about a dozen monster-big pippen apple trees in sight of his house that bore the finest big yellow apples, as large as a baby's head and sweeter than the lips of the local beauty.

Out in front of the Miller Mansion, to the banks of the Missouri River, laid a strip of fertile bottom land, about 300 feet wide. Here one year Grandpop Miller planted his melon patch. He raised hundreds of large melons, but one big yellow-striped dude outgrew anything in the patch, and finally it became one of the "Big Sights" on the Miller plantation.

One day when this monster melon was over-ripe, two big, hard-looking characters, landed at the mouth of Lora Dora Creek in a houseboat. They came up to the Miller home with two empty buckets for fresh water and induced Grandma Miller to cook them a big meal, which they were glad to have and did pay for. While Mother Miller was preparing their meal, they filled their buckets and went down to their shantyboat saying, "Mrs. Miller, we will be back by the time you have dinner ready." She called back, "All right, be here in half an hour."

As they passed down through the melon patch, they saw the big melon, at that time the proudest possession the great horticulturist ever raised. They could have had a dozen big melons gratis, by just asking for them, but this big fellow was too much of a temptation. One of the men took the two buckets of water, and the other plucked the big melon from the vine. It was a fair-sized load even for a big man.

They did not see little Willie Heckmann sitting on a big chair behind a bunch of lilacs. As soon as they were out of sight, the young detective reported to "Colonel" Uncle Pete, and he in turn summoned two of his big brothers, John and Sam. We held a council of war.

Grandpop was taking his afternoon nap. The older men ordered that he should not be molested and that they would tend to this theft. They ordered young Bill to go up to the house, where he was always a pet and a favorite, to borrow Grandma's monster-big butcher knife. This accomplished, we waited until these men went up to the house for their dinner.

Then Uncle John left our hideout, some 300 yards up Lora Creek, and he came back with the big melon from the shantyboat. They cut it in half, cut out the heart. One of the Miller cows, Old Star, was hanging around like she wanted to take part in this jubilee, and about this time when they were debating further proceedings, she unloaded a monster paddy of fresh cow fertilizer on a bunch of daisies that were enjoying the midday sunshine. Uncle Sam said to his brother Pete, "Run over to the barn and get a shovel. Be quick about it."

They carefully emptied this fresh bunch of cow paddy into the open halves of the big melon, and Uncle John was ordered to take it back to its place on the shantyboat. When he came back, he had a small, single barrel shotgun. He said, "I traded the melon for this gun. You two kids can have it."

This is how Uncle Pete and Willie, the detective, received their first gun, which they promptly named Shanty Boat Bess. More will be heard of this firearm as this story runs its course. It was not long until the thieves went to their shantyboat and started off down the Mighty Missouri. We did not have time to eat our melon, and when this boat was about one-fourth mile down the Bluffton Chute, they quit pulling near a flock of ducks. Sam said, "I wonder what they are going to do now?"

Uncle John's ready reply was, "Oh, well, I guess they are going to shoot them ducks or cut their melon!"

We went back to our hideout, and when we had stuffed ourselves with watermelon until our bellies were as tight as a tuned drum, we still had a large piece left. Pete said, "This we will take up to Ma and Pa, as a compromise gift, for things are going to pop wide open when Dad finds out he has lost his prized melon."

Sure enough, just as soon as we got back home and told Grandma about our enterprise, Grandpop Miller woke up. When we told him the shantyboat men had stolen his melon, he let all holds go and became a wild man. He cried, "Where's my gun and horse? I'm going to head those fellows off and shoot the daylights out of them!"

Grandma Miller was a quiet, unassuming woman, but when she put her foot down, it stayed put, and no one knew this better than her violent husband. She said, "You are not going to kill anyone on account of an overripe melon. When you hear the whole story, you will agree to call the case closed."

When told what had happened, his enjoyment was as happy as his tantrum of a few moments before. The case was now closed, but another trial was on the docket, and that was whether to let two boys, one an 8-year-old and the other 11, have a gun.

Now almost all the family members were present, and they voted on this proposition. All voted in favor of the boys except Grandma, but she said the majority wins. "But," she said, "mark my words, that little blunderbuss is going to bring trouble to this house. Them boys are not old enough to handle a gun, and you only have my consent if that grinning little detective Willie promises to back up every shot that comes out of that blunderbuss."

•

The big Wright Store in Bluffton burned to the ground, and in the excitement of saving some of the stock, someone spilt the cash drawer into the flames and some $300 in paper money and a lot of coins, like a few gold pieces, some silver, nickels and pennies, were scattered in the ruins. Some weeks after the excitement had died down, Uncle Pete and I started to explore the ruins. Before they found out what we were doing, our treasure box contained quite a bit of loot.

In Bluffton there was not much for two energetic boys to do, and this was our first chance for profit and excitement. Before we gave up, we had dug up half the north shore of the Missouri River. If we had dug as much on the beach at Nome, Alaska, where they made the gold strike, then the Miller and Heckmann clans would all be millionaires.

•

One evening along about the shank of the day, just below the mouth of Lora Dora Creek, the river bank had commenced to cave in, and another discovery was coming to the Bluffton Biographical Co. A coffin was sticking out of the river bank. We could not reach it from the bank, but we soon had our skiff Mary under same, and we found the skeleton of a very large man. Beside him in the coffin we found a tomahawk, some arrows, a clay pipe and some coins.

About that time the bank caved in just below us and another coffin came into sight. Uncle Pete said, "It is getting dark. Let's go home and come back here at daylight." We stored our treasurers in our big strongbox that we hid in the big cave in the bluff behind our house. The next morning, at the break of day, we were present, but the bank had caved in about 20 feet during the night, and both of our coffins had been gobbled up by the Mighty Missouri.

Our next adventure was to build two dozen rabbit traps. We set them on Miller's Island one evening and the next morning we had 23 rabbits. We took them over to Morrison and sold them for 5 cents apiece. More spondulics for our treasure chest.

A blizzard came along the next morning, and the river was full of ice so that we could not go to our traps. We went into our hideout in the cellar. While one of us stood as a "gigger," the other balanced our books, and we were satisfied. Uncle Pete said that if this weather kept up, the river would block with ice and then we could take care of them rabbits, and we did just that. We soon had them pretty well cleaned out. A financial depression came along, and we were despondent.

•

One day Uncle Pete and I were sitting on our favorite woodpile contemplating the story of the nymph they call Lora Dora Lee. Some say she was a ghost, some say she was beautiful—and about that time our dog Towns (named for a noted Osage River pilot) let out a big yelp up on Grave Yard Hill. We jumped up, boredom forgotten.

Uncle Pete said, "Go run and get old Shantyboat Bess, and meet me at the crossing up on Lora Dora Creek." That bellow sounded like he had jumped a deer, which he had, a monster buck. He ran right past us as the senior member of the firm fired point blank at him. This did not seem to bother the buck, and he ran down to the river and swam across to what was then known as Lora Dora Towhead.

Uncle Pete cried, "That was that damned Lost Creek Buck. He has a charmed life, they say, but I'll get him yet if only I had a larger gun."

About that time the deer in Montgomery and Warrenton counties were just about extinct, but the old Lost Creek buck hung around for

CHAPTER 1 ≈ WEE WILLIE'S BLUFFTON BOYHOOD

some 10 years in what was once perhaps the greatest deer, turkey and bear country in the state of Missouri. Many shots had been fired at this old rascal, but the best shots in Missouri tried and failed. He finally ended his days trying to swim the river in the ice in front of his famous Lost Creek, the stream that bore his name.

Like the Lost Creek Buck, there was one old turkey gobbler that had strutted his stuff back of Bluffton, some eight years after all the wild turkeys had been killed in that neck of the woods. This old gobbler seemed to bear a charmed life and had outwitted all the hunters. On our first hunting trip Uncle Pete and myself climbed Montgomery Hill but did not see any game. We had started back home, and coming around the corner of a barn, there we saw the old gobbler sitting on a lower branch of a big black walnut tree, seemingly fast asleep.

I whispered in Uncle Pete's ear, "Shoot, you dummy, shoot!" Up came old Betts, he popped away, and down came the old gobbler on the ground as dead as a doornail. Two prouder boys never came down Montgomery Hill. This old beauty weighed 38 pounds, and we took turns in carrying him down the hill.

At one place, in a short turn of the road, Wee Willie was ahead carrying the gun, when he ran into a big black and white polecat sitting in the middle of the road on his hind haunches. He seemed to say, "So far and no farther." Not having time to consult Uncle Pete, his partner up and blazed away, killing Mr. Skunk deader than heck.

Uncle Pete said, "You should not have done that. If you had missed or crippled that thing, we would smell for a month, and besides we would have ruined the turkey. The next time you are carrying that gun, you wait for me to tell you when to pull the trigger. They have put a penalty on me, and you are no better than me. Now that is final and don't forget it."

By the time young Will was 9, his father was running steamboats and was seldom home during the season. When he did come home for the winter, his son rejoiced.

Now we had a real buddy for what was left of that winter. Dad brought with him from the steamer Colossal a fine double-barrel gun, a fancy Bantam rooster and two hens, presents from the gang. He also had one dozen big cowbells, which were to be a secret until the river opened in the spring.

•

That winter my father brought home a red clipper sled for a Christmas present. My enjoyment with that speedy contraption was short. A big snow was followed by a rain that promptly froze, coating everything with ice. I sneaked out of the house, just at the break of day, with my Christmas sled. By walking and crawling, I finally made it to the top of a very steep hill in one of my grandfather's peach orchards. Not having any previous experiences with such a flying monster and without any gloves, I got aboard and started the downhill run.

In just a second I had knocked considerable bark off one of Grandfather's peach trees, but there was no stopping then. Another tree damaged the port runner. I then headed for a third tree that was sloping down toward the river, and I climbed that tree to its first branches. The sled came to a halt and fell on one side while I tumbled off the other. Undaunted, I pointed the sled downhill again. This time it never stopped until it went right into the Missouri River. Fortunately, I was not aboard at the moment. I was wrapped around a big tree on shore.

No one ever saw a more battered-up boy; the blood running out of my nose and mouth; my ears, hands and feet frozen. Finding no broken bones, I crawled home. Upon seeing me, my mother cried, "Where in the world have you been this early in the morning?"

"Oh, sledriding," I replied.

"Where is your sled?"

"It went down in the river."

After dressing my wounds, my mother put me to bed. When my father got up and heard the story, he came in to see me. "You should have had more sense than to try to sledride on a hillside full of trees. But maybe it was for the best. That contraption was too fast for you. I will build you a substantial homemade sled and will go out with you next time so you can see how it is done."

•

Old Shantyboat Bess was left at home pretty much while Dad was at home. Uncle Pete, myself and our old hound dog Towns did the driving for Dad, and carried most of the game. When we thought of this in our later days an old poem came to mind: *Come back again, Oh time in thy flight, And make me a boy again, just for tonight.*

CHAPTER 1 ≈ WEE WILLIE'S BLUFFTON BOYHOOD

If we were to tell what we killed in three months, no one would believe us, but we sure brought home the bacon. The Heckmann and Miller clans ate well.

•

At last the days lengthened out, the sun shone more brightly, and in the latter days of February, we had a big breakup in the Missouri. We had no floating property but our skiff, Mary. In early March, one bright sunshiney morning, Dad says, "Now boys, I am going to show you what we are going to do with those cow bells."

Our skiff Mary was in fine shape. We had caulked, finished and paid off our bills and launched same. It did not leak a drop and was as dry as an Indian's Powder horn. We got the oars, a minnow seine, a hand ax, and the fishing expedition was off to a good start. Uncle Pete pulled the stroke oars and was seconded by Wee Willie Heckmann. This is one of the reasons these two boys were destined to become two of the best oarsmen on the Missouri.

We went over on the head of a big sandbar and seined out about 50 Missouri River minnows, known as shiners, the best bait in the world, and went down to a towhead that laid out in front of Lora Dora Creek. We went in Lora and cut five big willow poles and one extra large one. We started on the head of the Towhead, and about 100 feet apart we put out five trot lines with three to five hooks on each line. On the end of each pole, we tied a cow bell.

This done, Dad said, "Now we will set big Mamma. I have a friend who claims you only need one big hook if you place it in the right place to catch a big fish in the Missouri River. This looks like the place to me."

He pushed the big pole way into the gumbo bank and put three extra-big hooks on the line. He secured three big shiners he had been saving, and we laid out the line. On the way back home we killed two big Canadian honkers. We never left home without the big shotgun.

"Boys," Dad said, "do not be disappointed with the big line, but if you keep it baited some day you will catch a Hell's Rauncher."

The next morning, just at the break of day, Uncle Pete came running up to our house, knocked on the door and said, "Get up quick, the bells of Lora Dora are ringing like the chimes of Normandy. Hurry up or some of my big brothers might steal our skiff and fish."

Willie's reply was, "They will not take our skiff while Dad is at home." All the bells were ringing on the first five lines, but Big Mamma was silent. We took six big catfish off those lines and never even raised Big Mamma.

The steamer Spangler was laying in port loading railroad ties, and we sold the fish to Captain George Keith for five bucks, and we were glad to get it. This same amount of fish would bring on the market at Hermann, the sum of $80 today. When Dad made us a present, we had some more money for our strongbox.

•

One day, Uncle Pete took Old Shantyboat Bess and went out back of town by himself. He ran across one of the hardest characters we had around Bluffton, and this man's dog followed him until the owner was out of sight. Pete, for sheer devilment, shot the dog and left him lay in the road. A native nearby saw this killing and reported same to the young desperado.

The next Sunday after this episode, the Millers had a house full of company, most of them sitting and talking in the recess of their old house. The young man whose dog Pete had shot. who was at that time not over 15 years old, rode up in front of the Miller house with all the latest fine trappings on his horse. He tied his horse to the hitching post, walked through the crowd, went back in the yard where Pete Miller had his dog tied, and shot him in the head. He calmly walked back to his horse and galloped away. He never said a word in this transaction and when out of sight one of the big Miller boys said, "If I had my pistol, I would have shot that son-of-a-buck."

Grandmother Miller said, "I told you from the start that little blunderbuss would get us into trouble. From now on none of you have anything to do with these terrible men, and the gun will be taken away from these two young squirts until they get old enough to have some sense."

That ultimatum was the worst heartbreak that ever happened to Pete & Co. We were sure down in the mouth. The next day, sitting on our favorite tie pile watching the driftwood pass by, Uncle Pete got another one of his moody spells.

"We are sure in a hell of a fix with our gun in hiding. What are we going to do without some kind of a shooting iron? It was all right when

CHAPTER 1 ≈ WEE WILLIE'S BLUFFTON BOYHOOD

we killed that big turkey gobbler and they had a big feast for their fancy friends down around Rhineland. It was hunky-dory when we brought in the rabbits. But when I kill a lousy old dog, all hell breaks loose in Bluffton."

After some more contemplation, he finally jumped up and cried, "I know what we'll do. We'll get brother Bob to build us a bow and arrow, even if we have to pay him something, for that money in our strongbox is turning green."

So down to the house we went and entered into a contract with Uncle Bob to build a real bow and arrow. It took only two days until the task was done and a demonstration was in order. We found that bow much too large for us. After trying every which way, even both of us tugging away at the same time, we refused to pay for same. Uncle Bob said,

Bob Miller as a boy

"I'll make you a smaller one, and you need not pay for it until it suits you."

We took the monster bow out to demonstrate to Uncle Bob what the problem was, and he soon found that as strong as he was he could not pull the arrow back. Along about this time a big woodpecker perched himself on a big tree about 30 yards away and commenced to peck away. Uncle Bob laid down on his back, put both feet against the bow, took both hands and drawed back the arrow and let fly. He tore that old woodpecker into fragments, and the wind blew the wreckage all over the county.

"How's that for a shot boys?" he shouted. "I wouldn't take a hundred dollars for that thing. The old Lost Creek Buck is as good as mine."

Uncle Bob wore out a pair of shoes, wore the backs of several coats ragged, shot that old bow some 1,000 times, and to the best of our knowledge never killed another thing. He finally threw the bow into the junk pile in disgust. The smaller bows he made for us were not much better, but in deep snow we did do damage to a number of rabbits.

Uncle Pete and I were seldom punished for our misdeeds and were usually backed to the hilt by Grandmother Miller, but the removal of Shantyboat Bess was the worst possible punishment we could have imagined. The dog shooting episode seemed to hang on forever.

When we were allowed to use our gun, most of our hunting trips were up to what would later be Uncle Bob's place on Montgomery Hill. Why this place is called a hill is unknown to me, for they have never told me what really is a mountain. To me, it seems if you have to go up a steep hill for over a mile you are getting pretty close to being on top of a mountain. Uncle Bob was my Uncle Pete's brother and would soon be my brother-in-law. He later married my half-sister, Justina, Dad's daughter by his first marriage. This made for some interesting attempts to explain the relationship in understandable terms.

On our trip up this mountain with our old hound dog, Towns, we often had seen a monster-big groundhog, but the old bustard always got down in this hole in the bluff before we could get a shot at him. We had just got up on the top of the hill when old Towns barked, "treed."

"That must be old Groundy," yelled Pete. Some folks claim that a groundhog cannot climb a tree, but old Groundy did. When we got in sight of him, he was sitting in the top of a walnut tree about 30 feet from the ground, with a look on him that said, "Come and get me if you dare."

Uncle Pete cried, "That's old Groundy all right, but he looks as big as a bear, and by the gods, he may be one!"

We were soon under the tree, which was standing on a steep slope. By getting on the upper side of the tree, we were not over 20 feet from this old scoundrel. We had only one load left in old Shantyboat Bess, having peppered our ammunition away coming up the hill, shooting at wild geese, crows and everything that came along.

Willie yelled, "Look at that old son-of-a-buck, he has only one eye. Take a good aim at the glimmer and you may blind him, for that No. 8 shot will never penetrate his hide."

Pete blazed away, and when the smoke cleared off, old Groundy was grinning like a jackass in a thistle patch. We both had pretty good throwing arms. So we gathered up a pile of rocks, and the bombard-

CHAPTER 1 ≈ WEE WILLIE'S BLUFFTON BOYHOOD

ment was begun. After bouncing about three dozen rocks off his head and back, the old scoundrel was still grinning and seemed to enjoy our efforts to bring him down off his perch. Pete then said, "I am going over to get brother Bob's gun or some instrument to cut that tree down. This is one time we are going to take that monster home with us."

Uncle Pete was hardly out of sight when old Groundy decided that this was the time to come off his perch. My partner had left me with a big club and our hound dog to guard that tree. The old scoundrel came slowly and carefully down the tree and about four feet from the bottom made a mighty leap and lit on top of our dog. What a battle there was!

As they rolled down the hill, Willie would sock him as hard as he could with his big club. It soon became evident that the smart critter was slowly fighting his way down the hill to his den in the bluff. Just then Uncle Pete came into sight carrying a big ax.

He, being older and stronger, took one mighty swing at old Groundy, and this half-blind and toothless old monarch took his last breath on Montgomery Hill, where he had held forth for so many years. We had a heck of a time to drag our prize to the top of the hill, but from there on it was down grade, and we dragged our meat downhill and into the Miller mansion.

When Grandma Miller saw our prize, she absolutely refused to have anything to do with the oncoming feast. Uncle Bob now appeared on the scene and offered to skin, cook and serve Old Groundy. He skinned him and hung him up in the smokehouse, saying, "I will be down here in the morning and will dish you up a feast you will remember all your life." That was one time he told the truth!

Uncle Pete whispered in my ear, "This is going to be good. It will be even better than when he made the big bow."

Uncle Bob left word to invite some of our friends to the feast. The next morning he was on hand bright and early. He found a big kettle, took it outside and built a fire under it. He boiled the carcass for three hours. He then took it out of the pot, pried its belly apart and filled the inside with apples, onions, carrots, turnips, celery and tomatoes. He tied a wire around the meat so the dressing would not fall out and put it in a large pan in the old Charter Oak cook stove and baked it until noon.

At the stroke of 12:00, he placed it in the middle of the table, saying, "We have nothing but bread and meat, and when you eat groundhog, you do like when you eat fish, and you do not need anything but bread."

Mother Miller said to her big son, "This is your show, Bob, and you will have to carve this critter."

He took the butcher knife that had carved the big watermelon and was as sharp as a razor. With all the power he had in his mighty hands and arms, he could not carve a piece of meat out of this critter. He then went and got a hatchet and borrowed a big iron fork from his mother, and he could not stick the fork in that critter either, even by hammering on the handle with the hatchet. Then, in disgust, he cut the wire that held the dressing inside, pulled the belly open and out fell some of the finest dressing that ever went down your throat.

After we had made a very fair feast, Uncle Bob took the carcass out to the chicken pen and threw it among the chickens. A monster-big game rooster was the boss of the flock. He surveyed old Groundy for a while and then flew on top of him, but he could not puncture the carcass with his sharp bill. He then flew down and again surveyed his chance for meat. He took a big run and hit old Groundy with both his big spurs, but once more he failed to draw meat or blood. The old rooster, who till now never suffered defeat, walked away in disgust.

Then Uncle Bob threw old Groundy into the hog pen with two huge boars. One of the hogs got hold of the front end, and the other grabbed its stern. With superhuman effort they finally pulled the old son-of-a-buck apart. The Miller hogs then had a feast. Uncle Bob, grinning, walked away, saying that a "tame hog likes wild meat, even if it is some of their kinfolks."

Uncle Pete then put in his oar by saying, "Capt. Heckmann wants a chief cook on the R. W. Dugan. Why don't you apply for that berth? You are sure some chef!"

Early one morning in the spring of the last season the Heckmanns were to spend in Bluffton, Dad got word to take out the steamer E. Hensley. Before he left, he picked up his gun and said to Pete and me, "Get your coats on. We are going to pay a visit to the bad men around these diggings." First we went to the hardest family, real devils. There were three men in this family, and the youngest member was the boy who shot Pete's dog.

CHAPTER 1 ≈ WEE WILLIE'S BLUFFTON BOYHOOD

Dad shook hands with the mother and her three boys. He said, "I am going out on the river, and my family will be left alone. This 9-year-old boy is all the protection my wife and the children will have while I am away from home, and we want to be your friends. The Miller family, too, wants to be your friend. They ask you to come out and get your mail like men, buy at their store, and they will trust you and grant you credit."

The young man of the family said, "Pete Miller shot my dog, and I do not know what to do about this."

To this Dad said, "Well, you shot his, and you are even. You two young squirts shake hands, and you'll be even." Dad then told them that anytime they wanted a ride on one of the boats he was on they were welcome, and he would see that it did not cost them a cent. He now asked, "What do you say about this? Shall it be war or peace?"

The oldest boy replied, "You go on out on your boat Captain, and if any of these so-called bad men around here molest your family, send that boy up here, and we will take charge. Your family will live in peace."

We went to three other families, and they all gave us their word of honor that as far as the Millers and Heckmans were concerned they were perfectly safe. This agreement was kept for many long years, and Uncle Pete and Willie Heckmann were never afraid of these bad men.

The Miller family had taken over the local Bluffton store, which housed the post office. Even though he was barely a teenager, Pete took over the rural delivery route, a job he kept faithfully for the rest of his life. The mail had to be brought across the river from Morrison by skiff, then delivered to the store and around the countryside, where roads were scarce.

Uncle Bob Miller and a man by the name of Moody caught a runaway flatboat in the spring ice break-up, and the Miller-Moody Transportation Company was born. Grandpa Miller had cut eight cords of wood up on Hussman Hill. He had men throw this wood over the bluff and carry it across the 200 feet of bottom land and stack it up on the river bank. But the Missouri River changed, and boats had to quit running the Bluffton Chute. Instead, they came up Straub's Bend and back to the bluffs above the town. This left Grandpop's wood in a place where it could not be sold

Uncle Bob kept after his father to let him take that wood 14 miles down the river to Hermann and sell it there for $3 a cord. Finally, Grandpop consented, and one day Bob and his partner went down and loaded the wood on their flatboat. They put up two sweeps for oars and were ready to start early the next morning for Hermann.

Mother Miller fixed them a nice breakfast, and they were off to their barge. When they got there, they found that the bank had caved in during the night and a big hunk of some 10 tons fell smack dab across their loaded boat. It had been well-tied and only the front end stuck out of the water. The wood was scattered in the river from Bluffton to Washington, Missouri, some 44 miles down the Missouri River.

When the Heckmann family moved from Bluffton to Hermann the Miller/Heckmann team was broken up. This did not keep the Millers from having more adventures that their grandson later recorded. Bob, especially, seemed prone to inventive ideas. Steamboat Bill kept in close touch and enjoyed the adventures instigated by his creative relatives.

Uncle Bob never ran out of ideas. Even after his mishap with the wood, he was willing to try again. He said, "I am going to build a sidewheel boat and have a place to run same by hand power. I'll see brother Sam and get the mail route from brother Pete. He is too young to handle that skiff, and it takes a man to fight that river and them wild dogs of Thees."

This started a big row among the family, and all were in favor of 14-year-old Pete. Mother Miller started to argue for her favorite son, but the boy got up in the middle of the floor and made this statement, "Bob, since you spent a year with Barnum's Circus and you came home and whipped the big bully back of town, you think you are a big shot around here. Now, let me tell you something. That mail route is my bread and butter; not only that, it is my life. You should be ashamed of yourself, and when the time comes and you try to take my job from me, you will be met by me and Old Betts. I'll shoot you, even if you are my brother.

"Furthermore, you are always bragging about those hand-powered engines of yours. Why don't you raise that sunken flatboat, build three pairs of engines and put yourself, John, and Sam in harness and start a Gasconade River Packet! I do not see any good of you all laying around here doing nothing."

CHAPTER 1 ≈ WEE WILLIE'S BLUFFTON BOYHOOD

That just about settled the argument, but Uncle Bob went on with his plans to build a small one-man, sidewheel boat. He picked up enough engine material from the wreck of some boat that sunk near Bluffton, picked up lumber out of rack heaps, caught some floating down the river, and talked his sister (my mother) out of some lumber we had left from building our house in Bluffton. He could not borrow or beg anything more from his old bank, Miller and Evans (his parents), since he had misfired on the wood contract.

Despite his troubles, early in the spring he started his building plan, and in about a month had one of the darndest contraptions that ever was launched on the bosom of the Missouri River. He set the day for the trial trip for one Sunday morning. The word got out, and he had a crowd of some 40 people to see him on his trial trip. He cut loose from the bank, got between his two big wooden levers and started out across the river.

The thing was moving along across the river, but his caulking was too faulty, his lumber too short, and, all in all, the construction was too weak. The Mattie Belle, for such he had named her, commenced to leak, leaned off to one side or the other until she turned turtle, fell over on one side and broke in two.

The Skipper did not go down with his ship but untangled himself from the wreckage and swam ashore below the mouth of Lora Dora Creek. A very crestfallen man came back up the river bank and up home to change his clothes. Uncle Pete said that he would be a fine specimen to carry the mail!

•

Uncle Bob's adventure into boating was probably no worse than the one Uncle Pete and Wee Willie tried. Indirectly, Uncle Bob had a hand in this adventure, too.

One hot summer day, Bob, John and Sam Miller were in swimming and playing leap frog at the mouth of Lora Dora Creek. Uncle Pete and Wee Willie were spectators and were never let in on the doings. One of the boys would scare the other and he would leap in the river and dive out of sight.

When it came Uncle Bob's time, he dove in all right, but he never came up. His feet were just under water, and he was kicking up the water like a 100-hp diesel boat on her trial trip. Uncle Pete jumped up and cried, "One of you damn fools go in there and pull him out! Look at them bubbles! Don't you see he's drowning?"

Both of the big boys jumped into the river and pulled him out on the sloping bank. Water, sand and corruption was coming out of his mouth. There was a big barrel laying there that was used to tar nets. Master Pete now ordered him to be laid across that barrel and rolled back and forth. This helped a lot, and when he was about to come back to life, the barrel got away and rolled over him.

Uncle Bob came back to life like a wild bull. He picked up a big switch, saying, "You lunkheads, I'm going to switch the daylights out of you."

John and Sam got up the bank first. John took off up Lora Dora Creek, and Sam went around the house heading for the great open spaces. Bob caught up with him just as he was going over an old-style rail fence and gave Sam the switching of his life. And that really hurts on naked hide!

Grandma Miller, hearing the commotion, came out of the house and said, "What are you naked Indians doing now?"

Uncle Pete, who had been watching this show, replied, "He is whipping Sam because he helped save his life."

The barrel that they used to tar nets with was a very large one, so Uncle Pete and Wee Willie decided it would make a dandy bullboat. We got a big crosscut saw and sawed it in half. All we needed then was two paddles, and we were ready to go.

The next day we made our maiden voyage. We decided to go over to McGirk's Island, but our progress was very slow. The swift waters of the Missouri River carried us down the river faster than we were going across, but finally we landed on the island, some two miles below our starting point.

Pete decided that while we were here we'd see if we could find some mushrooms. We found plenty, but we didn't have anything to put them in. We took off our shirts, tied up the sleeves and neck and soon had them full.

We now started back across the Big Muddy and, by heroic efforts, made it back to the north shore at Jones' Landing, some four miles below our beloved Bluffton. When we shoved our boat out into the muddy water of the big river, Uncle Pete said, "There goes our bullboat down the river without a brave nor a squaw in charge."

It was late in the afternoon when we finally trudged our way back home. Grandma wanted to know, "Where have you river rats been today?"

"Oh, we made a trip in a bullboat." Nothing more was said, as she always had confidence in her two pets.

Steamboat Bill was writing about his Miller relatives as late as 1952. In "Muddy River Snapshots," under the subtitle "An Early Polar Bear Club," he reported:

Three of my big uncles named Miller lived in the little hamlet of Bluffton, Missouri. They were all big, husky young men, and one winter they went across the river to Morrison to celebrate some event. They imbibed in too much tanglefoot and on the way home were hilarious and happy.

As they crossed through the big Morrison bottom, they came to a pond partly frozen over. One of them said, "Boys, this will be a good place to take a swim. I am hot as a fox." They jerked off their clothes, and in they went. Samuel, (no kin to the great Prophet), in water up to his neck, said, "Look at that poor farmer out there cutting corn this hot day, and we are here enjoying ourselves in this cool water."

•

The bell-ringing trot lines were not doing quite so good, but one morning Uncle Pete came running up the bank hollering, "I think we have a big fish on Big Mamma."

Sure enough, the bell on Big Mamma was playing a fine tune, but when we were about halfway across the chute, the noise stopped, and we soon found out that a big fish had torn the pole out of the bank and gone down the Bluffton Chute.

The next day two commercial fishermen were pulling up around a big tree that had fallen in the river. They saw one of the big branches shaking and stopped to investigate. They found it was a big fish on a long pole and commenced to pull it into the boat. When the bell came out of the water, one of them asked, "What the hell is going on now?"

The day after this, Dad came along with his steamer R. W. Dugan and landed at Quick's Landing to have a chat with his good friends, the fishermen. In the course of the conversation, the subject came up

≈ STEAMBOAT TREASURES ≈

The Steamer Dugan with the little Light Western, circa 1873

about them catching the big fish. When all was told, Dad told them about our Bell Fishing Co. at Bluffton, four miles up the river. They then offered to give him the pole, line, hooks and bell back. He said, "No, but I would like to have the big hook you caught that fish on. I am rigging up a jug outfit, and we have a lucky pear-shaped jug that catches as many fish as all the rest of the jugs put together. I want to hang that hook on that jug.

A trot line outfit consisted of 12 jugs. You can believe it or not, but on jugging trips this jug would catch as many fish as all the rest of the set would catch all together! We kept that jug in the family for years and caught many a large fish with it. My brother Sam and I lost old Lucky while passing the Steamer Bright Light, out from the mouth of Little Tavern Creek, two miles below Portland Missouri.

•

One of the largest events around Bluffton in the old days was a gander pulling. Let me describe one of these social affairs. They would hang a big tame goose in the limb of a big tree, just about the right height for a horse and rider to ride under. The goose was hung by his feet. The competitors were supposed to ride under this tree at a gallop and snatch the goose by the head. If he pulled the head off, he was the champion and could choose anyone in the audience as his girl.

This might seem to some an easy task, but we had several picnics when more than two dozen men tried before it was accomplished. The secret of this feat was in catching the head at the bill, and, no doubt, when this was found out it took the sport out of this entertainment. It seemed utterly impossible to pull the head off a gander if you caught it anywhere above the head of the target, no matter how strong or how good a horseman you were.

•

Grandpop Miller was always interested in mysterious things. One day we "explorers" brought into his parlor a dynamite cap. No one, not even Grandpa, knew what it was. It was dead in the winter and very cold. He told Uncle Pete to lay it on the red-hot, pot-bellied stove, and they soon found out what it was. Result: a lot of black minstrels from the soot, a new stove and new wallpaper.

This wasn't the only one of Grandpop's experiments that caused havoc. Another time, the Millers had a lot of company sitting down to the table in the dining room when Grandpa came in late. The parlor door was open, and he saw a strange animal parading around on the carpet. He rushed into the dining room, all excited, "There's an animal in the parlor. Let's catch it."

None of the boys offered to help until Pete said he would go down to the river and get a large dip net. Grandpop agreed. Then our gladiator stepped into the parlor, and the hunt was on. The big black skunk did not like the proceedings, made a couple of switches with his bushy armament, and hell broke loose in Bluff House. The company left. Grandpa and the parlor were under suspicion for months to come.

•

Our time in Bluffton was rapidly coming to an end. Winter was coming, my father was coming home from a successful season on the steamer E. Hensley, and we were making preparations to move in the spring. That winter, one fine moonlight night, father, mother and sister Tina were not at home when Uncle John, Uncle Sam and Uncle Pete came up to our house on a visit. It was too lonesome in the house, and we went outside. There was not much doing in Bluffton, and we always had to look for something to turn up. We found it.

Dad had put one of the steamer Clara's smokestacks in the center of our outdoor cellar for ventilation. This cellar had been built in the bluff just back of our house. Someone said to get a stick or a club and we could play a tune on the four guywires that helped hold this old smokestack in position. We started on "Way Down Upon the Swanee River," and although we were a little out of tune, things were going along fine. Then Uncle John said, "Now we will sing to this music." Along about the time we got to "The Old Folks at Home," there was a terrible racket, and the big stack fell to the ground, knocking part of the roof off our house and a panel off the fence. It just missed Uncle Pete and me by inches.

This certainly made one heck of a fuss. The four kids in the house commenced to bawl; the three Millers ran home in a roundabout way, and 9-year-old Wee Willie Heckmann was left alone to face the music. Believe me, there was some music to face, for my parents who had heard this racket, were soon home. Wee Willie always blamed this accident on Uncle John, for he had part of a rail for a bow, and his guywire was the first to let go. This is the first time this secret has been let out, and that big smokestack fell in 1879, some 74 years ago.

When the rumors began to fly around that the Heckmans were going to move to Hermann, 14 miles down the Missouri River, it was sad news to Uncle Pete and his pal Willie. All the time we were together, our only arguments and sometimes fights were when Willie Heckmann spent too much time with his Aunt Alice, who was just my age.

Early one morning Aunt Alice and myself took it upon ourselves to make a sightseeing trip by Cynthiana Creek. We mosied up the creek, fishing, picking wildflowers and throwing rocks at everything we seen. Soon we were at the home of one of our real "woodsie" families, and we picked up company. The young man, Jonnie Deno, took along an ax, and we cut down several trees that looked suspicious and shook the nests to scare out the squirrels. His girl, Cynthiana McCafee, took her pistol. Results of this chase: one coon, seven squirrels and one chipmunk. When we got back, Mrs. McCafee had a big lunch ready, and no meal ever tasted better.

While all this was going on and we did not come home for the noon meal, our mothers commenced to inquire and search for us. Soon the cry went up that we must have drowned. Brothers, sisters and citizens started on an all afternoon search up and down the river bank and up

CHAPTER 1 ≈ WEE WILLIE'S BLUFFTON BOYHOOD

to the head of backwater on both Cynthiana and Lora Dora Creeks, but no children.

We finally got away from our hosts, and when we came down the pike that leads into Bluffton from the north, old Sol was ending her hot day in the west. When our mothers saw us, instead of tanning our hides, they picked us up and clung to us like a lamper eel hangs to a German carp.

Uncle Pete left the crowd in disgust and said, "I sure wish I had met them first and they would have gotten the darndest beating any fool kids ever went through. What fools our parents are."

•

On another adventure, Aunt Alice and I stole away and went to the head of Lora Dora Creek. On our way home, we got to what was known as the Big Spring. This was the only hole in this creek of any consequence. There was a big rock in it, and a large amount of water formed a cave under this rock big enough to hide a cow.

As we came up to it we heard a big commotion in our favorite spring. With much splashing of water we saw a big tail disappear under this rock. We never really knew what it was but it could have been a beaver. Anyway, Aunt Alice, who always sort of stretched things, cried out, "That was the mermaid, Lora Dora!" And when we got back home and Alice told her story, Wee Willie seconded the motion.

Childhood without a few fibs, to me, never seemed worth while. As far as we know, Lora Dora is still playing ghost along our favorite creek.

In the old Bluffton days, on each side of the flower-bedecked Lora Dora Creek, there stood about one dozen extra-large maple trees, monsters for this part of Missouri. No one has ever completed childhood up to 100 percent until they have helped prepare these trees and tapped them for maple syrup. Uncle Pete and Wee Willie did this for a number of years, around where the pretty maiden Lora Dora Lee held forth.

The Bluffton cellars were built back against the hill on the west side of Cynthiana Creek, and on the east side of the same creek, there was a level piece of bottom land of about four acres. Here the Wine Company had built a large number of tanks in the ground, about six feet deep, 8 feet long, and 5 feet wide. As young explorers we could not figure out what these tanks were built for, unless it was to brew and ferment their wine. *[In fact, they were the old propagating pits.]* Anyway, these tanks were always partly full of foul water and bull frogs, from the wee little frogs to the big yellow honkers. We would gather our hats full of just the right kind of rocks, and then the big hunt was on. Many a big croaker went to the Happy Hunting Ground because of our unerring aim.

•

When the Heckmanns had lived in Bluffton for several years, our combined stock of animals was our old cow, named Star, seven bantam chickens and 11 hens with two roosters. One fall, Dad came home from the big steamer Collosal and brought us 10 guinea hens and two roosters. Why a guinea is called a domestic fowl has always been a mystery to me. Our one dozen spotted chatterboxes were no exception, and they soon proved to be one of the biggest nuisances that ever landed on the Heckmann Ranch.

They seemed satisfied during the winter, but when spring came they got restless and soon were spending most of their time along the high steep bluffs below town. Mother took me along one day to help drive these sons-a-guns back home. We would get below them and try to drive them up towards home. They would go along all right for a while and then fly out over the river, make a big turn and fly back under the bluffs. This would have been all right, but most of the time they would fly back down the river and we had to do the job all over again. One day after they had us both worn out, we sat down on a big log to rest up, gave up on chasing for the day and just watched the steamboats go by.

We continued having trouble with these stinkers, and along about high water, Dad came home from his charge on the river and stayed with us for several months. One day, when several of us failed to round up our wild life, Dad said, "Tell Pete to be ready, and we will at least bring some of them rascals home, dead or alive."

We started out early the next morning. Dad had his big gun, and Uncle Pete and Wee Willie went along as drivers. We found the guineas about one mile below town. All went well for a while, and we were nearing home when they started to fly out over the river and turned the wrong way. Dad let go with both barrels, and three of them never had to be bothered about any more. After that, about twice a week, we would go and get three more, and finally there was only one old cock left. He seemed to bear a charmed life. Dad, like all rivermen who have fought the Big Muddy, never gave up. One morning he picked up his big double-barrel and said, "We are going to get that old buzzard this time."

We soon scared him up, and he flew right over Dad's head. He let loose at him twice, but when we saw the last of the old rascal, he was clean across the Missouri River and flying south to return no more to the Bluffton shores.

Sadly, it was also time for the Heckmann family to leave Bluffton forever, but for one small boy it meant leaving his heart behind, only to lose it again to steamboats. The Miller/Heckmann families continued to visit at any given opportunity.

The Miller family remained at Bluffton. All the offspring married local young men and women. Grandpop Sam Miller became the local Justice of the Peace and was elected to the state legislature. He was called Judge Miller by all, and he wore many hats. He was at times the postmaster, storekeeper, hotel keeper and judge. First and foremost, he was a horticulturist, making a veritable Garden of Eden out of the hills and dales of this little community.

Even after the failure of the Bluffton Winery, Sam Miller continued to work with George Husmann in grape propagation. For a time he was in Sedalia, Missouri, on this work, but returned to Bluffton to spend the rest of his days. During his varied career, his first love remained horticulture, and he wrote about it on a regular basis, writing for *Colman's Rural World* and other farm journals.

He wrote in longhand and was a very poor scribe. He sent a long article to *Colman's*, and they could not find anyone who could read it. They sent it back to him, asking that he write a little plainer. He had forgotten what subject he had written on, and as he could not read his own writing, he bundled it up, put a rubber band around it, handed it to his daughter Alice and said, "Take that darn thing down and throw it in the Big Muddy, the receiver of sorrow, pain and failure."

•

When the Philadelphia Exposition took place in the state of Pennsylvania, a lot of Samuel Miller's old friends invited him to attend the powwow. They wined and dined the old horticulturist to such an extent that he came back home in the year 1901 and layed down and died. His beloved wife, Martha Evans Miller, preceded him in death some eight years before he went to his home above the clouds. A wonderful life well spent; a talented man has gone away, and nobody but a ragged-pants old steamboatman to take up a pen and paper to try to tell some of his wonderful work here on earth.

Uncle Pete Miller married Ida Monnig and was never a rich man, but he was the most interesting man this little hamlet ever saw. In his time he was a mail carrier, a boatman, a railroader, a farmer, a thresherman, a stock breeder and a fruit grower. He failed in some of these and was a success in others. Pete Miller fell dead alongside his beloved MK&T at Bluffton in the year 1947. He was the last of the original Miller family in that little city.

Uncle Pete Miller's motto and ambition, or whatever you want to call it, was, "The mail must go," and for some 75 years it did go. This faithful service alone, done for a pittance, put him among the immortals, and Uncle Sam can say to this, "Well done my good and faithful servant."

Before he went to the Happy Hunting Ground; he and this writer batched together for over a month, and we did a lot of fishing and caught some mighty nice fish. The largest one was a 53-pound channel cat, so we ended up where we started, with our cowbell lines of 74 years ago, but we never caught as many fish as when the cow bells tolled.

The Miller family kept the name of Bluffton on the map long after the little town had, for all practical purposes, disappeared. That once-thriving community with a store, hotel and even a bar at one time, centered around a bustling wine company, lives today only in imagination. Judge Sam Miller and his wife, Martha, are at rest up on Graveyard Hill.

CHAPTER 2

The Parting
Farewell to Childhood

The winter preceding the Heckmann move to Hermann was a busy one. Young Will was often out hunting with his father and helping him catch ties out in the river. Time did not hang heavy on his hands, but the impending move was on his mind.

Eventually, spring came in 1879, and the parting of the ways came along, a sorry time for the Miller and Heckmann Exploring Company. We divided the spoils of our strongbox, in tears. Uncle Pete bought a big gun, some fishing tackle, ammunition and other trinkets with his half. Wee Willie kept his in a secret hideout in the new Heckmann home in Hermann, and he, too, when 15 years old, bought his first shotgun.

We moved to our home on Wharf Street in Hermann; actually, we moved into the home of our paternal grandparents. We made the move on June 19, 1879. Here in Hermann, my father and mother were to raise a family of 14 children, to become famous as one of the most successful owners and operators of steamboats on the Missouri River. In addition, Capt. William L. Heckmann Sr. was considered to be one of, if not THE best pilots on our mighty river. We were a bunch of green country kids when we came to Hermann but were destined to become men and women of note. Seven of the boys became licensed river masters, pilots and marine engineers.

We moved in June when the flowers were in full bloom. Life changed for all of us. While we had grandparents in Hermann, we hardly knew them, and they were old and ailing. It was not the same as the Miller grandparents who had been with us all of our young lives.

Life at Hermann was a rude change for young Will. Not only was his Uncle Pete gone, but so were the woods and the freedom to roam at will. Hermann presented another aspect of excitement though. The new home on Wharf Street faced not only the wide Missouri River, but also the Missouri Pacific Railroad. When the family first arrived, the Wohlt/Heckmann interests were running the little steamer Light Western and the old stiff-shaft steamer Washington. The 10-year-old Will wasted no time finding a way to catch rides on the two steamboats.

In early January, Grandpa Heckmann died, and, simultaneously, the little Light Western was caught in ice and wrecked. Working frantically to try to save the Light Western, Will Sr. barely had time to get home for the funeral. Already, steamboats were exerting their power over the Heckmann family.

The boat disaster prompted the Wohlt/Heckmann interests to go looking for a new boat. By January 20, they had bought the steamer Hope in Kentucky. The whole family, even mother Mary Heckmann, eagerly awaited the new boat's arrival in Hermann.

Grandmother Heckmann died in February, just a month after her husband. On April 9, the steamer Washington burned, so now the steamer Hope was, indeed, true to her name. The Wohlt family took the remains of the little Light Western and built the trim little steamer Fawn. With the acquisition of the Hope, finances began to improve rapidly. After some sprucing up, the little steamer was busy towing ties to the port of Hermann.

We were still poor, but with the Hope, fortune began to smile on the growing family. (There were seven of us children by that time.) To my mind, the officers of the boat and even the 20 Negro roustabouts were one big family with the Heckmanns. Into that family one day came our first "town" dog. How he came no one seemed to know. He just arrived without an introduction, without a pedigree, no particular kind of a dog— just a little black pup with long wavy hair and a snow white belly. We named him Nick.

Nick divided his time between the home family and that of the boat crew. He paid attention to no other boat call save the Hope. If he was in Hermann when the Hope blew a landing whistle, he would make a record run for the wharf. If he got there in time, he would dash to the edge of the water, only to race up the bank with the big roustabouts who jumped out with the headline. After that line was fast to the big hitching post, he would jump on their legs barking his greeting. And

CHAPTER 2 ≈ THE PARTING

The Hope was captained by William L. Heckmann Sr.

when the running board was put out from the boat, Nick was the first aboard. He would pay attention to no one until he had dashed to the pilothouse to salute my father. After that he was eager to play with any of the crew that had time for him.

When the bell rang or the "nigger whistle" blew, Nick would leave the boat and trot back home to stay with the family. We always believed that he did this to watch over our house at night, for no one ever prowled around our home without Nick giving shrill warning.

On one occasion some of the roustabouts aboard the Hope went on a strike and the company sent some 20 German immigrants up from St. Louis to work a mixed crew of rousters. Dad had a big Calloway County Negro named George Jackson working for him at the time. He was a young giant. When the boat landed at Hermann, Nick came aboard and got in the way of one of the Germans who promptly kicked him. My father was coming down the forward steps and started for the fellow like a wild bull, but Jackson was nearer and blocked his way say-

Railroad tracks and the Missouri River were Steamboat Bill's front yard.

ing, "Cap'n, this is my job. I owe that lil dawg somethin', and I'm going to pay it." The German was big and strong, but when Jackson got through with him, he was, to put it mildly, soundly whipped.

Nick was with us three years. He had to cross the railroad tracks to get to the boat, and one night a fast passenger train caught him and cut him to shreds. Soon after the death of Nick, Dad began to look about for another dog. One day, while they were loading wheat at La Barge's Landing, some 15 miles above Hermann, the old man who ran the wood yard kept boasting about his yellow female squirrel dog. Dad offered the man 10 dollars for the dog, which he agreed to take if his wife were willing.

The man's wife however, refused to sell the dog for any consideration. Old George Jackson came up and said: "Cap'n, if you want that dawg, I can get her for you. Them folks owes me a debt, and I'm going to collect— I kept them Day boys from burning their shack. You give me that 10 dollahs, and I bring that dawg. This boat has just got to have another Nick."

Jackson made good, and another dog came into the family. But she was not another Nick. Sally would have nothing to do with steamboats or anything else that did not resemble a squirrel. Out in the woods she

CHAPTER 2 ≈ THE PARTING

had no equal. When she barked, the squirrel was either in the branches or in a hole or nest in the tree where she was barking. This dog could take a cold trail and run along the highest fence following that trail until in sight of the squirrel, never losing sight of it until the squirrel was treed. When she was through, it looked as if half the population of the area was treed. No matter how wild the squirrel, it had no chance to get away from Sally. We had Sally two years before the Missouri Pacific got her in much the same manner it had gotten Nick.

•

Many years later we had another dog, one named Dick, a jet-black beauty. He was a smart but lazy rascal. He was strictly a steamboat dog, spending about 90 percent of his time on the steamers Kennedy, Lora and Julius F. Silber. We taught him to swim and dive off the boiler deck and hurricane roof. He developed into a fine retriever in the water but was too lazy to go hunting on shore. Dick was a double-crosser deluxe. Whenever a visiting dog came aboard, he would treat him very friendly until he had maneuvered him to the deep side. He would then suddenly lunge toward the visitor, knocking him into the river.

One day brother Fred shot at a very large blue heron and broke its wing. Dick was lying on the boiler deck asleep but hearing the shot jumped up and leaped into the river. The heron was standing in about two feet of water on solid bottom. As Dick swam up the heron made one or two pecks at his eyes. Dick saw that he was no match for the bird and turned to swim back to the boat. The long-legged rascal followed him, and every time he stepped, he struck Dick in the back. He kept following and pecking away until the water got so deep he could go no further. When Dick had swum clear of the heron, brother Fred shot and killed the bird.

When Dick got back to the boat, he was a pitiful sight. Blood was running down his back and stern end. He whined and cried for help. Aunt Susan, the cook, threw about a half gallon of New Orleans molasses over his back and then sprinkled it with about two pounds of flour. In about 10 days he was well again, once more enjoying his lazy existence.

Dick had a sweetheart in the old Independent Stock Yards in North St. Louis. He went ashore on a visit one trip while the steamer Kennedy was unloading stock and failed to come back. There were few regrets over his leaving, and yet it is impossible to forget that no-account black beauty.

•

Soon after the arrival of the Hope, the older boys in the family, ranging from 6 to 11, began to stow away on the boat. If we were found within three or four miles of town, father would pick us up by the seat of the breeches and pitch us into the river saying, "Swim home, you whelp, and ask me next time you want to ride on the Hope." No father ever thought more of his boys, but he was raising us to be resourceful and self-reliant, to fear nothing, especially connected with the river.

Steamboats and trains were not the only dangerous things in Hermann. Life in town turned out to be scary at times.

One July night six of the Heckmann kids were in one big room in our new house. Mother and father and sister Tina went out to the Fourth of July celebration, and we were left without a babysitter. Along about 7 o'clock that evening, a big explosion took place. Brother Sam said, "What is it?" Wee Willie, 10, the oldest present, replied, "That must be one of the boilers at the mill." The mill was at the end of the block behind us. In about half an hour another monster explosion took place.

"What's that?"

"Oh, that is the other boiler," I answered with authority.

Arren Eberson who worked at the mill had become a buddy of mine, and I knew the old mill had only two boilers, and when sometime later a third explosion took place, Wee Willie did not know what to say. We staged one of the biggest bawling sprees that ever took place in the City Beautiful. About that time Mother and Dad came home, and the contest was over when they gave us some candy and crackerjacks and told us the community was celebrating the Fourth of July by firing a big brass cannon that had been left from the Civil War.

The indulgent father was not entirely subtle in his wooing of his son to the river.

My father built a fancy skiff. We named it Lottie in honor of my sister, Charlotte. Frank Rebsamin, nicknamed "Donniemit," one of my new companions, joined me to form our first business venture, the Lottie

CHAPTER 2 ≈ THE PARTING

Skiff Transfer Company. We were both 10 years old, and we used the skiff in salvaging railroad ties that were worth 27 cents each, fishing in the river and selling the catch, and running a skiff ferry across the Missouri at Hermann after the regular ferryboat had been laid up for the night.

Most of our passengers were drunks who had missed the last trip of the regular ferry. Our best two customers were a young white man who was always accompanied by a big strapping colored man. It seems the young white man had undertaken the project of drinking up his inheritance in short order. While drunk, he was insulting and abusive, but first would employ the colored man as his bodyguard. They paid us $1 for daylight crossings and $5 for night trips.

The ferry business lasted three years, until Frank decided to learn barbering with his father and I left to go with my father in order to learn the river. By that time we had lost our best customer anyway, he had accomplished his mission. He got a tankfull of Metzler's Cherry Bounce and saw so many snakes that the fright killed him. The skiff Lottie was turned over to my next oldest brother, Sam, who catered mostly to hunting and fishing for the Heckmann clan, who were growing up and crying for game, fish and groceries.

Mary Miller Heckmann, mother of the Heckmann brood, apparently became accustomed to the skiff as a form of transportation early in her married life. She reported Bill rowing across the river at Bluffton to go to the store in Morrison for eggs when he was just 9. In later years she simply forgot about her children as soon as they headed to the river, something her husband encouraged. Other parents might have looked askance at such little boys braving the Mighty Missouri—there was never any thought of life preservers. But in her diaries Mary makes no mention of her boys being out on the river at Hermann.

CHAPTER 3

Cub Pilot

Steamboat Bill wrote his own version of his "professional" approach to steamboating. In it he tells just what it takes to be a pilot, giving full credit to his father for his early training. The father had some interesting ideas on how to toughen up a boy for service on the river.

My father, Capt. William L. Heckmann Sr., was one of the most successful boat owners, masters and pilots the Missouri River ever saw. Besides being a skillful navigator, he was an ardent hunter and fisherman. In the fall of 1883, when I was learning the river under him, he took me along on one of his hunting trips. He was a very large man, weighing 240 pounds. His 14-year-old cub was a strapping boy for his age, and had to be, to follow old Rough Head, one of my father's nicknames.

We left the steamboat at the mouth of Third Creek in a small tin duckboat to float some 45 miles down the Gasconade River to our home at Hermann. During the shank of the evening, after our first day's float, we landed at the mouth of Lost Slough, some 15 miles down the river.

Pin Oak Lake was a quarter of a mile from the river, and in early November the wood ducks would come in to this lake to feed and rest for the night. We pulled our boat and tarpaulin out on the bank and made a hurried camp; we then dragged our duckboat out into the lake for the sundown flight of wood ducks to this same lake. Among water lilies, scrub oaks, yonkapins, wild rice and muskrat dens, we placed our boat in the middle of the lake, surrounded by stately pin oak and water oak trees. The wood ducks would drop down out of the sky and through these trees like rockets, and it took a good shot to make a kill.

The old duck boat was laying low in the water. Dad did most of the shooting, and his cub retrieved the game and maneuvered the boat.

CHAPTER 3 ≈ CUB PILOT

We bagged several ducks, and all was going fine when two ducks came in and made the old navigator try for a double shot. In shifting his position, he turned the boat bottom side up and left two surprised hunters standing out in the mud and water up to their waists.

We will leave out the profanity and abuse of the cub to see how we got Pop back into the boat and back to camp. We each got a grip on an end of the double-pointed boat and held it up in the air to let the water drain out. Dad was too heavy to wade ashore. A moving picture of how he got back into that boat would go over big. Anyway, after turning the boat over three times, he managed to crawl up on a sapling and step in from there. It depended on me to reach down to the bottom of the lake for our guns, which made me wet all over.

The old war horse paddled to shore while his cub waded shoreward. We got the boat and all to camp, stretched our 'paulin across some saplings and built a monster fire to cook our supper and to dry our clothing. We both had old-style, high-top leather boots. After supper and after dark, we sat half naked at the campfire with our boots, socks and most of our clothing hanging up around the fire.

Dad said, "We will stand watches until our outfit is dry. You stay up until about 10 o'clock and then wake me." He shortly was in dreamland, and soon the cub on watch went to sleep, too. When I woke up about midnight, the fire had died down, and some of our clothes were ashes. For our two pair of boots, we had four hard balls about the size of your fist.

One would have to know my father to know how his firstborn felt when he had to wake him to view the ruins. We had no change of extra clothes along, our boots were gone, our socks, too, and part of the splash bulkhead was burnt out of Pop's big breeches.

Daylight came crisp and cold, and after the war, we held a council. The cub had to walk around the big lake and up a big hill back of the lake to a Mr. Leimkuehler. Did you ever walk two miles barefooted on frozen ground?

Our good friend Leimkuehler fitted me out the best he could, but when we left Lost Slough, we were a motley-looking pair in that old duckboat. Dad's starboard shoe had the forecastle cut out to make room for his foot; one of my shoes was a wooden one, and we had to confine ourselves to river shooting, as we were not equipped for much land traveling.

It turned bitter cold for November. We picked a granary, partly filled with loose wheat, for our second night's lodging. We had lots of blankets, but that loose wheat was the coldest thing anybody ever picked for a bed. Long before morning we had to get out and build a fire for the rest of the night.

When the next day's float was nearing an end, I pleaded with dad to stop overnight with one of our many farmer friends who lived near the river. He said, "No, we are on a camping trip." However, in running the rapids at Powell's Dam we had another slight mishap with the duckboat, and we decided to stop over night with a Mr. Lalk.

Lalk had two big strapping hired hands working for him, and Old Rough Head asked them about squirrel hunting. They said that squirrels were plentiful and wished they could go out hunting with us. Mr. Lalk objected to this, but dad asked, "How much do you pay these men?"

"Well, they get $8 a month." Dad paid him one dollar to let the men hunt with us until noon. He also paid a dollar for a better shoe. I traded my wooden one for one that at least looked like a shoe. The two hired hands each had a long muzzle-loading rifle and had been bragging the night before what good shots they were. Pop put me down along the river bank to hunt for myself and took the two guides with him.

He put one on each side of him, about 50 yards apart, and the three of them went up and down through the big river bottom. Dad watched the trees close and at every move of a squirrel, his big Parker barked. They got back before noon with 13 squirrels. The boys had never fired a shot, saying that Dad never let a squirrel sit still.

After dinner we gave Mr. Lalk another silver dollar, and he said, "If you fellows would stay awhile, you would be a profit to me." The cub killed seven squirrels and we had plenty of game of all kinds to take home. We paddled the old duck boat home over the other 15-mile stretch, contented and happy. A riverman learns to forget quickly. Some farmers, too, it seems. No one could ruffle old Rough Head for any length of time, and no boy ever had a better father.

Steamboat Bill wrote more than one version of the following story. He evidently did not keep a file and often forgot what he had previously written. Or perhaps he just liked some stories well enough to repeat them.

CHAPTER 3 ≈ CUB PILOT

Steamboat Bill served his apprenticeship on the Steamer Vienna.

In the spring of 1883 my father was running the steamer Vienna on the Gasconade River, and his oldest son, Bill, was his champion roustabout, deckhand, hog catcher, steersman, game driver and devoted offspring. No task, no work, no command was too big an order for Capt. Heckmann's boy, Bill, and the older man expected and made his boy take chance after chance he would not ask or could not expect of any other member of his crew.

One night we were slowly making our way upstream on this picturesque Gasconade River with the old Vienna. The night was pitch dark, the riverbank full, and the old boat was laying low in the water with all kinds of merchandise for the merchants and farmers along the upper reaches of the stream. All went well. Dad was sitting back on the bench in the pilothouse, his eagle eye catching all mistakes of the young navigator, who was steering this old craft under the kindest, sternest and most skillful master and pilot I ever saw.

We had just pulled out under Scott's Island when a mighty rumbling like thunder was heard in the engine room and the engineer called up that both big drive chains had run into the river.

Dad jumped up and said, "I'll stick her nose in them big willows at the foot of the island; get downstairs and jump on one of those willows right now with a line. Get it fast in a hurry and tell them lunkheads not to check this boat up too soon and part the line."

Dad got her headed into the willows while his boy grabbed the end of a line and made his leap correctly to light in a big willow and get the line made fast all right. But a loaded boat in a current like we had in the river that night will not hold her headway long. She glanced off the willows, her head hit the current, and the men held the line too tight on the bitts; it snapped and almost threw me out of my perch on the tree. Before they could heave the anchor overboard, the Vienna had drifted downstream, out of sight and hearing.

Scott's Island was all under water, and midnight found me hugging my friendly tree. Under the island was some dead water, but on both sides of me this little river was sure in a hurry to reach the sea. On the bluff side of the river a catamount was letting out some blood-curdling cries; on a nearby tree on the island, a big horn owl was giving a concert; and over on the bottom side of the river some 'coons were fishing and letting out their strange language to furnish their share of this night's show. This, with the surging waters rushing through the tree tops, made the young pilot rather nervous, and he thought of Ma and the kid brothers and sisters in their snug beds at home.

Did you ever spend six hours in a tree top away out in what was then a wilderness, with blackness all around you? If not, you have no idea how this 14-year-old boy felt. My feet and clothes up to my waist were already wet from making the line fast to this friendly tree. Along towards morning I felt something slimy trying to share this tree with me, which felt so much like a snake that I let all holds go and swam to another tree close by and waited there for daylight, all wet, shivering, and scared, knowing that nobody, not even dad, would venture out on such a river and night with a yawl or skiff to rescue a sweet-water sailor like myself.

With daylight, two men in a skiff came and took me back to the boat. After a big breakfast, I was ready with another man to row father back to Hermann, our starting point, 65 miles down river, to order a new set of chains. The good old Vienna was out of commission 10 days, and this was an early lesson on geared machinery for Steamboat Bill.

CHAPTER 3 ≈ CUB PILOT

Steamboat Bill never sank a boat or seriously damaged a boat or cargo, but he had an early introduction to what a sunken boat was like.

Having never gone ashore from a sunken or burned wreck, it is hard for me to fathom the failures of boatmen and mishaps galore that never should have happened. But in my time I was one of the first to see the big sternwheel Montana that hit the Wabash Bridge at St. Charles and sank near the right shore, a total loss with a valuable cargo of 685 tons for Kansas City.

About the old Durfee we can tell a much longer story. This good old three-boiler, sternwheel, 800-ton boat made quite a name for herself before sinking out in front of the Gasconade Boatyard on May 31, 1881. She made quite a number of trips from Pittsburgh and St. Louis to the mountains. Then when the iron horse got out West to Yankton, South Dakota, this boat ran in connection with the railroads from that place to Fort Benton and the Yellowstone River.

After the railroads got across the mountains and there was no more business for this class of boat on the upper Missouri, one could buy a craft of this kind for a song. Capt. George G. Keith and others bought the Durfee and put her in the St. Louis and Kansas City trade. Coming down one trip loaded flat (as only Capt. Keith knew how to flatten them out), her head hit a bar near Gasconade. She swung around and when square in the river, her stern hit, her hog chains parted, she broke in two amidships, and for several hours the river was full of hogsheads of tobacco, hoop poles, chicken coops, pumpkins and, in fact, everything that was loose and would float or swim off the heavy-laden craft.

My father went to this wreck with the steamer Hope and took myself and a friend along. We salvaged a lot of freight, but it was a dangerous undertaking, as the boat was breaking up fast and was sinking in the sands of time. My friend and I made it our business, at a great risk, to get into the office. We salvaged a big pile of stationery, like way bills, bills of lading, letterheads and everything that was loose. For many a year afterwards, the Fischer and Heckmann kids had Durfee stationery at home and in school to scribble on. And each fall and winter when the river was low, scavengers secured all the copper piping, the brass and everything that could be pried loose, providing it could be used or turned into money off this wreck.

≈ STEAMBOAT TREASURES ≈

•

When I was about 12 years old, I made my first trip to St. Louis, accompanied by my father. We were to bring back to Hermann the ferryboat Fawn that had been on the old Sectional Dry Dock at the foot of Poplar Street.

Late one evening we arrived at St. Charles, on the Missouri River, and saw the big sternwheel steamboat Montana sunk above her boiler deck. She had struck the Wabash Railroad Bridge at St. Charles, on June 22, 1984, while coming upstream with 680 tons of freight on board, most of which was a total loss. When we saw her she was beached about half a mile below the bridge. The crew was living out on the bank in tents.

My father landed the Fawn alongside the Montana, and we lay there all night. That evening young Bill Heckmann sat with open mouth listening to Capts. George G. Keith, William Rodney (Bill) Massie, Hanson Chadwick and my father spin yarns and cuss the railroads and their bridges. Capt. Massie had been the pilot on watch when the Montana hit the bridge pier. She was the only boat that ever sank while he was acting as pilot.

Steamboat Bill told this version of his cubbing days in "Steamboating Sixty-five Years on Missouri Rivers."

Despite my mother's acid warnings, admonitions and outright pleas, I knew very early that I wanted to go on the river more than anything else in the world. I also knew that my father would be pleased and would aid and abet me in this desire. So, when George Riddle, pilot aboard the steamer Hope said, "Come aboard, Bill, and I will teach you how to steer the Hope," my 12-year-old heart was thrilled and eager. I left school for good to become a cub pilot.

To secure a pilot's license, one must work 36 months on the river as a deckhand, which means doing almost everything there is to be done aboard a steamboat. In olden times, when the boats went to the mountains on the Missouri River, a 2,300-mile trip from St. Louis to Fort Benton, Montana, a cub pilot, generally a young man, would get in touch with some first-class pilot and work for nothing, paying his board and paying the pilot from $250 to $500 for a round trip to the mountains. Between 1835 and 1870 the crack mountain pilots made as much

CHAPTER 3 ≈ CUB PILOT

This 1880 photograph of the Steamer Montana was taken at St. Charles, where she later sank. The Montana and her sister boats, the Dacotah and Wyoming, all made the trip to Fort Benton, but their large size made them impractical for the upper Missouri and the mountain trade.

as $1,500 per month on a trip and from $7,000 to $10,000 for an annual trip to the mountains. At the present time (1950), a young man wanting to learn the river gets a deckhand berth, and a great number of our present-day pilots are proud to help them secure their license this way.

I started cubbing on the steamer Hope on the Missouri River and finished on my father's boats. A cub pilot starts out by doing practically nothing but watch the main pilot on watch for several months. Then some day, when the big shot is in a good humor and the boat is in very good water, he will say, "Take her, Buddy, and see what you can do with her."

After the cub has tried this until he can steer a boat with reasonable safety, he will learn to "run a shore" and "run a point." (There never was a cub that tried to take his first point but what he tried to turn the point too soon.)

Next the cub is allowed to land the boat at some good landing, but only on her upstream trips. If progress continues well, he will be allowed to run a shallow crossing and, still later, to turn an empty boat around and make a downstream landing. (A downstream landing without turning the boat around is known as a French Landing.)

Further along in the training, the cub is permitted to "flank a bend" where there is a big set in the river. Then he may run several bridges downstream. And finally, when he can land a heavily loaded boat downstream after nightfall in a close river, he is a pilot.

In learning all this, the cub will have been "cussed out" a thousand times and will have learned more philosophy than he could have obtained in almost any other profession. While he is learning to handle, maneuver and land a boat, he has to study several dozen other things.

In reading water in the Missouri, Arkansas and Yukon rivers, the waves are highest at the point of deepest water, if the wind is upstream. If the wind is downstream, the waves are highest where the water is shallowest. When it is raining, all water looks alike. Such things as these make the pilot's profession a gift from the gods, or at least a gift of the sixth sense.

A pilot on an uncharted river must have a remarkable memory to keep hundreds of marks in his memory for both day and night work. My cubbing was in the tradition of the old mountain pilots, who could remember all their marks from St. Louis to Fort Benton— thousands of them. These men would take their marks on the upstream trip and run by them coming back three months later.

One of the hardest things I had to learn about the Missouri River was "running a rainbow reef." Pulling my boat over this reef at just the proper place, the break in the reef, bothered me. Heavy rushing boils on a crossing or a swift, shallow bend means the deepest water; slick boils, like a girl with a fresh-powdered face, means look out for shallow water.

A crossing on the river is the place where boats cross from one side of the river to the other, and as a rule these are the flattest places. Some crossings are long; some are square.

Flanking a bend or bridge means holding your boat back and letting her drift slowly through a place where the pilot is running a close place in the river, or a close bridge. It is called "making it on the run."

A set in the river is where the water draws more heavily toward one shore than the other and it is in these places that a heavy boat is generally flanked.

Reading the water means telling the deep water from the shallow— a gift that is given but few men.

By marks are meant trees, rocks, houses, hills, hollows or anything

CHAPTER 3 ≈ CUB PILOT

The Royal sometimes carried excursion parties up the Gasonade River.

that is not a man-made marker, such as government lights.

A reef on the river is a place where there may be one foot of water on the upper side and the water drops straight down at some places under the reef to as much as 15 feet. In other words, there may be one foot of water at a particular spot in the river while three feet away from that spot will be 15 feet of water. This has caused many drownings.

A rainbow reef starts on one side of the river and crosses clean to the other side in the shape of a rainbow. The break in the reef is the place to look for the deepest water.

A boil is a rough surface on the river caused by the water running over an uneven bottom. A break is a submerged snag that shows on the surface of the water. A sawyer is a whipping snag that sticks up out of the water and bobs around like a cork in the wind.

The different watches a pilot stands at night are called long watch, supper to midnight; after watch, midnight to 4:00 ; and dog watch, 4:00 to breakfast.

A job on the river is always known as a berth.

In another article, written in 1956, "Steamboat Bill Recounts 77 Years as River Pioneer," he told more stories of his adventures as a cub pilot.

While learning the river, as a cub pilot, I knocked the steamer Gasconade's smokestacks down twice in one day on overhanging trees on the upper reaches of the Gasconade River. Both my father and Capt. Wohlt were on board at the time, but neither censured me.

My first charge was the sternwheel Royal. She was the only steamboat that ever went up the Gasconade River to Arlington, 107 miles from Hermann. My father was my partner pilot. With the scow bow steamer Pin Oak, I made a half dozen trips on the Gasconade that were the fastest and most profitable ever made on that stream. It was my pleasure to take this boat, loaded to the nosing, down through Pryor's Bend, a three-mile stretch of crooked, swift and dangerous river. This was a feat never before attempted by a Gasconade River pilot.

The Steamer Arethusa
January 2, 1957

The Missouri River Commission, in 1894, built two sternwheel towboats at Gasconade and named them Arethusa and Atalanta. They were sister boats, as near alike as two peas in a pod. As had often happened in similar cases, one boat, for some strange reason, was the better of the two, and that was the Arethusa.

Capt. S. Waters Fox called me to his office one day and said, "Will, I have a stack of applications a foot high from pilots who want a berth on our new boats, but I don't have none from you."

"I am satisfied with my berth on the steamer Gasconade," I told him.

He then told me that the berth on the Atalanta was going to Bob McGarrah and that a well-known, capable man was suggested for the Arethusa. However, this latter man drank a good deal. Capt. Fox did not like that and said he wanted me to take charge of the Arethusa because my work on the chartered Gasconade had been very satisfactory.

"Give me a chance to talk to my father, and I'll let you know tomorrow," I told him.

"All right, Will," he said, " but my advice is for you to come with us. There is a great future for government improvement on the Missouri."

In talking it over with Dad, he wondered why the job had not been offered to my brother, Sam. I told him that Capt. Fox had over 50 applications from men who were better pilots than Sam and yet had picked me for the job.

"Well, go ahead," my father said. "It will do you good to work for

CHAPTER 3 ≈ CUB PILOT

somebody else besides our company. Sam can take your place on the Gasconade."

Most of my years with the government were spent as master pilot of the wonderful Arethusa. However, I did put in some time on the government towboats Alert and Golden Gate, the sidewheel towboats Sabrina and Melusina, the Atalanta, the Thetis and Titus, sidewheel misfits, and also the big sternwheel towboat William Stone.

The Steamer Arethusa

My reputation was made on the Arethusa. By the time I was 23 years old, Capt. Fox and many others said that Bill Heckmann was the best pilot on the Missouri River. Capt. Fox was the best authority we had, since he had hired all of the stargazers at one time or another. An engineer named Day said to my father, "Do you know that young Bill Heckmann is classed to be the best pilot on the Missouri River?"

My Dad's only reply to this was, "Well, look who learned him the river!"

Capt. S. Waters Fox, who was in charge of the improvement work on the Missouri, had, at one time or another, hired most of the first-class pilots. He was an authority on the subject of Missouri River pilots and often said, "I used to say that Capt. Billy Ball was the best towboat pilot on the Missouri, but I will have to change my mind because young Bill Heckmann is out there every day, doing practically everything with the Arethusa that Capt. Ball would have feared to do."

All the government boats had orders that when working around or above the dikes in dangerous places, they were to drop their tows in safe spots and let the Arethusa place them. In carrying out these orders, this little boat did less damage to herself and barges than any of the other boats.

Capt. Bud Spar, who was a very large, strong and dangerous man, had a grudge against me and did everything he could with his big towboat Alert to disquality me and my little boat. We always carried a sporting crew on the Arethusa. They had confidence in themselves and were not afraid to tackle anything. We carried a punching bag, a pair of boxing gloves, and we were the champion oarsmen among a thousand employees of Uncle Sam.

One day the Alert and the Arethusa were lying alongside a cornfield in Mokus Bend. Some of the boys were boxing, and Capt. Spar saw this. He had an enormously big deckhand working for him called Big Bill. He asked Big Bill if he knew anything about boxing. Bill said, "Well, down home they say I am pretty good."

"I'll give you a dollar bill if you will go over there and challenge Bill Heckmann to put on the gloves with you."

The match was on. We had hardly got going when Big Bill let go a right punch that hit me under the jaw and the next thing I knew I was lying flat on my back in the cornfield. I did not stay there long, and when I got up, I threw off my right glove. Before Big Bill knew what was happening, I drove my fist in his right eye and partly blinded him. We then called it off and went back to our boats. Don't let anyone tell you that you can't see stars; I saw thousands of them that day. The very next day Big Bill fell overboard while wheeling coal. He became exhausted when only 10 feet from shore, went down and never came to the surface again.

One day we steamed down the river from Rocheport just before the worst cyclone in history. The wind blew all day just about as hard as I ever saw it, and the little Arethusa bobbed around like a cork. When we got to Gasconade, Capt. Fox said, "Take your boat around into the Gasconade River and tie her up in a safe place. It is getting blacker and blacker, and we are going to have a very bad storm." The storm started below Boonville, Missouri, and went down the south side of the river. When it came close to St. Louis, it broke. What it did to that city, in 1896, is a story in itself.

In 1894 and 1895 we laid up all winter at Cambridge, Missouri, behind a long dike with a big fleet of government equipment. It took 10 men to watch this outfit, and it was my duty to carry the mail each day from some three miles away. My Winchester pump rifle was always with me, and the crew had rabbit, squirrel and quail all winter.

During my years on the river, I have been called everything from a

CHAPTER 3 ≈ CUB PILOT

philosopher to a river rat, as well as some other things not fit to print. But I have never let any such talk affect me in one way or another. Some jealous rivermen have even said that neither my father nor myself could be called real pilots.

In the last days of February, 1895, the ice went out only as it can on the Missouri, but we were all safe behind the dike. Jim Stoddard, our cook, fixed us up a farewell dinner that included a big platter of fried rabbit. He asked our wit, Frenchy Oliver, to ask the blessing. He complied with the following:

We have rabbit hot and cold,
We have rabbit young and old;
We have had rabbit stewed,
We have had rabbit stuffed;
But now, dear Lord,
We've had rabbit enough.

In August of 1939, Steamboat Bill wrote of his pay as a cub pilot.

Some 58 years ago I was working for the Hermann Ferry and Packet Company, at that time owned by my father and a man named Talbot. We were running on the Gasconade River, and my only duties were roustabout, mud clerk, steersman and head deckhand. For these duties I received from Mr. Talbot, at the end of the season, a $6 overcoat. From my father, I received nothing in salary, and during the few Sundays I was at home during the boating season, mother gave me 25 or 50 cents for spending money.

Every chance that came my way, after working an average of 18 hours a day, was devoted to baseball. Dad often said if it was not for baseball that damn boy might amount to something. Today, on some waters of America, I am informed that deckhands who can hardly speak United States receive as much as $185 per month for eight hours of service and overtime for holidays.

Getting back to the old and present times, let me say that from 1894 until 1900 I worked for Uncle Sam on the Missouri River. In those six years I was either master or pilot of boats like the sternwheel Alert and Golden Gate and on the sidewheel towboats Sabrina and Melusina. But most of this time I was master pilot of the famous U.S. sternwheel towboat Arethusa.

We ran with what was called a daylight crew and worked from four o'clock in the morning until eight o'clock at night. The deck crew was composed of three men, at $35 per month each. Lots of nights we came in at nine o'clock, and there was no kick coming when these willing men were asked to work some two hours more to coal up the boat so it could put in a full day tomorrow.

Today, the crew on a government boat works eight hours per day, draws about double the wages we did 40 years ago, and they come home in the fall with enough overtime that they can loaf around all winter. I am writing this to show the two extremes. We used to work too hard and too long, and now we are trying to get by without working. In another 20 years, if the bubble does not burst, nobody will work.

•

In 1894 and 1895 we laid up all winter at Cambridge, Missouri, behind a long dike with a big fleet of government equipment. It took 10 men to watch this outfit, and it was my duty to carry the mail each day from some three miles away. My Winchester pump rifle was always with me, and the crew had rabbit, squirrel and quail all winter.

Going after the mail and hunting did not fully occupy his time, so a writing career was born. It was here that Steamboat Bill wrote his first story, "Wilburn Walton," for the Glasgow Missourian, of which Bill Ruffel was owner and editor.

Steamboat has been writing stories ever since, mostly for *The Waterways Journal*. Our superintendent, John Auld, was a very determined man. Once, when a big barge got caught on a falling river and was balanced on top of a dike, he said, "Bill, we've got to get that barge off there, or Capt. Fox will fire both of us."

So we tried it with the Arethusa and only succeeded in damaging our bitts, tearing off a cavel and breaking up our lines. We were ordered to the U.S. boatyard, 13 miles downstream, to get the damage repaired and to pick up some larger line. I found a half-coil of 3-1/2 inch line, which seemed to me to be satisfactory for our purpose. Returning to the barge, we secured the line on our bitts, capstan and two head cavels. Engineer Hal Danberry had orders to "throw it into her," and we went out under gong. We had about 500 feet to go when we took up the slack. When we did that little boat shook and trembled and

CHAPTER 3 ≈ CUB PILOT

almost turned over, but the barge moved off its perch.

The sudden jolt knocked Johnnie Grimm, one of our deckhands, off the barge into the river. Mr. Auld, who had been sitting on the pilothouse bench, got tangled in the pilot wheel. My uncle, Pete Miller, who was one of the deckhands, said, "If you are going to pull any more stunts like that, let me know, and I'll jump overboard and swim ashore."

Irish Jimmy's cookhouse was a mess, with the floor covered with broken dishes and groceries. He cried out, "When you get down to the office boat, have my money ready. I am after going to quit."

The barge was afloat, and Mr. Auld said we should try not to let Capt. Fox know about it. But somebody snitched. The next day Capt. Fox came aboard. Seeing the big coil of line, he said, "Will, what is that doing on here?"

"Oh, we'll use it to pull off sandbars and stranded equipment."

"Take it down to the boatyard and leave it there," was his instruction. When we unloaded it, Uncle Pete remarked that it was a good thing somebody in that outfit had some sense.

The Arethusa ended her career by turning turtle on the railroad bridge at St. Joseph. Fortunately, Bill Heckmann was not aboard. Capt. Fox lost his life when the steamer Norman turned over below Memphis in 1925. He lies buried in the Glasgow, Missouri, cemetery. Peace to his ashes.

Steamer Royal
Only Steamboat Trip Ever made to Arlington, Mo.
November 2, 1935

In the latter '80s my father made a trip up the Gasconade River with the steamer Royal to Arlington, Missouri, where the Frisco Railroad crosses the Gasconade River. It was my pleasure to be on this trip, the only one ever made by a steamboat above Vienna, Missouri. Steamboats had been running to Vienna for some 10 years, but no boat had ventured above that port. When we did get up in the upper reaches of this river, it seemed we were entering a new world, and we were naturally very excited.

To the good people ashore it meant more, for most of them had never seen a steamboat. We had a heavy load of wagon timber, the river bank was full, and progress was slow up this swift stream. We could see the people crossing the side bottom fields and taking short cuts through the woods to head off and get a look at the boat. Whoever was on watch, the Dutch captain or his cub pilot, their feet were on the big whistle treadle at intervals of every half hour.

At lots of places we would see 100 people viewing the old boat. She was not much of a boat among the floating palaces on the lower Mississippi at that time, but up this little stream, to these people, our staunch Royal seemed colossal. Some of these good folks would follow the boat for miles along the bank, and at one place a boy and a big fat girl followed us for three miles, shoving vines aside, knocking down brush piles and skipping through the underbrush, overcoming all obstacles until they came to a large stream where they could not wade and it was too cold to swim. To me this picture is still in my mind. I often wonder what became of that boy and the big fat, red-cheeked girl. Hope they are still living and can see their beautiful little river rolling along.

Strength was prized, and roustabouts, black and white, were constantly in competition. Steamboat Bill wrote the story "Three Strong Men" in March, 1931.

One fine morning we landed at Portland, where an elderly man had a wagon and team of white mules. On the spring seat beside him, perched away up in the air, was a beautiful girl. He wanted his outfit ferried over to Chamois, Missouri, four miles up the good old river. The wagon was loaded with an old-style walnut cupboard, a monstrous big cook stove, a six holer and an old-style oak trunk, locked with a big iron lock for keeps.

The bank was very steep and slick from a late rain. Old Rough Head, the captain, said to me, "Go out and unload that wagon, unhitch them mules, get a line and snub that wagon down the bank; them jugheads can't come down that bank with that load." After I got one good look at that gal I told the boys to put that cupboard on my back and I would tote it down on the boat. The path was now lined with cinders from the boat's ash pan. To this the girl objected, saying it had to be handled carefully and that there was no man living that could carry such a load.

Knowing we had some strong men on the old Royal and knowing it was the lightest of the three pieces on the wagon, I took first choice

CHAPTER 3 ≈ CUB PILOT

and without any effort carried this cupboard down to the head of the boat, where they eased it off my back safely onto the deck. The fireman, seeing the girl all aflutter and praising my strength, came out on the bank with us and said: "I'll carry that stove aboard. Put her on my shoulder and back."

Here the man spoke up and claimed it could not be done. The fireman was an elderly man, a short, stocky-built man, with powerful strength, so the old cook stove went down the bank and on the boat on his shoulder. This good man later drowned off the U.S. steamer Arethusa, just above the Chamois Landing. In the joys I have seen along our rivers, some sadness has come. The memory of seeing this good old friend drown, without being able to render any assistance, has been with me always, a never-to-be-forgotten loss.

We had now got to the strongbox, the treasure chest, the last package locked and laden with something heavy indeed. Into the picture now stepped my old partner, mentioned before in some of my stories, Obediah Bledsoe, the big, tall, handsome giant. "Put that box on my back; that boy and old man have only been carrying chicken feed. Watch Obediah."

Here the captain of the wagon came down and objected, saying it took eight men over in Indiana to put that chest in the wagon. The girl was bobbing up and down on that spring seat, laughing and clapping her hands and saying, "Oh, what fine big strong men!" The little man now developed into a conscientious objector and was delaying the show, saying, among other things, that the box dare not be dropped. Bledsoe gave him a push with one of his big paws, and he staggered off to one side and out of the way. This seemed to tickle the girl more than anything we had done this far.

It took all of us, except Old Roughhead, to get this package on Bledsoe's back, and he carried it aboard without any apparent effort at all. I have seen this man carry many big loads, but never anything heavier than that treasure chest.

Times were slack on the river that season, and three of our old roustabouts were standing out on the bank watching this performance of strength. Marshall Harris, a big, wide-shouldered man, built low to the ground, stepped up saying, "Them white folks ain't so hot. I carry the wagon." Big George Jackson, with the help of Eli Perkins, another big man, offered to carry the mules aboard.

Old Roughhead cried out, "This farce has gone far enough. Roll the wagon and let them mules walk." Dad would have been out there himself; he liked to show off, too, but he now had a bay window, and his star as a strong man had then already set. We had been running the little old boat early and late, so Dad turned the wheel over to me and went back in the cabin to take a nap.

Big Obediah, always out for a lark, had no trouble enticing the girl up into the pilothouse. Both of us were sold to this beautiful creature. The Royal, not a very fast boat, soon had covered the four miles upriver to Chamois. Still our personal progress was fast, and when we landed at that place, we had that couple's history. We also had that girl ready to leave her kidnapper, and had her hired as a cook on our boat.

She told us she had run away from a good home in Indiana with that man. He had promised her, when they got to Camden County, in Missouri, he would open the strongbox and dazzle her eyes with the treasure it contained. She would never want if she would then marry him. It seemed she was now tired of her bargain, of him, and of the trip. Nobody ever acted more sensible or innocent than this girl.

When we got the old man and his outfit up on the bank, he yelled, "Come on Margaret; we are ready to go."

"Go yourself; I have gone far enough and am staying right here," she said.

All might have gone well, or perhaps worse, but about this time Dad woke up and came into the pilothouse. "What does this mean, and what are you waiting for? What is this girl doing here?"

Obediah had now deserted us. The girl, in her innocence, said sweetly, "I am going to stay here and cook for you. Show me the kitchen, and I will do the rest." Dad said, "No, you are too good-looking to cook on this boat. Get out there to your father, you are delaying this boat."

"That is not my father," she said. "I'll have you understand I am good enough to cook or do anything for your boys, but you are the boss, and I will obey, but please give me your address. I will fulfill my contract with that piece of a man out there, and if that box is not full of treasures, I'm coming back to throw myself on your mercy and strength. God knows I can never go back home now."

CHAPTER 3 ≈ CUB PILOT

Dad gave her our address. This she put into her bosom, down next to her heart. She left that boat crying, never to be seen again. My father was a good old sport, and I am satisfied if he had heard all of this girl's story that old man would have left without his girl.

Funny things happen along our rivers. In the time of less than two hours this girl's light heart turned to sorrow, and she left some sadness on that old boat. Youth's adventures make us ponder as the years roll by.

The work of a roustabout was never done. All boats burned fuel, and in the early days this was wood. It took enormous quantities of wood to keep a steamer running.

Making a Woodpile
June 24, 1950

Now let's see what old Steamboat knows about cordwood, which should be a lot, for my father and myself handled or burned some 100,000 cords of wood in our time on the river. When the old packet boats laid at the bank, loading or unloading freight, in some way or other the money was coming in. But when they landed to load wood for fuel, they were losing time and paying out money. For this reason, a mate that could not make a woodpile in a hurry was not wanted, and the poor roustabouts that loaded this wood were abused, humiliated, cussed and whipped to see how fast this wood could come aboard. A master would never say, "We will load or take some wood" at some designated place, but would say, "We are going to make a woodpile, and I want to make it quick."

One mate had a reputation as a bad man, and was especially mean when making a woodpile. He did not let his men stop at a rank to put the wood on their shoulder a piece at a time, but he stood at the end of the stage and the trotting or running roustabouts in an endless chain would pass by the woodpile and make a grab of three or four sticks at a time, and they were on their way. He would address them in very strong language, and say, "Give me the wood, and if you can't get the wood, give me the bark." And they sure had to bring something and bring it quick.

A Missouri River mate by the name of Dick (Windy Dick) Norris could make more noise at a woodpile than any other mate that ever came up the river. John Winn or Alex Shay would not say much, but the wood would come in much faster. Just as they say, "Still is the water where the brook is deep." Leroy Cook of Chicago tells me the steamer Eclipse burned 100 cords of wood in 24 hours, but when you figure wood at less than two dollars a cord, she was cheap on fuel at that, and that Old Baby was so fast that she should be a long way up the river in 24 hours.

When my father first commenced to deliver wood to the Jefferson City Penitentiary, they loaded the wood aboard on their shoulders, and my father allowed his men to stop at the pile and put all they could carry on their shoulders. In his time he had three white men that could carry 24 sticks of hardwood or 36 sticks of dry cottonwood, just as it came off the pile. Thirty six sticks of wood is almost one-quarter of a cord, and it seems unbelievable that this had been done. We never found a colored man that could do this, although we offered 25 dollars in gold to any that could do this stunt. Later, when we got more scientific, we used wheelbarrows. If the old packet boats come back, we may have atomic wheels on same. About the largest wood yards on the Missouri River were on Bates' (Rush) Island and on Dodd's Island. Both Bates and Dodds became wealthy in this business. They owned barges and kept them loaded with wood. The boats would pick them up, and when unloaded, several men would float them back for more wood for the next boat that came along.

Charles D. Eitzen and my father were the two biggest men in Hermann after the Civil War. They were neighbors and enemies and lived on Wharf Street. Eitzen, as the old steamboat agent, wanted room on the levee to store freight. Dad needed the same room for cordwood for the flour mill, the two brickyards and for the Hermann public.

At Portland, Missouri, a man by the name of Macon charged 10 cents a cord for piling or ricking. He was an expert, and when he got through piling up a cord of wood, you could throw your hat through the cracks. Wood piled up this way would not have sold at a way-landing, but the merchants and big shippers bought this wood from the farmers and sold it to the steamboats. Portland was a big shipping point, and the boat that did not buy some wood did not get much freight.

On the upper Missouri River they had what they called wood hawks.

CHAPTER 3 ≈ CUB PILOT

Some were Indians. They went up on the old boats for the sole purpose of cutting wood for the steamboats. I have often wondered if these so-called wood hawks operated on other rivers. (Let's turn this question over to Capt. Fred Way Jr., the Ohio River historian.) Perhaps the cheapest and best cordwood ever sold was cut on the banks of the picturesque Osage River. The finest hickory, hill white oak and ash was only $1.25 a cord. A cord of this kind of wood was equal to more than a ton of coal. Most of the firemen on our boats refused to use sassafras wood, claiming it was unlucky and led to disaster.

Loading cordwood at the Hermann landing

One of the last and largest timber movements and destruction of forests around here happened at the Aux Vasse River, 25 miles below Jefferson City. The steamer Gasconade in the spring of 1901, took 60,000 railroad ties, 1,500 cords of wood and 500,000 feet of lumber out of this little river to Jefferson City. The wood and lumber went to the penitentiary, and the ties were loaded in boxcars at Cedar City.

One could write for days about cordwood, but if you really want a red-hot fire under your kettles and plenty of fog, gather up some pine knots off the slopes of the Ozark hills on the upper White River and put them in your furnace. The steamer Kennedy, a two-boiler boat, was one of the hardest boats to fire on Western Rivers, but she was plenty fast. In fact, she was one of the fastest small boats that ever turned a wheel. While on the upper White River the fireman filled the furnace full of pine knots. She ran up the river two miles and laid up for the night, and the engineer spent several hours cooling her down, from that one application of pine knots. He said, "I never pumped so much water in two boilers in my life. That fog buster must be crazy."

The Heckmann men, even Steamboat Bill, loved to take a dig at education and seldom missed an opportunity to do so. Excerpts from "Heckmann's Way," published January 22, 1944, illustrate:

One of the most noted passengers that ever rode on a boat with me was from the University of Yale. Early one morning he came up in the pilothouse, and he was all excited. We were, and were supposed to be, going downstream. The fast steamer Lora was stepping down a big river full of drift at better than 20 miles an hour. He insisted, and wanted to bet, we were running upstream because the drift was coming toward us. Further down the river he spied a big house some hermit or nut had built up in a big tree. "How did that house get there, Captain?"

"It lodged there in the 1881 flood."

Now the house was at least one-fourth of a mile above the river bank. His reply to this was, "Well, well, I never thought this river got that high."

After he swallowed that one like a hungry crappie swallows a Missouri River shiner in Chariott Creek (when the big scattered rain drops fell in April), this old man thought to himself, "I am really glad my father yanked me out of school before becoming a professor."

It did not take a college education to load a bull, an occupation even a college professor probably could not have improved on. In "Heckmann's Way" Steamboat Bill tells one story of a boat and a bull.

Your story of the big bull brings back memories of Charley Cook's Sandy Hook bull, which the steamer W. H. Grapevine transported from Sandy Hook Landing to St. Louis, some 160 miles downriver. We loaded this bull one trip at Sandy Hook without much trouble. The stockyards there were full of shippers, sightseers, roustabouts, passengers, hogs, cattle and calves. The old boat was headed square into the bank, and her stern was away out in the river.

We had no trouble loading this bull, but for some reason his majesty did not like his surroundings. He broke the ropes, knocked down the bull rails and executed a perfect head dive into the big river. He went clear to the bottom and stayed down there so long we thought he would never appear alive again. But this was not to be, for up the bank he came, snorting, bellowing and spitting mud, water, blood and corruption out of his nose and mouth.

When he got to shore and secured a good foothold, he decided to go back up through the stockyards and on back home. As he went through gates, fences and the middle of the stock pens, no one ever witnessed such a scatterment of men and beasts. The last we saw of him, he was flapping his tail and went up over the hill towards home.

On our next weekly trip down, we landed at Sandy Hook, and Charlie Cook said, "Well, Cap, we have the bull here again; you had better tie him up better this time."

Again, the old boy did not object much to being loaded, and when we backed out from the landing after night had come, all seemed well. But we had hardly got turned around and straightened out down the river when a deckhand came running up on the roof and said the big bull jumped overboard.

We turned the old lugger around, switched the headlight on and located the big fellow swimming toward a cutting bank. He had some trouble finding a place to get up the bank, and in the meantime, we had landed the boat. My brother, Fred Heckmann, and three husky roustabouts were waiting for him. When he climbed the bank with two big ropes still fastened to his legs, they grabbed them, and the race was on.

Mr. Bull, with these four husky men hanging to the ropes, started on through the bottom and the hills towards home. With the big headlight playing on this group, red, white, black and yellow, they made a weird sight, indeed, in a nasty black night. Soon another headlight appeared on the scene and a fast Missouri Pacific train came busting along. Mr. Bull paid no attention, but crossed the track in front of the engine by inches and, of course, the men holding the ropes had to let go. After the train passed, the bull was out of sight and on his way back home, unmolested.

Our third trip down, the old boy was again ready for passage, and this time he had a ring in his nose. We put a rope on each foot or leg and tied him five different ways to put him in the stockyards at St. Louis. This mammoth specimen of bullhood weighed 2,480 pounds. A St. Louis butcher bought him, put him on exhibition and took in a small pile of dimes before turning him into sausage.

William Lewis Heckmann Jr. at age 16. "A lady killer, but he did not know it," said Steamboat Bill of this photo.

CHAPTER 4

Return to Childhood Haunts

Young Will Heckmann remained homesick for his boyhood home, returning there off and on as long as his pal, Uncle Pete Miller, lived. He wrote often of these visits.

While we lived in Hermann, every chance we got we would go up to Bluffton for a visit. To go to see Grandpa and Grandma Miller was one of the greatest pleasures and enjoyments of our lives. Grandpa Miller was a great host and entertainer, but among the boys, Pete was even more so. In the hollow of his bones there was no marrow, but this place was filled with hospitality. Whenever anybody from Sedalia, Rhineland or Hermann came on a visit, business stopped as far as Uncle Pete was concerned, and the hunting and fishing expeditions were on.

Time went on, and we became older. Pete married Ida Monnig, but as far as Wee Willie, now known as Steamboat Bill, was concerned, our relations became closer and stronger. Pete worked with us two seasons on the steamers Gasconade and Arethusa. About this time, Pete and I were some of the best skaters, oarsmen and swimmers along this part of the Missouri River.

We were pretty good shots with firearms but were outclassed by the Mosley brothers, Arett and Carl. (Arett Mosley was to marry the second youngest Miller girl, Alice, one of my childhood companions.) Brothers Fred and Johnny Heckmann, too, could outshoot us, especially with a rifle. Now, all these characters are gone to the Happy Hunting Grounds, and only Steamboat Bill is left to tell these tales. Our stories still go on, but like everything else, will someday come to an end.

•

Along about 1891, the Missouri River froze over tight, and along came a very deep snow. Then on top of this came a freezing rain and bitter cold weather. Everything, everywhere you went, even our old river, was as slick as glass. Will Heckmann Jr. was now a grown man, just turned 22, and he had a world of confidence in himself.

Early one morning at Hermann, he strapped on his skates, picked up his gun and was on his way to Bluffton, 12 miles upstream on the Missouri river. He skated right up the middle of the river to the town. After greeting the folks there, he was not satisfied and decided to skate *up* Montgomery Hill to Uncle Bob and sister Tina's. He stayed there for dinner, but did not take off his skates. When Uncle Bob asked him to do this, his reply was, "Oh, it ain't worthwhile. I am going to skate down the hill." This brought forth a protest from both my uncle and sister. Bob said, "Nobody but a fool would undertake this."

Along about two o'clock in the afternoon, the downward descent was on, and believe me, it was one of the greatest mistakes of my life. It was more than a mile to the foot of the hill. All went well over the first downward hump of the hill. A big gate was open when the mighty man went through at about 30 miles an hour. He then struck a cornfield with high ridges in it and fell down.

After that he went humpty-dumpty over the ridges to go through a rotten rail fence into the steepest hill, where there was a lot of big standing timber. He bumped from one tree to another and was mighty soon down on some level bottom in Lora Dora Creek. Here another big tree stopped his progress. With every effort he had in his system and the help of the good Lord, he was able to get on his feet again.

He was battered and torn, but no bones were broken, so he skated over to the Miller house and told his story, as he took off his all-too-trusted skates. Uncle Pete said, "You have accomplished something that will never be done again, and I am proud of my old partner."

Grandma Miller patched me up in good shape, and along towards evening a flock of about 300 wild geese lit alongside of an air hole in front of Bluffton. Uncle Pete said, "Do you see them? It is too bad you can't go along."

I snapped, "What do you mean I can't go along? You get your expedition ready, and we will see about me going along."

Pete answered, "All right, I have a plan that I have had in mind for several years, and we will try it out tonight."

Just before dark a young man by the name of Graber showed up and

CHAPTER 4 ≈ RETURN TO CHILDHOOD HAUNTS

said that he wanted to go along, too. "All right," we said. "Be here right after supper."

Uncle Pete borrowed Grandma's big dishpan and fastened a lantern inside of same. We put on heavy woolen socks over our shoes so we would not make any noise or slip on the ice-covered snow. With a pocket full of matches, we were ready to go. We walked up the river about a quarter of a mile above the geese. As luck would have it, there was a slight wind blowing from the east. We lit our lantern. Uncle Pete took same and got in the middle. Then, three abreast, we walked down towards the geese. Our captain's orders were, "When I count three, fire, and no sooner."

Our gleam was not too bright, and after walking quite a distance, the birds commenced some kind of a conversation among themselves, which, too, was in our favor. We hit the head of the air hole just right, and going down the north side of the air hole, it was not too long until we saw a big black streak ahead of us. These geese were still chattering among themselves.

Uncle Pete said, "One, two, three!" All three of our guns went off like one shot. The lantern was blown out, and we were in darkness. We fired three more shots; then holding hands, one of us got out to the edge of the air hole, and picked up three geese. We knew we had killed more but decided we would wait until morning to pick them up. Poking around an air hole on the Missouri River is a dangerous operation after dark.

The next morning, at daybreak, we met near the bend of the air hole. Ed Graber had a big gander he found coming from home. We looked down to the lower end of the swift water and saw a lot of black spots, which proved to be geese. Uncle Pete said, "These are crippled, and no one knows how many dead geese were sucked under the ice." The man substituting for Uncle Pete, carrying mail, found a goose on his route. We now had 11 geese accounted for.

We went home with our kill, ate a big dinner, and then I started back home on my skates with four geese. Some distance below the air hole there was a black spot that proved to be the largest goose of our killing. Going just a little further, another black spot over towards the north shore proved to be another Canadian Honker.

Let me tell you, pardner, six big geese proved to be quite a load on skates, and Will Heckmann decided to take the evening train from Gasconade to Hermann, seven miles downstream. When boarding the train, I bumped into a lady who apparently did not really like geese, especially dead ones. The hard-boiled conductor yelled at me, "Get out of the way of that lady with your ganders." Not being in a good humor I yelled back, "If you will just keep your big mouth shut, you can have one of the ganders."

He took same, saying, "You look pretty well bunged up already, and for that reason I will take it home with me instead of wrapping it around your neck."

•

The older Miller boys did quite a lot of trapping and caught a number of beavers. The largest specimen of this kind that they caught weighed 70 pounds. In 1872 the upper island out from just below Bluffton was known as the Bluffton Island. Beaver Chute ran between Bluffton Island and Holschlag Island. Along about 1875, this chute filled up and these two islands became one body of land, some 900 acres. Dad homesteaded the Bluffton Island and then bought the Holschlag Island. Then this large island was and still is known as the Heckmann Island. Many beavers were caught in Beaver Chute, hence the name.

Steamboat Bill later disputed an article in the Missouri Conservationist, claiming credit for re-establishing the beaver from releasing a pair into the Meramec River in Dent County, Missouri. He said if John Coulters, who stayed behind to trap after Lewis and Clark left the headwaters of the Missouri River, could travel 2,000 miles to St. Louis in an Indian dugout canoe in 30 days, fast-swimming beavers could certainly make the trip.

A beaver could have made a trip of this kind, for he is no slouch when it comes to paddling his own canoe. There is no doubt that the beaver has made a real comeback, and the Conservation Commission deserves a lot of credit for their help in this survival, for the beavers have come back almost as fast as (when conditions are right) ticks on an old cow.

•

On one of my visits up to see Uncle Pete, he invited me to go up to Pea Ridge, saying that this is one place we have never been. What possessed Grandpop Miller to add this strip of land to his collection of

CHAPTER 4 ≈ RETURN TO CHILDHOOD HAUNTS

mountain possessions, we do not know, but it has been said that he raised peas on that barren ridge the size of our average cherries.

When we got to No Man's Land, we sat down on a rock and ate our lunch. Uncle Pete unburdened himself by saying, "It is questionable if my father ever added this God-forsaken place to his possession, and what if he did raise peas here as big as radishes? That did not mean anything. If they had been as big as pumpkins, he could never have done anything with them. This place is about as far from nowhere as a human being can get. They say God has put everything here for a purpose. Let's go home; we have seen it all. No, let's wait to see those buzzards fly over and see what they think about it. A Bald Eagle would never light here, and a coyote could not dig a hole in these rocks."

Eventually the river ensnared Pete Miller, as well as the Heckmann men.

Infringing on Uncle Bob's patent, Uncle Pete Miller built a sidewheel, gas-powered boat. He had better material and workmanship, and this little sidewheeler was quite a success. His longest trip was from Bluffton on the Missouri River to Arlington, Missouri, some 100 miles up the Gasconade River. Friends with him on this trip had a wonderful time hunting and fishing and entertaining the natives and fishermen on the upper stretches along this scenic little river.

CHAPTER 5

Romance

From all reports, Will Heckmann Sr., came into the world with enormous personal magnetism and a great talent for using that charm. His namesake son was tall and handsome but lacked his father's talent for impressing the ladies. In Steamboat Bill's copious writings, he often refers to his inordinate shyness. He never wrote about any conquests, only about abysmal failures with the fair sex. Even as a little boy, he was already the target of the feminine wiles.

When Wee Willie was about 10 years old, just before the move to Hermann, the Miller family was trying to run the hotel at Bluffton. Mother Miller had a 17-year-old hired girl to help out. This young lady was wise beyond her years. Willie was not, but he was large beyond his years.

She had been raised by a German family, and her talk was interesting and cute. She took a shine to young Bill, and this bashful character was too young to understand her ways or intentions. One day when the wagons were loading peaches, we all went up on the hill to help load a caravan of peaches. For lack of help, Grandpa Miller had let the grass grow high and handsome in his peach orchard on Hussman's Hill.

The hired girl would get away from the crowd and holler, "Oh, Willie, here are pretty peaches." She kept this up until everybody but the writer knew that she wanted to make love to young Bill. He, the bashful kid, did not find this out until years later. But as long as he remained in Bluffton, he heard his Miller relatives giggle and call, "Willie, here are pretty peaches."

Young Bill's bashfulness did not improve much in the early years in Hermann. About 1882, at the age of 12 or 13, Bill left school to go with his father on the steamboats to "learn the river." As such he was cook, roustabout, fireman and, finally, a cub pilot.

CHAPTER 5 ≈ ROMANCE

Young Love

In the spring of 1883, dad was in charge of the steamer Vienna, running up into the foothills of the Ozarks on the beautiful Gasconade River. I, at 14 years of age, was cub pilot on one of our first upstream trips. We landed at Fredericksburg, Missouri, one evening. The sky overhead was dark. Continued lightning flashes and crashes of thunder promised a storm as we tied the trim little craft securely to the bank.

The store and warehousekeeper at Fredericksburg said, "Say, Captain, my niece is up at the house on a visit from the East and would like to ride up to Kilpatrick's Landing with you."

Dad replied, "Well, Ed, I would like to accommodate you, but we will get to that landing in the night. We have no empty bunks, and it looks like we are going to have a pretty bad storm." To which Ed replied that the young lady had no other way to get up the river and that he would trust her to our care, storm or no storm.

"Well," said dad, "if she goes along, she will have to ride almost all night in the pilothouse. How old is she? And is she good looking?"

"She's about the age of your boy there. I'll leave her looks to Bill," responded Ed.

A bit later the young lady came aboard without any maids, no barge with golden oars, but with all the fashions of the East and other accouterments that made the sweetest picture my 14-year-old eyes had ever seen. She took her seat on the pilothouse bench, and she and the cub pilot used what daylight was left to cast shy glances at one another.

The Gasconade is not very wide, perhaps 300 feet at its widest stretches, but it was never too dark for "Old Rough Head" and his cub to run upstream. We put a torch on each side of the boat forward of the engine room so we could see the outline of each shore, and the old Vienna paddled along without any navigation difficulties.

With the rain pelting the pilothouse sash, the coal fire in the stove crackled and cracked. The old tiller rope rattled in the sheaves. A romantic setting, indeed, for this bashful boy and girl! The night wore on; midnight came in its inky blackness, and still the flood poured down. Dad, the old salt, offered no help at steering the boat or entertaining the girl. Whether he was "pounding his ear" or staying away from the pilothouse through design has never been discovered.

Past midnight, speech had not come to either of us. Along about one o'clock in the morning we rounded Butcher's Bluff. A catamount let out a weird cry from one of the river bluffs, and the girl began to cry softly. A bit later a horned owl out the port side of the river saluted us with a greeting, "Who, who, who are you?" We gave no answer, but watching her tears fall, called sympathetic tears from my eyes.

From then on for three hours, we took turns at letting the tears fall with the pelting rain, yet not a spoken word came to our spellbound lips. We were now nearing the landing where this creature, who grew momentarily more fair, was to leave the boat. The dark hour before dawn was approaching, and our parting, for me at least, loomed even darker. I have often wondered what might have been if this had been a moonlight night, or even a starlit one—surely the moon in its fullness or the falling stars would have loosened speech instead of tears!

The landing whistle now sounded, and as we swung into Kilpatrick's Landing, the Dutch captain, always dutiful and a favorite among his passengers, crew and skippers, came into the pilothouse and said, "We will lay up here until daylight. Get a raincoat for this young lady, and you and Johnny Bowers take the girl home. It's a mile through the bottomlands and swamps. See that she does not get her feet wet, and get back as soon as you can."

On occasions like this, Fortune generally furnishes a character to do justice to the undertaking. Big Obediah Bledsoe stepped up and said, "Captain, I will take the girl home. That redheaded fireman does not know the way, and besides he let the last girl fall into the river when he tried to help her over the stage plank. We will take young Will along. It will be good for his heartburn." The big giant made good his words.

In going through the lonesome swamp, we heard the lone cry of the loon. The raccoons were having a frolic, and no noise sounds queerer than this in the tail end of a rainy night. Through swollen branches and miniature ponds from the all-night rain we tramped. The girl, high and dry, in Obediah's arms, was as talkative as a Havana parrot. But she only talked to the big boy, and the cub pilot was left clean out of the picture.

When we set her down on her own front porch at the house that stood on a hillside, daylight was breaking through. A few stars had shiningly opened the heavens to stop the rain. In her own simple way

CHAPTER 5 ≈ ROMANCE

she thanked Big Obe for bringing her home. As she turned into the house she said, "Come to see me before I go back home. Both of you."

For the cub pilot this vision had vanished for life, as he never saw Sally again. Obediah paid the princess one visit. On his return, an elaborately unconcerned boy found the big, good-natured Obe on the head of a barge away from the gossiping crew.

"What kind of a visit did you have Obe?"

"Nothing much. She didn't seem to like me in my store clothes. That gal is in love with you, boy. Buck up and get over the bashful stage. All that magpie talked about was you. If you do not go to see her, she will die of a broken heart. I knew all the time that she did not care for me, but if I had put her in your arms in that flooded wildwood, you would have let her fall into the water, and your dad would have run us ragged. From now on that gal belongs to you as far as I am concerned."

Nothing is more wonderful than bashful love, but by the time the cub pilot had mustered up courage to pay a visit to his vision, she had gone back to the shores that are washed by the salt water of the Atlantic Ocean. Obediah raved; I mourned and, secretly, wept. But the tears did not wash away the bashfulness of 14.

The advice of my big friend was to work hard, save my money and visit the girl when the winter's blasts had frozen our rivers and the old Vienna was taking a rest. It was wonderful advice for a boy who worked hard all that year on the river for the price of an overcoat!

The following winter the Old Dutch Captain had invited himself up on the Gasconade River to see a family named Winterbottom. The head of the house owned a mighty fine pack of deerhounds. Dad managed to put in at the best stands and killed three fine deer during his visit. Consequently, he was feeling expansive. Among the many promises he made was one to the 16-year-old daughter of the family that he would introduce her to his big son, Bill, when the boat landed in the spring.

The very first trip next season, we were landed at Rich Fountain Slough loading wheat when a girl appeared on the opposite side of the river and asked to be crossed over as she had a basket of eggs to sell. Dad sent me over with the boat's yawl, and in silence we paddled across Ole Man River.

She was a comely miss, the picture of radiant health. Even as one can often see sunsets on our rivers that no artist can paint, this girl's lips and cheeks were the color no cosmetics can simulate. Unlike the other girl, she had no silences but, instead, a most wonderful gift of gab.

After disposing of the eggs, she asked the Dutch Captain to introduce us, which he got out of by saying, "If you two cannot get acquainted by crossing the river twice in a skiff, your case is hopeless."

She replied, "Well, if he is going to take me back, I'll do my part." She did. Her tongue tapped her best thoughts to drag the cub pilot into conversation, but she had no luck. The oarsman was deaf, dumb and blind so far as she was concerned. He had payday and a trip east on his mind. She stepped out of the skiff to the banks of the river all ruffled up in anger, saying, "I know what's the matter! Your Dad thinks I'm not good enough for you! Wait until I see that old Dutch Captain again! I'll tell him something!" Later she made good her threat, and the senior Heckmann had to look for new deer-hunting grounds.

After this maiden's visit Dad asked, "Will, why is it that you do not like the Winterbottom girl? Her Dad lives in the heart of the hunting woods, he has some of the best dogs I ever saw. They are nice people, and the girl is a peach. Besides, she will make a fine summer girl for you." But the cub couldn't stir up any enthusiasm, in spite of all her father's possessions, so he just hung his head without answering.

It was not until eight years later that the cub pilot found a really great partner to go with him down the stream of life. And he picked her himself!

•

Steamboat Bill is always writing about himself, so you might as well listen to his courtship days. His first four girls were brunettes, and the next two were redheads. Then Steamboat Bill and a cowboy chartered two Texas ponies and rode out in the country about five miles back of Hermann, Missouri, where they met two real blondes. One of these girls is still going down life's pathway with Steamboat Bill. He has made thousands of mistakes in his life, but here old Steamboat hit the jackpot.

The local newspaper noted the event by acknowledging a gift.

One of our most esteemed ladies, Mrs. Will L. Heckmann, brought a large piece of wedding cake to the A-C office. This was from the wed-

CHAPTER 5 ≈ ROMANCE

Newlyweds Bill and Annie Heckmann, setting off "down the stream of life."

ding of her son Will Jr. to Annie Buddemeyer. This event took place at the Heckmann home on December 29, 1892. Our thanks and best wishes for the happy bride and groom.

Steamboat Bill could never pass up the opportunity to doctor a story. These might be called Whoppers, but the author put these fits of creativity down to Spontaneous Combustion!

Now let's say something about one of my girls, a brunette, who was rightly nicknamed "Long Annie." How Barnum ever missed her or how Young Bill ever fell for her will remain a marine mystery.

Like the White Eagle, she was all out of proportion. She weighed less than 100 pounds, was short-waisted and had the longest set of legs Young Bill ever saw hooked to a female human body. Her feet were all out of proportion. Bill's own height at that time was just short of 6 feet. But when she stood alongside of him her hips were at his shoulders. Her height and her big feet would have made a hit in any side show.

But she was pretty, witty and smart. Your body does not make your mind, and if the writer ever did or said anything to lighten her burden, this is one thing for which he should receive credit.

For more than 60 years, Annie walked life's pathway with her big husband, Steamboat Bill. Tiny, no beauty, a great cook, at times downright acid, Annie was a loyal wife and mother of the four Heckmann children. Annie's great gift was that she was an astute business woman who could handle money. All four Heckmann children went to college. Three daughters attended Normal School to obtain life teaching certificates. Son Rodney went to Elmhurst for four years and then Eden Seminary for three years to be ordained as a minister in the Evangelical Church.

Annie was a devoted daughter-in-law; she enjoyed Mary Heckmann's company. Both women shared a great joy in their flowers and gardens. Mary had her 14th child at the same time as Annie was having her first.

But Annie's fondness for Mary did not blind her to the fact that Will Sr. immediately started "borrowing" money from her husband. She deplored her father-in-law's casual approach to money. When the sum reached $5,000—a great sum for newlyweds just getting started—Annie demanded and received signed notes, securing the debt with the senior Heckmann's home.

The Heckmann family owned a home on West Second Street in Hermann. The property included a block-long vineyard. Will and Annie bought a lot and built their house, which still stands today, on the southeast corner of the vineyard.

When her father-in-law died, Annie did not hesitate to claim the property. It was all honest and above board, but the foreclosure became a sore spot in the family. After this debacle, Mary Heckmann packed up her considerable brood and moved to St. Louis, with no real comprehension as to what she would use for money.

At first, she felt rich. She had $3,000 from an insurance policy. But after buying a house, new furniture and a new piano, she was stumped as to what to

CHAPTER 5 ≈ ROMANCE

use for the daily living expenses. She had a difficult time adjusting to paying for things. Before impulsively moving to St. Louis, water and wood had been free. A garden had supplied vegetables, chickens produced eggs and meat, the old cow produced milk and butter, the men of the family were avid fishermen and hunters, and the farm supplied fresh pork. Apparently, it never occurred to Mary these things now would cost money.

Three of the big Heckmann sons were married and contributed nothing to the mother and her brood. The two married daughters were having a hard time keeping afloat financially. The resident girls all tried to earn money, but the world was really not ready for the working woman.

Son Rodney inherited his father's strong profile.

Martha, widowed and with a little daughter to raise, sold corsets and sewed for the entire family. Lizzie occasionally went to help out in homes as a housekeeper. Mary, the giddy teenager, went to high school and took lessons on the piano and kept the house brimful with her friends.

Bill and Annie remained aloof from the family. But Annie lost no time in taking possession of the Heckmann home place and eventually reselling it.

Disaster was not unknown to Bill and Annie. Their youngest daughter was the apple of their eyes. Gladys taught at Syracuse, Missouri, where she met the man she married. Gladys Heckmann Carpenter, pregnant and despondent, died before her baby could be born. The parents shared their grief, and after a short while her father wrote an article for the local paper.

Mrs. Verner F. Carpenter
Hermann, Mo. Nov. 20, 1920

Time, the divine healer, has eased my sorrow to where I can write about our girl that died.

Some years ago, our third and youngest daughter came to us here in Hermann. She was christened Gladys Marie. She graduated with honors from public high school here; was confirmed and became a member of the Evangelical Church. One year of her life was spent at the Warrensburg Normal, and she taught school one term at Syracuse, Missouri.

In October 1919, Mr. Verner F. Carpenter, of Smithton, Missouri, claimed her for his wife. They lived in happiness one short year, and then death entered their home.

In our home here as just ordinary well-to-do people, our girl had everything that youth and life could ask for. In her beautiful home at Smithton, she fared the same. The many friends she made in this beautiful little hamlet of some 400 people and in that community for miles around loved and respected her for her beauty, sterling qualities and her work. Her parents, sisters, brother and husband idolized her. Every day and hour of her life since she went to Smithton was spent in preparing her home, her garden and everything the young couple had for the bountiful years that were to come.

Up until the last minute of her life, her actions never showed anything except that she was as happy as anyone could be who expected to become a mother in about four months. Our Gladys was a beautiful girl, and in her short life every minute had been crowded with happiness; she loved outdoor life, could row a skiff, was a fast and graceful skater, was at home in the water, a good musician and an unusually expert basketball player.

On Sunday, November 7, 1920, the second anniversary of the time she had the flu, when her life for days hung by a thread, Gladys became quiet and not just like herself. She had taken in her last flowers and bulbs from the garden she loved so well. The early severe weather had caused the leaves to fall more quickly than other years; her lawn was carpeted with dead and dry leaves; everything she loved in nature's home was dead or dying. It had been a dreary, dark day, and towards evening she asked her husband to take a walk while she prepared supper. When he returned a half hour later, his sweetheart was lying in bed gasping for breath.

He that giveth and taketh life, never stayed the hand that destroyed our girl just budding into womanhood. But my dear friends, you had to know this girl to feel that he left us here to grieve because they needed another angel in heaven.

Mr. Carpenter is a prominent Mason and the departed was to have

CHAPTER 5 ≈ ROMANCE

been initiated in the Order of Eastern Star in a few days.

The paper further reported:

Letters and reports from Smithton all bespeak a home where love and happiness abide and never a cloud to mar the bright and happy days. On Sunday, the second anniversary of the day that marked the turning point of the occasion when Mrs. Carpenter was critically ill with influenza, Mrs. Carpenter, who was looking forward to motherhood, felt indisposed and seemed very melancholy.

Gladys Heckmann Carpenter

Her husband remained at home with her all day until four o'clock, when she insisted that he, being indoors at the bank every day, take a walk for recreation. Reluctantly, he did so. Returning an hour later, he found his wife in bed, unconscious. The smell of carbolic acid in the room and in the empty glass on a table told the tale. He hastily summoned a physician, but it was too late. She died within a very short time.

She left a note in which she said that she knew what she was about to do was not right but that she simply must do it. All circumstances, the happy home, the happy vein of her letters to her parents, the devotion lavished on her by her husband, the happiness with which she looked forward to motherhood, then the return of the second anniversary of that critical moment of suffering, when during influenza her life hung but by a thread, and with the return of that anniversary, depression and melancholy, point without a doubt to a resulting mental attitude, and unbalancing of the mind, that with a suddenness drove her irresistibly to that awful act.

Whatever went through Will's mind during this trying time, it did not affect his devotion to Annie. After taking her to see the movies "When a Farmer Takes a Wife" and "Steamboat 'Round the Bend" he reported:

Janet Gaynor was the best cook on the old Erie, and glory be to her spunk, she was not afraid to say so. My wonderful wife is too modest to say this, but if a contest in cooking was staged on the river, she would come out the best cook on the Missouri—this with apologies to Capt. Bob Taggert's wife at Marion, Missouri.

On occasion, Will waxed eloquent about other aspects of Annie's character.

Things That Are Sacred
November 5, 1938

In my time on our rivers, there is no one who has had more chances to accumulate things that would interest river fans, and there is no doubt that there is no riverman who has kept or owns fewer of these treasures than I. Boat fixtures, pictures, river books, river and Indian relics, records, models and what not have slipped through my hands like aged liquor goes down a toper's throat.

They always told me a man with small ears was stingy, and my ears are small. But being a pilot overcomes this gift. Coal Oil Johnny had nothing on me when it comes to getting rid of things that to me should be sacred. In the last few years, fishing has been my hobby. Just let me tell you of my trouble around our home with Ma Heckmann.

Ma: "What are you looking for now? You have no fishing tackle in that bookcase. Look out for that looking glass; it is a wedding present from Mrs. Lessel, who died last year at 94. Forty-six years is a long time to keep anything around where you are at."

Dad: "Can I have this old dipper to bail out my johnboat?"

Ma: "I should say not. Capt. Ed Baldwin gave that to our daughter Monica in 1902, and it is about all we have left off the old Grapevine. You have not even got a fixture left of this famous old packet boat."

"Mom, do you remember when our boy Rodney went out and bought us that old tin dipper with a wooden handle for Christmas? Them sure were the good old days."

Ma: "What are you going to do with that knife? Leave it in that machine drawer. It has not left this room since our girl went away in 1920. It was your last Christmas present from Gladys, our dear departed daughter, the girl we dream of, the girl we again expect to see, or, if not, life is not worth our struggle here below."

Ma: "What are you going to do with that anchor?"

Dad: "Use it to anchor our hoop net."

Ma: "Leave it hang right where it is at. Your old friend Ed Roehrig gave you that in 1911 when you were together on the steamer John R. Wells."

Dad: "Can I have this old basket, Mom?"

Ma: "No, absolutely no. That's handmade and the only thing we have to remember Uncle Willie Wild by."

"Can I have this empty sack, Mom?"

"Take it. You have used a thousand in the last 50 years. Sacks cost money now."

Pop: "Times have changed since we were married and all the commission houses were sending out empty sacks gratis by the thousands. Our shed used to be full of them. You remember the stories you used to tell in the old days when women and girls still believed in covering up their shapely limbs. Why, many women and girls along the Missouri, Osage and Gasconade rivers had underwear made of empty grain sacks. You know, Ma, a dress in them days covered a multitude of sins."

Ma: "What are you writing about? River trinkets? Well, do you remember when you refused to pay five dollars for the backing bell out of the engine room of the steamer Boreas II? You pay as much as thirty dollars for an old fish net, but refuse to pay five dollars for a relic worth a small fortune. You are like that fish-eating fellow. He would do nothing but fish and eat nothing but fish. He married a fine young girl and they were married six years and had no children. One day Maggie said, 'Ben, I am going to see a doctor and find out why we cannot have a child.' After the doctor examined her he said: 'If you ever have a child it will be a miracle.' She went back to her man and said, 'Look here, you fish-eating fool, that doctor said if we ever have a baby it will be a mackerel.'"

Along in the early '50s the steamer Boreas II burned up one mile below Hermann, Missouri. She was on her way from the "Mountains" to St. Louis with over a million dollars worth of gold dust in her safes.

≈ STEAMBOAT TREASURES ≈

One man had $90,000 in gold dust that he refused to put in care of the boat's officers. Everybody got off this boat safe and sound but this man, who it has been said burned up in his stateroom without his dust, a black mark for some of this boat's crew. The backing bell we speak of had about four feet of partly burned engine room carling hanging to it. This bell is now used as a dinner bell at a farmhouse on Rush or Bates Island, minus carling and fame. [*This story of the burning of the Boreas II includes a lot of exaggerations and a few facts. Rumor was that the boat was indeed burned under suspicious circumstances, but no record exists of any loss of life.*]

Steamboat Bill was an attentive husband and often planned outings for his wife.

Saturday at high noon, January the 25th, in the 1930th year of our Lord, Ma and Pa Heckmann registered at the new Mark Twain Hotel on a sightseeing trip to the Mound City—St. Louis. The Mark Twain is a wonderful hotel, but how much more wonderful it would have been if the immortal Mark Twain could have come back to superintend the building of this place. He would have built and fashioned the building in itself along the fine lines of our old-time floating palaces. The cabin or coffee shop, in its white and gold, would have represented the old-time splendor of a real steamboat cabin, wonderful to behold. The afternoon of this day we spent at the American Theatre enjoying Ziegfeld's "Show Boat" in all its splendor, perhaps the greatest production ever offered the American public.

How much more beautiful this would have seemed to us had we known at the time that one of the stars as Magnolia of this cast [*Irene Dunn*], was the daughter of an old friend, Capt. J. J. Dunn, supervising inspector of this district, who died here some years back. Charles Winninger as Captain Andy played his part as only an old-time river captain of the Golden Era could have done.

Thank you, Edna Faerber, for starting the ball rolling with your novel that started our rivers on a comeback that nothing now can stop. After what we call supper and society calls dinner, we debated the question as to whether we should ask Captains Wright and Smith, of *The Waterways Journal*, and their wives downtown for a blowout at some show and some hot tamales after. Mom said, "I am afraid they are too high-toned for us."

CHAPTER 5 ≈ ROMANCE

"No, no, Mammy. I have met Mrs. Smith, and you know her husband and Mr. Wright , too; besides, the Smiths own a Ford."

"Well, have you ever met Mrs. Wright?"

"No, I have not."

"Now there's the rub, Daddy. You know she is from down South, and you know what a southern aristocrat is like. Look at our daughter, Monica, down in old Mississippi, and as far as I am concerned there will be no party until we meet Mrs. Wright."

"Well, well, that's all right. Let's go to the Orpheum and hear Henrietta cuss."

On the way to the showhouse, just as we passed *The Waterways Journal* corner, we saw a couple walking down the

Bill and Annie Heckmann. Her shrewd business sense kept Bill out of the financial troubles that had plagued his father.

muddy pavements ahead of us. I knew right away that it was Captain Wright and naturally supposed the lady he was escorting was his wife. As we walked along behind them, Mom said, "Now if Mr. and Mrs. Wright are as fine a couple as those two people ahead of us, I would say all right, throw your party, you old sport, and see if I don't keep up with all of you."

"Well, well, let's speed up some, or we'll be late to the show, and after we had passed Mr. and Mrs. Wright, I flanked my old sweetheart around and we stopped in front of this couple.

"Mama, meet Capt. and Mrs. Wright."

Such a meeting of surprise and goodwill is seldom witnessed by the U. S. Custom House. Compliments flew thick and fast. Among this quartet I believe Captain Wright was the one most pleased. Whether it was the fact that this lucky editor was again glad to meet us or whether he was happy that we found him with his own talented and beautiful wife, I do not know. Anyway, the two women fell in love at first sight, and that settled the party. Of course, it is still in the shadows, but it's coming as sure as the bright lights shine on Old Broadway.

At the Orpheum we all saw a play called "The Royal Family." No steamboat appeared in this play, but one of the characters in this play could and did cuss like an old-time steamboat mate. This degrading habit hurt our boats, and it will sink our modern plays still lower than what they are, if that is possible.

Sunday afternoon we went out Grand Avenue way to the new Fox Theatre. This great man may at present be in financial difficulties, and he has lots of company, but he surely does know his stuff when it comes to building a showhouse. Here we seen and heard more river lore and picturesque river scenery with boat pictures. We even heard our old boat blow her horn just like the old steamer Joe Wheeler did down in the Ozarks on upper White River. This boat had the most melodious whistle I ever heard. Here we saw a good, clean show and more signs of the present popularity of our river.

Sunday evening we spent at the Capitol. This is just a one-boiler showhouse, but we seen a fine show advertised as Ziegfeld "Glorifying the American Girl." To me it looks like Mr. Ziegfeld has been busy the last few years in glorifying our old steamboats, and no one is more thankful for this than Steamboat Bill.

On the way back to our boarding house, Ma got scared going over a busy crossing and made one of her Chinese trots for the sidewalk. "Can't I break you of that hop, step and a jump? You can move just as fast by taking long steps like I do. Besides, these people will know we are from the country."

"Well, I may be from the country, but not green enough to ask for toilet articles at the glove counter in a 10 cent store like you did the other day."

Monday morning we started on a visiting and shopping tour. At Nugents, Ma bought some curtains for our shack up home, which she paid for with a check. The sales lady called one of the cabin boys over to see if the check was okay. He said, "Madam, you look honest, and the check looks good, but you should have a bank book or something that would help us identify you. Ain't you got nothing with you?"

"Well, nothing but my husband setting over there; he knows me real well."

We tried to get some toilet articles here, but could not find them.

CHAPTER 5 ≈ ROMANCE

Mom said, "The only place we can get what I want in St. Louis is at Kresge's 10-cent store."

"Why not go to a drugstore; what is it you want, anyway?"

"That's all right. I know what's wanted; take me to Kresge's."

"All right, all right, come ahead and have it your way."

We discovered the place, all right, on Washington Street, but we got in the wrong building, and after we had explored the whole first floor, Ma says, "We will find it in the basement."

"Well, why not ask somebody about this junk?"

"Ask for the basement, and we will find them by ourselves."

I picked out a good looking elderly lady (just a habit), and said, "Madame, how do we get to the basement?"

She said, "You are in the wrong building. The basement is upstairs in this place. Perhaps you will find what you are looking for in our 5- and 10- cent store in the next building."

"Ma said, "You go over and look for those things; I want to buy some stockings for Ruth."

"No, we will find that stuff together. A house divided amongst itself will fall; besides no one knows what you want."

"Well, I want something in white; those black things they sell up home stain the enamel."

"I thought all the time you wanted something feminine."

In searching for the other building, I was looking up for another Kresge signboard. Ma said, "What are you looking for now?"

"What do you think? Another Kresge building."

"Look down at your feet; you're stepping on it now; their name is on the doorstep, hence the basement is downstairs in this building." Here we found the basement all right and after a short search found these nameless toilet articles in white, marked five cents per dozen.

"Buy a bushel of them, Ma, we are not coming back to get any more of them rubber bumpers, a go between a wooden seat and the white painted iron superstructure."

Monday afternoon we spent at the Grand. Here we saw no river scenes but saw some gobs in questionable quarters in Shanghai, China. Just before we checked out of the hotel, while walking in one of the gangways, Ma said, "I wish you would quit rattling that money in your pocket, something will happen to us yet before we get out of this town."

"Well, well, don't worry, Mamma, our return ticket does not rattle, and that is about all we got left."

My ever-changing partner now said, "Let's stay here another night; I want to see Eddie Lowry."

"Nothing doing, I saw you kissing your pillow last night—what did that mean? I am getting you back home. We may come back to see some of them Shakespearean plays at the American next week."

Ma: "Yes, *Much Ado About Nothing* would just about suit you where the hero says, 'If it proves so, then loving goes by haps; Some cupids kill with arrows; some with traps.'"

Pa: "You sure used traps, Ma, when you lured me out on that stone bridge in that moonlight night about 37 years ago. What a speech I made then, and as a girl you sure knew when to keep still. While you are talking of what would be suitable, what's the matter with *The Taming of the Shrew* for you? How I wish I had done what Petruchio did from the start; then things would have been different. 'Well, come my Kate; we will go to our home; Our purses should be proud, our garments poor; for it is the mind that makes the body rich.'"

Ma: "Well, just keep on quoting your old Shakespeare. I may be another Katherina, but thank God, I am honest. What's that piece of soap doing in your pocket? I never saw you buy any. If you did, why did you not get it at Kresge's?"

"That's not the question. What were you doing in my pocket? Kate would never have done that, and it did not take no 37 years to learn her either."

CHAPTER 6

The Contest

*"The time has come," the Walrus said, "To talk of many things:
Of shoes and ships and sealing wax, of cabbages and kings..."*

By 1930, when Steamboat Bill was in his 60s, he had a rival in writing steamboat stories for The Waterways Journal. Capt. Frederick Way Jr. was coming on strong, and readers could anticipate fresh stories each week. In "Mark Twain and Others," Steamboat Bill put forth a proposal that produced interesting results.

From Steamboat Bill:
  The advantages Mark Twain, as a writer, had over Captain Frederick Way Jr. and Steamboat Bill were many. In his day he had the fine, big floating palaces to write about, with the territory between St. Louis and the Crescent City, which he made famous for all time. In his day, a boat could run around an island in the fog and load cordwood several times at the same landing without knowing it, until told by the landing keeper. Today, most all our islands are fenced in on one side or other by dikes.
  When he told how you could tell a girl from a boy in how they caught something in their laps, the girls at least wore enough clothes to catch something with in that day and age. Another thing, he had to go to the Old Country to write "Innocents Abroad." I often wonder where he would go now to find innocence.
  But leaving Mark Twain to rest in peace, I often wonder how it would

take if Captain Way and myself, respective river champions, would stage a story contest. Each of us would write a story about steamboat roustabouts, and then let the subscribers of The Waterways Journal cast their vote for their champion, or, better still, let's start a Waterways Journal vox pop page, so they can knock as well as boast.

Now, Captain, you are a good loser, and if you do lose this contest, I hope it will not mar our long-distance acquaintance. For myself, I will say I have lost everything but my appetite, and it, with a poor stomach, is bad, so you see losing will not hurt this Old Codger one way or the other. Quite a few years back, it was told that John D. Rockefeller offered $1 million for a new stomach. It seems he is getting along all right with the old one, but we are getting off the subject.

Now, if this strikes your fancy, answer through the columns of The Waterways Journal with any suggestions you may have, for this should create more interest in our river paper than anything that has happened since you were the youngest subscriber and the German police dogs first came to Hermann, Missouri, to tear a piece out of Steamboat Bill's trousers.

From Capt. Way:

To the Editors of The Waterways Journal,

Notice is hereby given to Steamboat Bill the chip is knocked off his shoulder, and if he will look in the July 26 issue of The Waterways Journal he will discover a brainstorm entitled "Liverpool Blues." It is a rouster story. Not written for a contest, true enough, but a rouster story just the same.

So get hot, now, Bill. Do your stuff. When it comes to getting licked, that's the best thing I do. The Chris Greene, Tom Greene and even bigger shots than that have walked all over my toes and the Betsy Ann's toes, but we still go up and down the river and whistle for all the landings.

Everyday, in every way, things get better and better. The Waterways Journal opens an office in Pittsburgh, and at the same time the Betsy Ann has 65 round-trip passengers, with eight more getting on at Wheeling. And that rouster story is written and printed. You brought this on yourself, Bill Heckmann. You surely must have a rip-snorter up your sleeve. So spill the works.

CHAPTER 6 ≈ THE CONTEST

Liverpool Blues
July 26, 1930

I don't know just who started the begging, but first thing I knew, Slick and Paddle Foot commenced mouthing and signifying about a dollar a day wasn't enough. First thing I knew, everybody humbugged. Everybody! Even old Soldier and Country. Then Mister Charlie came out with the shipping tickets and said, "Boys, what's the matter?" Nobody opened their face right away, but pretty soon Slick stuck his foot in his mouth and said, "Mister Charlie, us boys want a dollar and a half a day. You know, Mister Charlie, a dollar ain't enough. No man can live on just a dollar."

Well sir, Mister Charlie looked awful mad and said, "You characters aren't worth a dollar and you know it." Then he took on about how us boys was only old women dressed up in pants and a lot of that stuff and then he ended up with saying that the pay was going to be a dollar. And no more! Just a dollar. "You fellas can work for a dollar or starve. I don't care which. STARVE if you want to," says Mister Charlie.

If it hadn't been that the Coahdill had just been in and got a lot of the boys rich, maybe it wouldn't have turned out like it did. Them boys had toted chickens and eggs off that boat for near on to 11 hours, and most of them had right sore feet. All of them was hungry. Good and hungry. But the worst part was that they had some jack in their pockets. And the Lord knows when a roustabout gets rich he ain't no account to himself or nobody.

Mister Charlie was the head mate of the Betsy Ann. He always gets the boys to work for him without no beefing, but this time he was mad over something and acted hard. Awful hard. I never saw him so biled up about us fellas wanting more money. Slick told Mister Charlie everything about how us fellows needed that money, but it didn't do no good.

Then the Captain of the Betsy Ann came out and said, "Charlie, what's wrong with these boys?" They stuck their heads together for a little bit, and then the Captain say, "O. K. boys, I'll pay you a dollar and a half for this trip."

Slick was about half lickered up and the next thing I knew, he says, "Captain, *we* cain't work with this mate. He's always abusing us fellahs. Talk bad to us and *we* ain't going to ship with him!" Nobody said nothing 'cause Slick always does the talk for the fellahs. There was a pretty good gang of the boys watching. I remember they was Half Pint and Soldier, and Pitty Pat and Zenie and Kate Adams and Rags.

Well, the Betsy Ann was late, and it made the Captain awful mad because we boys wouldn't take the tickets and go to work. Then Mister Charlie bent his head over and did a little whispering to the Captain. They mumble something and shake their haids.

"Boys," said the Captain, "We're powerful late with the Betsy Ann, and I can't stop for no arguing, so I'm putting the mate off the boat and getting another fellow down at East Liverpool to take his place. Now, boys, won't you go to work and load the boat?"

There's nothing more ornery than a roustabout who's got someplace! Just cause we boys got the best of the Captain and Mister Charlie, everyone of us commenced right away to get the swell head. We dragged our feet and just shuffled along about our work. Wouldn't shoulder-bone no iron. Wouldn't back and belly no heavy box. Wouldn't do nothing except beef and signify.

Mister Charlie came directly with his grip and got off the Betsy Ann, sure enough. First, we boys studied out they were playing us a trick, and we laid to quit if the Captain didn't pay off the mate. But he comes out in the wharfboat and looked black as coal at us fellers. He lay down his grip and said, "I know some fellers who are going to live hard when I get them on the next boat with me!'

Slick opened his big trap and said, "Never mind about that, Mister Charlie. We ain't working for you no more!" But the mate didn't say nothing. That looked funny to me. That right there looked funny. When some roustabout gets fresh with Mister Charlie, it is always *too bad*. And when this time he didn't say nothing, it looked funny to me.

Us boys dragged around half the night and bye and bye the time came we were hollering, "East Liverpool!" with the freight, and the second mate was tapping the bell. Time to go. Us boys had all shipped up for the trip down the river. And a big trip it was, too. Big lot of pipe for Liverpool. Big long pipe. Took three men to bring every piece in off the hill. Two on the ends and one in the middle.

The Captain told me to get back on the stern line. Paddlefoot come back to let the line go off the wharfboat, and I says to him, "Paddle, if we have any brains, you and me would get shut of this boat right here. I

CHAPTER 6 ≈ THE CONTEST

smell trouble here. Old Slick's all primed up with money, and he is going to make trouble. Looks bad to me. Certainly looks bad!"

But, us old roustabouts ain't got no brains, so when the bell taps and the Captain hollers, "Let's go," Paddle and me jumped in on the fantail, and there we were. Going down on the Betsy Ann. Big trip and no mate.

When the grub pile was dished out, Slick took his pan and looked hard at it. I

Capt. Frederick Way Jr. was owner, captain and pilot of the steamer Betsy Ann.

knew he was going to squawk. So, sure enough, he looks at the old watchman what was handing down the pans and says, "Old man, this here bread is moldy. Us fellahs cain't eat no moldy bread!" I smelled mine, and I knew it was good enough for the Captain to eat, but us boys had got contrary, and nothing looked good. Nothing a-tall. So I chirped up with the rest of the gang and said, "This bread is moldy, too!" Then the watchman said, "Boys, I can't do nothing about it. You will have to see the Captain or somebody."

"Come on, everybody!" yells Slick. "We are going to see the Captain about this!" So we went out around the boilers and tromped up the steps to the cabin door. Slick busts right on in there and jerked his finger to us to come on in. I felt sort of sheepish standing there in the cabin looking at that Captain feller. We all knew the bread was good. All this beefing and humbug, just because they give in to us fellers up on the wharfboat.

"Captain, us boys cain't eat no moldy bread!" says Slick. The Captain put down his paper that he was reading and looked hard at us boys. "Let's see that bread," he said. Then Slick reached out a hunk to him. The Captain looked at it a minute and then opened his mouth and ate a piece. Didn't say nothing. Just ate and ate. Pretty soon he had it all gobbled up. Slick was stuck. That tickled me, it did. Sure enough made me smile. Old Slick stood there and looked so dumb-like while the Captain ate that bread and didn't say nothing.

"Isn't anything wrong with that bread," said the Captain. Then he picked up his paper and went on a'reading. Slick looked mad and said, "Damn!" and went back out the door. Us boys didn't say nothing. We just trailed back down the steps. Down by the boilers Slick looked awful mad and say, "I'll fix that Captain. I'll fix him!"

Them boys got awful ornery. The Betsy Ann landed at Freedom for some oil and Paddle-Foot let his barrel get away from him and slide right in the river. The Captain hollered at Paddle, and Paddle sass back. And *no*body got the barrel. Just got sunk or something. I knew Paddle let go that barrel. He done it a'purpose. No old ragged roustah but what cain't swing a barrel down THAT bank.

So when we get to Liverpool, must a bin long about morning. Wasn't coming day yet, for I remember the breast lights were burning. Everything started wrong. The boys were getting tired and sleepy. Slick had got a headache and was mumbling and beefing and moaning.

Kate Adams and Zenie had a fight when we put out the planks. I don't know what was wrong, but first thing I knew, they were a woofing at one another like they were a couple of bulldogs. Then everybody stopped work to watch them two fellers mouth off. For they didn't fight none. Just a lot of mouthing.

Kate Adams says, "Don't signify with me, you big Ape!"

Zenie say, "Shut your damn trap!"

"I'll tear your head off!" says Kate.

"You'll tear whose head off?" says Zenie.

And that's the way they keep a'going on. Boat just laying there, and nobody doing nothing. The second mate wasn't a big fellah, and he was afraid to say "mush" to us boys because he thinks we might quit the job.

Then Slick shut everybody up and went up to the little second mate and said, "Mister, us boys has got to have labor money to unload all

CHAPTER 6 ≈ THE CONTEST

this heavy pipe off the head of this boat!" Imagine that! Labor money for unloading the pipe! So I see then how Slick is getting back at the captain on account of that bread business.

"Us boys were all standing there looking at Slick and the second mate and didn't notice nobody coming. But first thing you know, Slick look toward the wharfboat door and commence to shake and look fidgety. I look too. Everybody look.

There was Mister Charlie standing there. Looked black as night. In one hand he had a blackjack. In the other he had a big piece of wood. Everybody shut up. Everybody! Nobody said nothing. Just all stood there and looked at that big man standing there in the door. Then Mister Charlie said something. I knew what he was going to say. So did everybody. And I knew what we were going to do about it too. He said, "There's going to be some pipe took off this here boat." Said it slow and even like. Then he looked wild, with his eyes a'poppin' and yelled, "And it's going to start right now!"

All the boys jumped for the head of the Betsy Ann, and two fellahs commenced hoisting up pipe. It took three men to tote a jint of that pipe aboard the boat at Pittsburgh. There at Liverpool Mister Charlie make one man carry. "Raise up, old women!" say Mister Charlie. "Work, work like you live—hard!"

That pipe just flew off that boat. Just flew!

And rousters flew around. They sure limbered up!

And Mister Charlie was mate again.

I knew all the time it was going to turn out that way somehow.

From Steamboat Bill:
Old Mule, The Black Human Fly
August 19, 1930

The little city of Miami, Missouri, at one time was a very extensive shipping point by Missouri River steamers. It is one of the few places still left on the Big Muddy where the old river warehouses stand silent and empty in the grandeur of the past as far as river shipping is concerned. Quite a few years back, a good man by the name of McCoy bought up and filled one or more of those houses full of wheat. The price of this cereal went up, and he made something on the last transaction that filled those structures with grain.

Mr. McCoy was a white-ribbon man. [*A white-ribbon man was one who had signed the temperance pledge.*] We were under charter to Shobe and DeWitt, then extensive river contractors, with the steamer Julius F. Silber and barges. They released us from our towing contract long enough to bring a boat and barge load of this wheat from Miami to the Glasgow Milling Company, 33 miles down the river. In our crew of 20 roustabouts (one of whom it will be best to give a short description), our hero, Old Mule, was the most prominent character.

Old Mule, who claimed to be the black human fly, was a tall, sloping-shouldered, butt-footed braggart, with the largest mouth and two rows of the whitest and largest teeth I have ever seen in the mouth of a human being. Wingy, his partner, was a mean fellow, and handy with a razor; Rabbit was a fancy dancer and comedian par excellence; Rastus was a rare entertainer from Portland, Missouri, when in his cups; Indian Joe was the evangelist; Bad Eye was rightly named; and King Button was a big, burly-necked man of the worst kind, but a straight shooter, as he only used his fists in an argument.

Along in the early afternoon of a bright autumn day, we had the good boat and barge flattened out with grain, and we were waiting for a shipment of supplies still to come. It was cidertime back of old Miami, and someone had presented our roustabouts with a candy bucket of sweet cider. About the transaction, the donor, Mr. McCoy, said, "Captain, you know I am opposed to strong drink, but this will not hurt, and I want to congratulate you in the kind of a crew you carry and the way you handle them. They sure are obedient and industrious."

After all of the roustabouts had a good swig of that cider, I asked that they bring it aboard the boat and we would spike it. This we did by pouring a gallon of 100-proof, pure rye whiskey in the cider. The bucket was again full, and it was not long in putting a different color to the oncoming exhibition.

After several rounds of drinks and the smacking of lips, the richness of this mixture began its work. Old Mule, always the loudest, said, "I'm the only living human fly in existence. Wonder if there are any tall buildings in Miami? I'll show you how to climb."

Wingy spoke up, "Shut your big mouth. You don't need to go uptown. I bet you my trips wages you cannot climb that warehouse, and there is a ladder halfway up there already."

CHAPTER 6 ≈ THE CONTEST

Old Mule answered, "Your bet's covered like the flood covers the pebbles in the bed of a brook."

Wingy said, "Hold the deal. You owe me from that last bet. Get the Captain or clerk to ratify this transaction."

Old Mule replied, "Hurry, I'm a climbing fool, and I've got to go. That must be squirrel whiskey. Give me another swig, and I'm going heavenward!"

The warehouse stood on the side of a hill. Someone had opened up a rock quarry, and the riverside rested on piling. A ladder went up about 20 feet, and a wooden sack chute came out of the second story window, but the river end was rotted away.

Old Mule climbed up the ladder, made his way past one window and got a hold of the sack chute to make his way to the second story window, but just as he grabbed an old window shutter, the warehouse end of the sack chute crashed to the rocks below. Mule managed to hold to the shutter and actually made his way to the top of same. He then reached up and caught hold of an old tin gutter. This would not hold his weight, and it fell to the ground, too. This left Old Mule stranded, and only outside help would ever get him back to Mother Earth.

Wingy: "There now! I done won that bet. That bozo is hard aground on that shutter!"

Old Mule: "Wonder if they have a hook and ladder company in Miami?"

Wingy: "Where you think you are? In St. Joe where the polices and fire company took you off that last building you tried to climb? I saw them bust that club over your head when they got you back on the pavement. You sure will be lucky if you get out of this mess that easy. Listen Mule, was it previous before, or previous after you played human fly in that man's town that you stole those chickens on Duncan Street?"

Mule: "You sold dem chickens. Go get a ladder."

Bad Eye: "You get nothing, that big baboon comes down off that house like he went up, by his ownself."

Someone was moving across the river on the ferryboat, and in their junk was a big iron-tooth harrow about 8-feet square.

Bad Eye: "Those rocks are too soft for Old Mule to fall on. Some of you country folk fotch me that harrow over here, while I lay it down for that human fly to fall on. Turn them teeth up. I catch my flies, I do not swat them."

Here a big country man stepped up and said, "I objects to this performance." King Button got up and socked the country man one in the jaw, flattening him on the rocks, and he then turned to the crowd and said, "Anyone else who wants to help Mule, why step up, the ballroom is open." There were no takers.

Rabbit: "That gazaboo hanging up there is no human fly. He is a disgrace to us rousters. You sure are some human fly. Your mind must be warped to think that way. Actually, you are uglier than human sin. Still, if they bring me that old scale platform over here, I struts my stuff. Am I right, Button? Have your fellows bring that platform!"

Bad Eye: "Let Old Mule's last hours be happy. I'll sing and dance, its cidertime in old Miami, and I'm happy."

Wingy: "I sure do hate to set in an assembly like this where they all have to study so long to say something worth listening to. I'm going up town and mingle with some town folks, where brains count and force doesn't rule."

Bad Eye: "Hit the board walk while you're all together. Go and be quick."

Exit Wingy.

Rastus: "The evening shades are a'falling; the shank of the evening has come and gone. Soon that harvest moon, which is full tonight, will shine on that black fly hanging on that rotten shutter. Man, you are the ugliest human I ever saw with my two eyes. Look at those feet; it takes two cowhides to make you a pair of shoes. You sure are a dumb human fly. All I ask is when you fall I get your teeth. Man, that hole in your head looks like a granite quarry. There is ivory enough in your mouth to pedal a new piano."

Mule: "Bad Eye, please go get the captain and get me down offen here. I'll buy you all the beer you want."

Bad Eye: "Just another drink of that sweet cider, and I go get the captain's shotgun and if you do not soon fall, I'll sure shoot the hinges off that old shutter."

Button: "I second the motion; go get the gun!"

Bad Eye: "Captain, lend me your shotgun. I want to shoot a skunk!"

CHAPTER 6 ≈ THE CONTEST

Crap games were a constant source of entertainment for roustabouts and deckhands. This 1912 photo was taken on the Tennessee River aboard the Steamer St. Louis.

Captain: "Let me carry the gun."

Bad Eye: "Sure, Captain, let me tell you something; there is trouble brewing. You know Button is a bad man and he does not like Old Mule. If that nut falls before the liquor dies out in these folks, I look for trouble. Better hold on to that gun. Fill her full of buckshot and take charge of this comedy. Man, what did you put in that cider?"

Mule: "Joe, you will help me, I know."

Indian Joe: " Good Lord, look down on this gathering and bless us all. If Old Mule must fall, drop him lightly, for with all his faults, we loves him still, and Lord, if you move Button and Bad Eye, I move that harrow. That's all, Amen."

Mule: "Thank God, here come the captain, Mister George and help."

Rastus: "Captain, are you or are you not going to help that flying nut? I'd like to know because I want to be on the side of that Auto Matic for I've seen you in action with it before."

Captain: "Button, what's going on here?"

Button: "Nothing, boss, we're just waiting for that black fly to drop."

Mule: "Save me captain, you know I work hard for you. Mister George helped me out of that last scrape when these same fools tried to drown Old Mule."

Captain: "Bad Eye, you and Button go back down on the boat; you other men carry that harrow over where it belongs and get a tarpaulin off the boat."

Bad Eye: "Come on, Button, that's shotgun government and sympathy for that climbing fool now at work, and we're not needed here."

Mule: "Hurry, boss, I'm about all in, and I do not want to fall on them rocks. What time is it now?"

Rastus: "Why you want to know? You ain't going nowhere."

We stretched a big tarpaulin under Old Mule, and his eyes began to roll in his head. When all was ready that cowardly rascal did not want to jump. Only after threatening to let Bad Eye shoot him down, did he turn all hands loose to fall into the canvas below. Actually, folks, when we lowered him to the ground he was in a dead faint.

Rastus now took charge. "Bring me water and bring me plenty; the flying demon has done gone and fainted."

After throwing three buckets of cold water on Old Mule, his eyes again began to roll, his tongue began to wag, and the old braggart was himself again.

The day was now spent, and old George Jackson, of Calloway County, Missouri, came on watch. Jackson was respected and feared by even men like Bad Eye and Button. He said, "Go back on the boat folks and turn these monkeys and bad characters over to me! Go, Captain, Mister George and Bones; Old George is on watch now, go to bed and sleep like you were in your Mamma's arms!"

This we did on this occasion and on many others during the 40 years this faithful man looked over the welfare of my sainted father and the older members of the Heckmann family.

•

A Whistle Story
Captain Frederick Way, Jr.
September 20, 1930

There is nothing quite as satisfactory as having a good whistle on your steamboat. When you step on the treadle up in the pilothouse

CHAPTER 6 ≈ THE CONTEST

and listen to the hiss of steam and then ease down just the proper way and produce melody, it gives as a reward, sort of a superior feeling. Even though your musical education might be confined to the mere rudimentary knowledge of winding up a Victrola, tuning in a radio, or whistling with a warbling trill (done by moving the tongue up and down in your mouth while the lips are puckered), you feel that you have some kinship with the great artists when you can go under a bridge and blow the whistle of your boat in such a way that it will echo and make all sort of wonderful sounds.

When I first stepped aboard the R. Dunbar (No matter now, the name might as well be exposed, as the whistle was burned up in the fire when she went up in smoke down at the Canulettes), that boat had a good whistle. It was a ticklish sort of a thing and had been tuned to just the proper pitch by experts who are paid to do that sort of business. And, let it be said for them, they earned their money. By easing up on the treadle in just the proper way, it was possible to bring such harmony that there would be tears in the eyes of the roustabouts. Old ladies would weep, and the captain got letters from people on shore who sat up half the night to hear the old Dunbar blow for the landings. "Bless you," the letters would read, "and may God remember you. Blow that wonderful whistle a little longer next time you pass our home. It is an inspiration. Aunt Bella, who has been sick for years—paralyzed and bedridden—groaned and turned over last time your boat went up. It was a miracle. May the Lord reward you. We pray for you…" and so on.

Then, like a bolt out of the blue, we found ourselves one morning with a new chief engineer. The old fellow who got off left on account of sickness. The new man was a trifle younger in years and a mere calf when it came to knowing anything. That is, about whistles. He claimed to be an expert engineer. For that matter, he had all the credentials. His license was genuine, signed with the flourishing, bold penmanship of George W. Dameron and Mr. Peyton, the Cincinnati inspectors. He had a whole suitcase full of mechanical instruments. What they were, I don't know. And now I don't care. My only wish was that he get tangled up in them someday and come out in pieces.

It was my fault as much as any body's. I like to brag on good things, especially when I have some claim to them. If my watch is a good one and keeps pretty good time, then I like to show it off. But this bonehead, know-nothing was one of the sort who always has something a little better to produce. No matter what, he had something better. A man like that is treacherous. I should never have done what I did. God forgive me.

It happened up in the pilothouse. We had a landing for Cheshire, and I was on watch. This infidel of an engineer was sitting on the bench behind me and had just been redesigning all the boats, which were under construction down at the Marietta Manufacturing Company plant as we passed there—in his head, you understand—for this man could do anything with his mouth. I blew a neat landing whistle, and the old Crowder did it proud. The steam was right, the water was right, the air was clear, and that whistle certainly sounded fine. With a lump in my throat and tears in my eyes, I turned to the fellow and stammered, "Wasn't that wonderful, my friend?" I called him friend. There were witnesses, and it can be proved, if necessary.

"It needs tuning," he answered.

I might have known better, but it was too late then.

That evening he appeared on the Texas roof with two wrenches, a pair of calipers and a pencil and paper. There was an evil smile on his lips as he said, "Now I'm going to fix it." I jumped up and down and danced around and pleaded with the man to let things alone. But of no avail. The acoustics were wrong. The pitch wasn't right. Everything was loco about that whistle. It demanded his immediate attention. On up a ladder he went, bent for destruction. A helper was carrying his tools.

I stood there in the pilothouse and prayed a little, cried a little and tried in vain to build up a hope that the man was right. He is an expert, I argued to myself. Perhaps he knows what he is talking about. But then, the sound of stilson wrenches pulling with might and main came floating down to my ears. Rusty joints creaked and groaned and grated horrible up there on the roof. Every sound went through me like the wail of ghosts in a moonlit graveyard.

In 20 minutes time, the engineer, helper and all the tools were back down the ladder. He came up in the pilothouse and wiped his hands together. People who do that for no good reason need watching. They will steal things. I have noticed that after some observation. "Well, I'll

CHAPTER 6 ≈ THE CONTEST

try her out," I said, making a motion toward the treadle. "Tut, tut, never mind. It is perfect. No need to blow it until you have to," he said. Then he left.

We were approaching Marietta from down the river. The more I got to studying about what sort of a noise that whistle was going to make, the more thoroughly frightened I got. Finally I broke out in a chill. Then my head got hot, and the sweat was standing out in beads. My breath got to coming in hard, short pants. Feebly, I called down to the clerk, "Call my partner." That was the meanest trick I ever did, and may the good Lord forgive me for it.

I lived a thousand agonies waiting for my poor, unsuspecting partner to come up the steps. Finally, at the last possible moment, he came up blinking and coughing, fastening up his belt. "What's the matter, partner?" he asked. I reeled dizzily and managed to tell him that I hadn't blown for Marietta yet. Then I fell toward the bench. It was a dirty trick. Just like catching fish in a seine. He had no chance at all. With total ignorance, he blissfully stepped on that cursed treadle. There was a gurgle, a shriek—and I swooned.

A week later we got a letter from Manager Hoag, of the Lafayette Hotel in Marietta, complaining about making such an awful noise when we blew for a landing. "It wakens all the guests up. Do you think such a thing is necessary? I appeal to your intelligence," it said.

But it is a long worm that never turns. That dastardly scoundrel of an engineer spread all the destruction possible on the Crowder and then resigned. I will always claim that the boat whipped him, but he said that he had no cooperation.

He got a berth on the Tacoma, where there was a hard-boiled pilot. That boat had a pretty whistle, too. And had until her dying day. I heard later that this low-life expert tried some monkey business over there and that he died later of poison in his ice cream. He had no near relatives. I helped pay his funeral expenses, and gladly.

But, the Crowder's whistle never blew right to her dying day.

The reader may have noticed that the boat in Capt. Way's story started out as the Dunbar and then suddenly, without explanation, became the Crowder. Capt. J. L. Hacker had a few comments about that.

≈ STEAMBOAT TREASURES ≈

To the Editors of the Waterways Journal:

I will accept your invitation to comment on the stories of Capt. Frederick Way and Capt. William L. Heckmann, since they are written in competition and one challenges the other.

The whistle story of Capt. Way is a river story—steamboat story—by and of the crew of the boat, except as to the effect the whistle had upon people ashore, which does not detract anything from its merits, but there is one discrepancy in the story. There is no explanation as to how the whistle got from the Dunbar to the Crowder. That is poetic license, so to speak, and may be passed over.

There is real merit in Way's story. His engineer is a gentleman whom we have all met on the river. "An expert" who comes aboard with an air of superiority and proceeds to "fix" things. They often tear down the furnace on a good steaming boat and rebuild it in a way that Capt. Way's engineer fixed the whistle. His previous story, "Liverpool Blues," if I remember the title, was a better story than his whistle story. If he is as good a pilot as he is a writer, he will make lots more money out of it. It takes many years to gain a reputation and emolument as a writer, but *The Waterways Journal* is very indulgent to aspirants.

Somebody "swiped" my *Waterways Journal*, and I have not Capt. Heckmann's story before me. The action of his story was not aboard a steamboat, but centered wholly upon the action of the drunken roustabouts ashore. It is quite a thrilling situation for a drunken roustabout to be hanging to a shutter on a warehouse door, with an inverted harrow on the ground below him, but highly improbable, as the innate caution of a Negro would keep him from such an antic, drunk or sober.

There is no "Human Fly" about him. You would have to tie him to get him up on a flying machine. He loves the ground and would be hard to get off of it, and it is often hard to get over it. He has no equal as a steamboat roustabout or the man behind a mule in a cotton patch. Now if it had been some white stray in that gang of roustabouts, full of "squirrel whiskey," he might have performed this "Human Fly" stunt, but never a Negro—J. L. Hacker.

Steamboat Bill was quick to defend his "Human Fly" story.

Now you see, folks, publicity does not come unassisted, and if you want to be known you must blow your own horn. The police records

CHAPTER 6 ≈ THE CONTEST

in the City of St. Joseph, Missouri, of about 22 years ago, will show that Old Mule was arrested for climbing a building there, or trying to climb it. If the old warehouse at Miami could talk, it would tell many a stranger tale than my story about Old Mule, the Human Fly.

From The Waterways Journal:

Last week *The Waterways Journal* printed Steamboat Bill's story on roustabouts offered in competition with stories by Capt. Frederick Way Jr., who this week sent in one for comparison with Bill's effort entitled "A Whistle Story." Comments on the relative merits of last week by Steamboat Bill and this week by Frederick Way in the story line will be welcomed.

Undaunted, Capt. Way picked up the ball and came right back.

To the Editors of the Waterways Journal:

It is with genuine pleasure that I read the comments of Capt. J. L. Hacker on the contributions recently offered the readers of *The Waterways Journal*, by Steamboat Bill and myself. Let me say here, by way of explanation, that these tales come to me with much the same notions as Tweedledee had in the immortal "Alice in Wonderland." He explains his thoughts with the verse:

> "The time has come," the Walrus said,
> "To talk of many things:
> Of shoes and ships and sealing wax,
> Of cabbages and kings.
> And why the sea is boiling hot,
> And whether pigs have wings."

These stories are all part truths. There is some truth in all of them. A few were actual facts. Several others were deliberate lies. But no matter—they made stories.

Just a word about this contest. The notion has spread abroad that Bill Heckmann and I are trying to outdo each other. That is far from the facts. He suggested that we both write a "rouster story" and let *The Waterways Journal* readers submit their votes on the relative merits of each. As his contribution, I think the "Human Fly" tale was his choice. Mine, as pointed out in a previous letter, was "Liverpool Blues." One other rouster story that I have attempted was called "Once Upon a Time on the Lorena" and told of Uncle Tom Cabin troupe and the bloodhounds. And while speaking of this, let me relate an odd incident in connection with it.

When originally submitting the thing to *The Waterways Journal*, I hastened to explain to the good editors that the story was mine, but the idea was not. It came originally from a gifted newspaper correspondent who wrote up the tale when I was a boy. I read it, remembered it, and really just rewrote it several months ago for *The Waterways Journal*.

Imagine my surprise, about a month ago, when a Pittsburgh evening paper used the bloodhound tale, rewritten again to completely disguise the authorship, and taking up the full front page of the second section of a daily edition. Accompanying the story was a large illustration of the "dorgs" jumping from the guards of the Lorena into the cold, icy river with several frightened rousters in the background. So that story has become a valuable property. It has had three appearances in public, each time under the pen of a different author!

It is a good tale. If I ever make an attempt to collect my scattered brain-children into a single volume, that story is going to occupy a prominent place. But I'm going to tack a note at the beginning of it and disclaim any credit for the original idea.

Now fully fired up with enthusiasm for writing, Capt. Way delivered a book review, a veritable oration on good writing. Teachers of English and creative writing may profit.

A Few Random Shots
Capt. Frederick Way Jr.

After the Civil War was brought to an official close by the surrender of Lee, it is reported that a few random shots were fired back and forth by soldiers who had not heard the news. Do not be misguided then. This is not the opening gun of a debate. It is a little sharpshooting on the side. And it has to do with Professor Charles H. Ambler's new book, *Transportation in the Ohio Valley*. J. Mack Gamble efficiently reviewed the book in the January 2 *Waterways Journal*, therefore, the bids are in, and the issue closed. But, like a pack of firecrackers, this is the final "bang" with which the celebration is apparently over and forgotten. It is out of place entirely, had no invitation; but is just one of those things that are bound to happen.

CHAPTER 6 ≈ THE CONTEST

The new book is all Mack Gamble said it was and more. It is brim full of fact and fiction. It sticks to the Ohio River and tells the whole story in remarkable fashion. Professor Ambler has been meticulous in his attention to detail. Every fact is verified with the proofs laid out like a geometry text. But isn't it true that the author of "Alice in Wonderland" is remembered—not for his long list of successes in the realm of textbooks. Didn't his story of the immortal Alice eclipse any treatise on trigonometry he ever wrote? Won't it live when his studious calculations have been relegated to the dusty shelves of history?

How I would have cried for sheer joy if there had been a dodo bird or a mock turtle in Professor Ambler's book. What an innovation had there been a Mad Hatter or a cake labeled "eat me." But no; I searched in vain. Exposed were facts, facts, facts. Soon it became like a church sermon where the preacher makes the deadly mistake of saying, "In the first place; in the second place." That chills me to the bone. I wonder, always HOW many places before the last one.

I got up hope when the book got around to the time-race the sidewheel Buckeye State made up the Ohio River in 1851. That, most surely, was going to stir up some excitement. But listen:

Rivalry sometimes extended to packets of the same lines, that between the Messenger and the Buckeye State, of the P. and C. Packet line being the talk of the wayside in the early fifties. It is said that it was to show the Messenger a thing or two, she being a favorite with traveling celebrities and on this occasion carrying Jenny Lind, that the Buckeye State, in 1851, made her famous run from Cincinnati to Pittsburgh.

That's all. Positively all there is to it. The biggest event of the early packet days relegated to a sentence or so! Why, oh why, couldn't Professor Ambler have limbered up and said "on top of the pilothouse was a full-size stuffed deer." Why couldn't he have added that people blocked the Wheeling suspension bridge and cheered from the shore as the boat went by. Even old Tony Whitton, her pilot, got so enthusiastic that he climbed up on top of the pilothouse—stuffed deer and all—and waved a silk plug hat at the populace? Rode the deer under the bridge, that man did! That, in a way, was the spirit of 1851 on the Ohio River.

There is a chapter in this book headed "Floods and Disasters." Maybe, in that place, there is a realistic taste of adventure. Put me down for a prevaricator if the City if Louisville didn't get crunched to death (in the book), with a death-like silence, which would surround a graveyard at midnight. Even a "silent" movie of the event would be recorded the 'scape pipes pluming out volleys of white steam and the white-collared stacks belching black smoke as the "Big Dick" drifted to her doom with steam up and not a soul aboard. The Charles Brown sank right in sight of the Louisville, and the Greenland was lifted from the Cincinnati marine ways—when Capt. Gordon C. Greene thought he had her in the safest spot in the world—but such events as these are not mentioned. The old prison ship Success, in the mouth of the Kentucky River, proved the worth of her teakwood hull by ramming the Island Queen and sending the Princess to her grace—but why go on?

Two Fords coming together could cause more commotion than the United States-American disaster in 1868 did on page 386 of this *Transportation in the Ohio Valley*. The John Loomis and Scioto collided in the next sentence with a serenity that would have become two elderly ladies greeting one another. Wait a moment, I take it back—both collisions happened in one sentence.

My apologies, Professor Ambler, my sincere apologies. Perhaps you will want to fathom this thing down to the fact that you did not enlarge on the Betsy Ann-Chris Green race. But it isn't that, although an event that startled the whole United States and commanded headlines in the hard-boiled newspapers to the effect that "Rival Packets Race for Speed Supremacy Up Ohio River" was certainly worth giving one sentence of space. I thank you for that and honestly mean it.

I simply deplore the absence of enthusiasm in your book. It is a wonder, and in the wildest of my dreams, I never once dreamed that the Ohio River would ever have such a complete biography as you have given it. The book is a masterpiece of accuracy and should be in the possession of every friend of the Ohio River and its tributaries.

Once Upon a Time on the Lorena
Capt. Frederick Way, Jr.
June 14, 1930

Melodrama once in a while has its place on the river. Occasionally something will happen that tastes of all the sensation of the showboat stage of 30 years ago. Something that has its hero, its villain, the pretty dark-eyed, yellow-curled picture of feminine virtue, and even the frills of low-hanging clouds, snow storms and tragedy.

CHAPTER 6 ≈ THE CONTEST

So let us set the stage, then, in the cabin of the packet Lorena. The winter wind is whistling outside. Snow is pelting on the stained-glass doors at the front bulkhead there. Outside, the night is black and dreary as a long, low cloud partly hides a waning moon. The silver reflection on the cold, black waves of the river shows huge cakes of ice silently floating by, grim specters that threaten to gouge yawning holes in the sides of the plodding little packet.

A little group of passengers huddles around a huge, eggshell coal stove in the forward part of the cabin. It is colored cherry-red and looks singularly cheerful. Even sounds warm, as the flames roar through the silvered stove pipe. Below is the sound of rhythmically working machinery. The turning of the paddle wheel makes the boat shake and slightly tremble, there in the cabin. The small acorn appendages on the tips of the countless white, scroll-worked carlins down through the cavernous recess of the cabin sway in unison. A calf, somewhere below, bawls for its mother. A rooster, seeing the moon, crows lustily. Ducks make funny little sounds in their coops on deck.

A big man, his forearm on his knee, looks intently at the stove. He wears a huge, black hat, has a frock-tail coat, and his white necktie is set off with a brilliant, glistening stone. With one hand, he idly twirls the end of a huge, black mustache. It would not be surprising were he to open his mouth and bellow in deep, sad tones, "God help the poor sailors on a night like this."

Across the cabin, in a little straight-backed chair is a young lady. No yellow curls, to be sure, but braided plaits down either shoulder. And each set off with a light pink bow. A checkered gingham dress. She watches the stove, also, dreaming of other little boys and girls who don't have to ride steamboats on dark and stormy winter nights.

A big, fat lady, her chair pushed well back from the fire. And a short, bald-headed fellow, who is stretched out like a ramrod. A big hunk of tobacco in his jaw. Once in a while he will let fly a stream of juice with deadly accuracy toward a huge, shiny spittoon.

You have met no others than Simon Legree in person, Little Eva, Eliza and Uncle Tom. The latter couple are white folks now, but when they get their makeup on tomorrow night and show in the Palace Theatre at Baresville, Monroe County, Ohio, you will better recognize them. Several big, black trunks outside the cabin door are marked "Uncle

Tom's Cabin, Inc." Down in the deck room are packing boxes loaded with scenery, mechanism to float angels through the air, artificial ice of some sort and several pair of patented feather wings, which hook in some sort of a vest and make the wearer look pious and holy. Just aft of the boilers, with boxes set about them to keep off the wind, are three sad, mournful hound dogs. Their leashes are tied to the after mud drum leg on the port side.

The roustabouts, driven from their usual nesting place under the boilers by the intrusion of the dogs, sit on boxes as near the heat as they dare. Paddlefoot dismally regards the solemn eyes of the hounds and says, "Them poor mutts need exercise. That's what wrong with them."

Slick, a long, wiry boy, smiles from ear to ear. "Let's let them roam around a spell," he says. "Let's on-tie them dogs and let them stretch!"

And so, Paddlefoot is elected to crawl up in the darkness and unfasten the leash that holds each of the three pups to the mud drum leg. Sinister idea, this! Old rousters had a scheme for regaining their lost sleeping place.

"There you are, doggie!" says Slick. "You're let loose now. Walk around some and stretch your legs!"

But three solemn hounds sat still in the delicious warmth of the boiler heat and did nothing. The moon went under a cloud, and the wind whistled ominously. Cakes of ice were getting bigger as they floated by in the dark. Occasionally the Lorena would plough into one, and there would be a dull thud. The boat would shiver a little, and the actors in the cabin would look knowingly at one another.

Slick had an inspiration. He clapped his huge hands together and called, "Liza, Liza." Instantly, the three dogs perked up their ears and uttered low growls. For they, too, you must know, were trained to their actor roles.

"Liza!" called Slick in louder voice, spurred on with his initial success. The sleepiest dog stood up now. "Liza!" The others uncurled from under the boilers and came out by the packing boxes.

Paddlefoot and Zenie took up the call now. They all clapped their hands and called "Liza!"

The three dogs jumped up on top of the boxes and instantly espied the moon coming out from under a dark cloud. Saw the cold, dark river

CHAPTER 6 ≈ THE CONTEST

rolling by. Sniffed as they smelled the fresh wind.

"'Liza!" And just then an enormous cake of ice showed up ghostly white in the water.

The three dogs had got their cue. They uttered deep bays and sprang over the bull rails, and there was a sudden Splash! Splash! Splash! and then terrified howls, as the dogs found themselves in real river water and among cold, glistening blocks of unmanufactured ice.

The packet Lorena plodded her way wearily onward. The terrified roustabouts leaned over the rails and watched the struggling hounds disappear in the murky waters. The moon hid under a bank of black clouds and darkness settled down again on the scene.

If you should ever go down to Sardis Bend and walk aboard a little shantyboat there, it is likely that three old dogs will howl. For the lonely man who lives there owns three such creatures. They came to him one black, stormy night. One night when the winter wind blew and the moon was hidden under low, gray clouds.

The contest seemed to go on forever, as stories by both Steamboat Bill and Captain Way continued to appear regularly. However, no winner was ever declared, so the contest, as such, was apparently an unsettled issue. The reader may form his own opinion.

CHAPTER 7

Whoppers
Spontaneous Combustion

Steamboat Bill had a gift for embellishing a story. If the story was good, he tried to make it better. If it was bad to start with, he usually made it worse. He even dramatized his own birth—born on a steamboat on the Missouri River, he claimed! This was really a whopper, clearly refuted by the bare facts of the recorded birth in the county courthouse.

He even had to get into the act on reporting the Civil War. The little town of Hermann largely escaped the main thrust of the Civil War. The one and only Confederate raid (some called it a frolic) of Price's forces, led by Marmaduke, has become a staple of local folklore.

Women and children were evacuated to the safety of Graf's Island, and all the young, able-bodied men were away at war, which left old men to defend the town. They had exactly one big weapon, an old brass cannon, which is still on display in front of the Gasconade County Courthouse. This they dragged up the Catholic Hill and fired at the approaching Confederates coming around Kallmeyer's Bluff. Steamboat Bill wrote the following much-embellished account of the event for the Hermann Advertiser-Courier.

> Years after the Civil War, when major Marmaduke became governor of our great commonwealth, he said he would like to go back to Hermann and meet Mr. Valentine, who gave him the best drink of wine he ever tasted, and he wanted to greet the man that shot that old Hermann cannon. He meant Capt. Nebel.
>
> During the bloodless bombardment, Capt. Nebel made what was perhaps one of the most peculiar shots fired during the whole Civil War. In shooting at the rebel soldiers and cannon stationed on

CHAPTER 7 ≈ WHOPPERS

Schroeder's Hill from Catholic Hill, the ball from the old brass cannon went directly in and down the barrel of one of the rebel cannons and put it out of commission. No wonder Hermann is even today noted for crack shots!

It was Steamboat Bill's habit to start a story, digress, return to his subject, then digress some more. He had a penchant for stories of peculiar marksmanship. This particular digression was part of a story that appeared in The Waterways Journal.

Hermann's famous cannon

This one was told alongside of a potbellied stove in the pilothouse of an old Missouri River steamboat by a yarn-spilling steamboat captain who was along for a free ride. He said, "You see that big rock up there on the brow of that hill? When I was a young man, I stole out with my grandfather's old muzzle-loading rifle and went up there and sat down on that rock, looking for game that was plentiful in the woods at that time.

"I hadn't been there long until a big 28-pound turkey gobbler was strutting his stuff up the hill towards me. Overhead was a large bald eagle circling around and getting closer and closer; and just below the turkey was a large timber wolf sneaking up on his prey. I slipped down off the rock, got on my knees, cocked that old blunderbuss and was ready for war.

"Just as the eagle swooped down and the wolf made a leap, I pulled the trigger. When the smoke cleared away, I went down there and found that I had killed all three of them varmints with one shot."

You can figure that story three ways. Either it was about the best shot ever made, the biggest lie ever told, or the truth heavily laden with falsehood, for which the old captain was noted.

Occasionally, when a Waterways Journal deadline was coming up, Steamboat Bill unabashedly enlisted help.

The History of Aurora Springs
Written by C. N. Mitchell
For Steamboat Bill and Charles Jenkins of the
Steamer Eugenia Woods.

The season of 1881 was dry in Miller County, Missouri. Everything went dry in the fall, and a lone squirrel hunter was rambling to the head waters of Saline Creek that empties in the Osage River about four miles below Tuscumbia, Missouri. With parched lips this man was longing and looking for a drink of water, but all the branches and springs were dry in the upper stretches of the Saline.

He sat down on a log to wait for a squirrel to come out of a hole in a nearby tree, and in the forest's stillness he soon heard water trickling somewhere. Looking further up the ravine, he saw a tiny stream of water forcing itself up out of the parched earth. He hurried to the spot to find a small stream of clear water coming up out of Mother Earth.

He dug a small hole in the ground, waited for the water to clear, and drank his fill of this sparkling fluid. This man was subject to swelling spells after taking a cold drink of water, and he sat down to wait for this swelling that never came. After taking another large swig of this water without any after effects, he said to the solitude of the forest, "By ye Gods, I have found the fountain of youth right here in Missouri."

He hiked over to Preacher Downing, the man who owned the land the spring was on. Together they went back to the spring and after drinking their fill returned to their homes to report the find of fresh and healing water.

As press agents they both made good. They named the place Aurora Springs, and in three months' time some 1,500 people had gathered around these healing waters. The lame, the blind, the weak and the strong gathered here, in what then was a wilderness, to find the fountain of youth. They came in every known way, in what were yet pioneer days, and stayed anyway they could. No doubt some were benefited and these waters had healing qualities for some ailments; but their powers were not what some claimed for them.

CHAPTER 7 ≈ WHOPPERS

They told the story of a bald-headed man who went a long distance to this spring, as it had been reported to him that this water would restore lost hair. He took a keg, went to the spring, filled it up with this pure water, and when he got back home several days later, the keg was all sprouted out with shiny black hair. Whether the water grew hair on his head has never been told; but stories like these are what put Aurora Springs on the map, and we are still looking for the fountain of youth.

This history can be verified by Capt. William D. Earp, of the new steamer Bixby, as he was a boy in this neighborhood at that time.

Incredible as it may seem, Steamboat Bill presented this whopper as a true story in The Waterways Journal.

One Story Not in My Book

Before the government held the banks on the Missouri River and the banks still were caving into the river, the steamer Nicholas Wall, a very fast sternwheel boat, was making weekly trips out of St. Louis to Lexington, Missouri. This took a fast boat, and the Wall was the only packet boat in history that ever made weekly trips this far up the Missouri River.

One morning, while coming up Prunty Bend, the pilot on this high stepper, saw someone floating down the river on a peculiar object. This proved to be a beautiful girl named Till Turner, who had fallen in the river while pumping water out of a brick cistern.

The captain of the Wall was a tall, handsome, young Irishman from down on the lower Mississippi, and after questioning this beautiful maiden, he decided to tow the cistern back home seven miles upstream to the head of Hill's Bend, or Buffington Landing. This proved to be a tiresome undertaking, and if his boat had not been a powerful one, he never would have accomplished his purpose.

The pilots, the purser and the mate all objected to this undertaking, but to no avail. The captain said: "I know Mr. Turner, and with the reputation you Missouri River steamboatmen have, if we do not return this girl with the evidence that she floated away, he will swear we kidnapped her and will fill us full of shot." Mr. Turner was a Southerner and a slave owner, and Miss Till was the belle of Carrol County, very popular and handsome indeed.

≈ STEAMBOAT TREASURES ≈

The river had been encroaching badly on Mr. Turner's land. The servants had all gone to the emancipation picnic, and Miss Turner went to the cistern to get a bucket of water. It was foggy that morning, and having no idea the river was that close, she started to pump when cistern, girl, pump and all caved into the river.

Her cries for help were hushed by the raging water and caving bank, and on down the mighty river went this wonderful girl clinging to the pump handle. Her trip was uneventful until she was picked up by the crew of the steamer Nicholas Wall. Here her life's romance commenced, as handsome Capt. Riley captured her heart and fancy at once.

When the Wall landed at Turner's Plantation, a day late on account of towing that cistern, and after tying same up to the bank, Capt. Riley himself took the girl ashore. After Miss Till had explained her absence, her parents could not thank the handsome boatman enough, and they would not let the boat leave until everybody down to the roustabouts, had tasted of Southern hospitality in liquid form.

It was a happy crew, indeed, that left Buffington Landing that day. It goes without saying that the Nicholas Wall got more than her share of freight on all of Hill's Bend the balance of that season, and her captain more than his share of attention from the Turner family, especially their only daughter.

This cistern later broke loose in a fall flood and floated down the river some 217 miles, where it struck the head of Struttman's Island and broke or fell in two. When the river fell, Henry Struttman hauled these brick out on his Island and built a smokehouse out of them.

Steamboat Bill ran true to form finishing this story— chronology was never one of his worries. Having already recorded the Emancipation Picnic, he concludes with the Civil War.

The Turners lost all their land, and the Civil War found them back in the South. The steamer Wall and her handsome captain, too, went South that fall after that record-breaking and eventful season on the Big Muddy. Miss Turner's love for Captain Riley, was never returned, and after fighting through the Civil War, he drifted to Alaska, where Miss Turner later followed him, only to find that he had married an Indian woman. The broken-hearted lady returned to the States, where she died an old maid.

The last account of Riley was just after the mad gold rush. With the

CHAPTER 7 ≈ WHOPPERS

help and knowledge of his Indian wife, he had found his sack of dust, and when asked by his kin and friends (the old pilots of the Wall wanted to make a loan) to bring his wife and four children back to the States at least for a visit, he said, "I am now an old man, I want to see all of Alaska first. With all my riches, I could not duplicate the old Nicholas Wall, so here I stay, and here I die." And here ends a story more true than most readers will believe possible.

In "Lopsided Sal," published in 1948, Steamboat Bill stretched his imagination and storytelling skills—and perhaps his reader's patience.

Along about the year 1915, this old barnacled codger wrote an article in *The Waterways Journal* about a fisherman who was the father of a platinum blonde daughter whose looks and form would put anything in the shade since Hollywood became a movie center. *[The blonde has nothing to do with the story, so do not bother looking for her.]*

Some years ago, this man's son, while camping in one of the old river warehouses at Miami, Missouri, found an iron box containing historical documents worth millions of dollars. After reading the contents, he left the box lying around, until one day he needed a sinker for his trot lines. He set the trot lines some two miles below De Witt, Missouri, among the wrecks of such famous boats as the A. C. Bird, R. W. Dugan, New Lucy and 10 other wrecks of old-time packets. When he raised his trot line, the sinker pulled loose. What is perhaps the greatest historical document in history lies buried in the shifting sands of a great river, where treasures galore lie buried for all time.

Here is the story this young man told me of what he read in the document:

Long, long ago, before the age of the Mound Builders, there was in America a super race of men and women whose children at birth were larger and stronger than Tarzan ever dared to be. They were known as the Concrete Tribe, which in a way proves that America is the oldest country in the whole world and that we did pretty well with it before the Mayflower landed. In some 300 years, by manipulating foolish laws, corrupt politicians, who stayed up nights to give our country away and to collect taxes, have created a debt that never will be paid in the life of man or beast. By their tactics, the price of wild turkeys was raised from 20 cents to about $29 and other foods in about the same brackets.

These good-natured giants of old were not numerous. Only about 2,000 of them lived in what is now the state of California. Becoming crowded, they decided to migrate to some other sections of our country. They started their trek east with their pet rattlesnakes, white elephants, mammoths and all their other junk.

The leaders of this tribe were Oswald Shuffelbaum and his wife, Lopsided Sal. The latter got her nickname from building a levee (they built levees in those days, too.) In working with her big mammoths, she undermined a mountain, which slid down on her and broke her lower portside leg some 25 feet above the foot, halfway up to her knee. When the bone knitted and she could walk again, the leg was several feet shorter, hence her name Lopsided Sal.

Before leaving California these good people became steamboat-minded, and this has since happened to other people, to their grief and sorrow. The whole story of their migration, carrying material for building a mammoth steamboat on which all their 2,000 people could live in harmony, is told in the lost papers. With their animals and strong backs, they transported all the materials and tools to built this boat.

They wandered east for three years and finally found a spot on the banks of Salt River that suited their purpose to build this boat, the Lopsided Sal. They had with them their concrete mixers and large trees of California redwood, both solid and hollow. One can imagine the size of these men who could carry California redwoods upon their backs with ease. It took 10 years to build this boat.

When they decided to launch the hull, they found it was twice as wide as the Salt River. It took them four years longer to saw her in two lengthwise; then they floated both hulls out into the Mississippi River. Here they spliced the two hulls together with wooden pegs, then started to install the machinery and build the cabin.

She was a low-pressure, compound affair. They installed 27 concrete boilers with a working pressure of four pounds. The engines were made of hollow redwood trees. The larger cylinder was 97 inches in diameter, with a 24-hour stroke. The walking beam on her cold-water doctor was 223 feet long. Being superstitious, like all good boatmen, they could not put 13 boilers on one side, so they put 12 on one side and 15 on the other. They did not have any naval architects in those days, so they made another mistake and put the doctor and large, low-pressure

CHAPTER 7 ≈ WHOPPERS

cylinder on the same side as the 15 boilers. Of course, their boat was lopsided, too, and hence her name.

They did not know about the Cory system of engine-room telegraphs, so were up against a stiff proposition, until their head carpenter suggested using one of their big rattlesnakes to pass signals to the engine room. This old rattler was 487 feet long, and it took 27 deer hides to make a collar for his neck. On the end of his tail he had 42 rattles as big as cow bells. They stretched him out from the pilothouse, down under the boiler deck and to the engine room. His head was alongside the big pilot wheel, and his tail was near the throttle of the Lopsided Sal.

When the pilot wanted to come ahead, he would hit the old rattler on the head with a 47-pound sledge. This would make him shake his tail once in the engine room. To back up. the pilot would hit the rattler twice. In my day, only one boat had a more musical set of engine bells, the U.S. Minnetonka.

At first, all went well with this boat. She was very fast, a big carrier and a fine handler; but tragedy was in store for these good-natured giants. One day the pilot made a mistake and hit the old rattler on the head three times. The mighty engineer thought they wanted to come ahead strong, so he turned on all the live steam in the low-pressure cylinder. The boat shot ahead and became unmanageable.

The pilot, Possum Bixby, lost his head, and the boat hit a steep rock bank. One side tore loose from the other, slid back stern first and sank in the mighty Mississippi, drowning all on board. The other side, after breaking all the wooden pegs, started down the river, but her boilers burst, killing both humans and animals. They did not have a Coast Guard in those days, or perhaps some of these people might have been saved.

Perhaps it is better as it happened. When you stop to think that one of these giants ate a large elephant for breakfast, if America was now inhabited by 147,000,000 of these monster tribesmen, they would eat up everything, and we would not be able to feed starving Europe.

Steamboat Bill says that one of the main causes of this disaster was the many white elephants aboard this boat.

Rabbit, the great colored, story-telling roustabout, says that most of the islands on the lower Mississippi were first started by the two wrecks of the Lopsided Sal and the bodies of these big men and beasts. Some day, within the next 80 years, we'll try to get in touch with some good divers and find the box. We will sell it and build a steamboat that will make the Lopsided Sal look like old Rough Head's light draft Gasconade River packet Kingfisher.

Strangely, this story provoked a reply. Ralph I. Henderson came forward to swear that "Steamboat Bill's Lopsided Story Was True."

While reading a December issue of *The Waterways Journal*, I was quite startled to see the headline "The Lopsided Sal" and note my old friend Steamboat Bill's name under it. Some years ago, Steamboat Bill and I had often discussed the historical documents to which he referred as we sat around the potbellied stove at the Florence Yard during the long winter evenings. I was somewhat younger than Steamboat Bill at the time, still am for that matter, and was inclined to doubt the veracity of his stories of that ancient race of supermen contained in those old documents.

Steamboat could always spin a good yarn, but he was so explicit on this particular story and insisted that he himself had seen the contents of that steel box. Of course, he readily admitted that he could not read the documents, the characters of which appeared to be "so much Chinese" to him. In fact, his description of the writings led me to believe they may have been somewhat similar to the ancient picture writing, interspersed with characters and symbols, such as the ancient Mongolian tribes used to record their deeds and actions.

I was never acquainted with the young man who found these valuable old records, but Steamboat's account of the difficulties this young man had in deciphering the ancient record, the study and research it had required, together with the impressive list of eminent psychologists (Steamboat assured me that this five-dollar word referred to those specialists in reading the thoughts of modern men from "doodles," so who could be more proficient in interpreting ancient picture writing?) to which the young man had been referred in his efforts to read the document, convinced me that the stories he read from the manuscript must be authentic.

I know that Steamboat was sincere in his recounting of these ancient records, for at that time his mind was clearer and he could recall with vivid detail many more of the exploits of that ancient super-race than

CHAPTER 7 ≈ WHOPPERS

the specific instance he recorded in *The Waterways Journal*.

In those days I was much more athletic than at present and was very interested in Steamboat's tales of the sport of those ancient supermen. Of course, the conception of sport has changed very greatly over the centuries. For instance, hunting, today considered a major sport, in those days was considered work. Proficiency in wrestling and fighting was necessary for everyday survival, and the pitting of animal against animal in mortal combat was a cunning device to reduce the work necessary in hunting and not considered in the light of sport at all.

However, those old documents do tell of a game that I have no doubt is the origination of our game of golf. The tribe's leader, Oswald Shuffelbaum, realizing that if his tribe was to survive in the modern world of that time, knew that they must be provided with some form of relaxation after an arduous day's work. This, of course, was after the tribe had migrated from California to their campsite on the Salt River. While in California, their leisure time was occupied by swimming in the deeper parts of the Pacific Ocean.

Oswald tells how he considered many types of relaxation but finally decided upon a game something similar to our present day golf as the ideal sport, one which would keep his hunters and warriors keen of mind, sound of wind and limb and, at the same time, provide the relaxation they so desperately needed.

He called the young men of the tribe together and laid down the rules of the game, which were quite simple. Each player was to be given a set of five irons and a supply of balls. Starting from a given point, each player was to see how far he could knock his ball from the starting point, or tee. After he had teed off, the players lined up at the starting line and sprinted to their own ball. From then on, it was a race around the course to see which man could propel his ball to the "cup" in each successive "green," using the clubs only and be the first back to the starting line.

The first task, of course, was to lay out and build the course. Great credit is given to a young engineer in the tribe, named Bunion, who did the surveying for the course. The course consisted of only four holes, but it lay over some of the most difficult terrain then known. Reference points used in the survey for this course have long since been lost, but from the general description of the course, its location can still be plotted today. The first tee must have been located in the Smoky Mountains for the document mentions the difficulties the builders had in keeping the atmosphere clear while they were building up and leveling the tee.

Lopsided Sal herself finally solved the problem by holding her skirt above her head with both arms extended, then shifting her weight first to the long leg and then to the short leg, thus causing her body to weave from side to side. This action caused such a wind that the air remained clear for three days, during which time the men were able to complete the tee. Flat-top Mountain in the Great Smoky Mountains of today is probably the remnants of this very tee.

Sand greens were decided upon, since it was feared that grass greens would probably attract the grass-eating dinosaurs of that time and thus slow down the game while one of the players chased them off. The first green, constructed in what is now the southeastern part of the United States, was made by pumping sand from the Pacific Ocean through a pipeline of hollow redwood trees. The cup in this green was probably what is now known as Death Valley. Remnants of these three greens are also known as the Gobi Desert in Asia, the Great Sandy Desert in Australia and the Sahara Desert in Africa.

The construction of the course required six weeks by three of the best men in the tribe. While this was in progress, other men were at work molding the iron heads of the clubs to be used in the game.

The clubs had shafts made from the redwood trees and heads of iron similar to today's clubs. Five different shaped heads were made by scooping out the desired shapes in the earth, then melting iron and allowing it to run into three molds and harden. Since the blast furnace was unknown at that time, the tribe used the open flame method for melting their iron.

They piled up a huge stack of ore near their molds and built a large fire at the base of the pile. Two men were required to blow on the fire to produce the required heat, and, as the iron melted, it was led into the molds through open ditches, all the molds being close together and connected by shallow ditches so that all could be poured at one run.

The document gave the calculations of the quantity of iron required for the pour and adds that an allowance of five percent for overrun was made but not required when the actual pour was made. This op-

Tales of fantastic boats were a popular staple of river lore. These illustrations appeared in the January 6, 1923, issue of The Waterways Journal

eration took place in the region now known as the Great Lakes country and, without a doubt, the lakes were formed by water collecting in these molds, and that unused five percent of iron is doubtless the Iron Mountain of today.

The course was a success from the day it was opened; its greens were magnificent; its rough was really rough, and those water hazards were something to talk about. However, its very creation probably contributed in a large part to the final annihilation of the tribe.

After 36 holes on this course, the men would come in hungry enough to eat two large elephants, which they did. This heavy consumption of food caused a sharp increase in the market price, and commercial hunters immediately started killing the game faster than it was produced, eventually causing a famine, which so reduced the tribe in numbers that they decided to migrate to Africa, where it was reported that a large herd of elephants was still in existence.

It was during this migration aboard the Lopsided Sal that the pilot, Possum Bixby, made a fatal mistake of tapping the wrong signal on his engine bell resulting in the tragic drowning of all souls, as Steamboat Bill has already told you.

At times Steamboat Bill's readers must have wondered if a story was true or a whopper, a product of what the author called "spontaneous combustion."

Up between Glasgow, Missouri, and Kansas City, on the Missouri River, a colored bootlegger had a large batch of mash for whiskey in a monster of a big feed trough. A female hog, after wallowing around in the mud and slime of the horse lot, got a whiff of this stuff and decided to investigate. In wandering around she got too close and fell into the trough of mash and drowned. Someone said to the bootlegger, "That must have been a big loss for you." He answered, "No, sir, boss, we ate the hawg and those river contracting boys working out there bought every drop of the likker."

Steamboatmen seemed to take great delight in concocting stories about imagined steamers.

The Story of the Steamer Cackler

In the year of 1832 the monster steamer Cackler came out to run exclusively between Happy Jack Hollow and Chicken Point, a distance of 299 miles on the Missouri River. This boat was very fast, but only

CHAPTER 7 ≈ WHOPPERS

made monthly trips between these points, as her captain and sole owner, Chick Bantam, was a peculiar kind of a cuss. He only ran his boat on Fridays, Sundays, holidays and the 13th of the month, which was his day of departure from Happy Jack Hollow. This boat came out late in the fall and only made one trip in 1832 before the ice drove her into the mouth of the Sni River for winter quarters.

In 1833 they made eight round trips, but on their ninth trip her big 18-inch copper steam pipe burst and killed 800 roustabouts. This pipe ran clean across the deck and connected the two big batteries of boilers on each side of the colossal craft. Besides killing these roustabouts, many claimed this explosion is what made all the stars fall in the year of 1833. Among this number was our very learned and smart man named Darrow, but Capt. Chick said this was only monkey talk.

The Cackler was a monster of a boat. Your imagination would have to be all intact and just off dry dock to grasp the size of the boat and the wonders to be seen there. She had an immense stateroom for every one of her 1,600 roustabouts, with running water and a barrel of whiskey standing open with a tin cup hanging on a nail in each room. A Texas tender got lost in the Captain's room and was gone three days before they found him. The farmers would drive aboard with their ox teams, go right up the steps and drive clear around the cabin. They carried lots of eggs on the boiler deck.

The captain found two big gooseberry bushes, which he had dug up and put in monster tubs, and they grew to be 50 feet high. When these millions of berries, big as an apple, were ripe, horticultural eyes expanded in wonder indeed.

The Cackler was a hard boat on fuel, she turned her monster wheels 40 revolutions per minute, and every time she exhausted 17 cords of wood went up in smoke. She was the only boat up to that time that had a pilothouse on each side and four pilots on a watch at the same time. She was so wide that they loaded wood and other freight underway from both sides of the river.

The roustabouts would hop off ahead of the boilers and come back aboard on the front of the fire doors to drop their wood and go back after more, a constant stream of humanity traveling around these boilers night and day, feeding these boilers whose fire doors faced aft. This was one of the first boats built that gave the high-pressure boats the name of fuel hogs. This boat had a battery of 13 Jonestown boilers on her starboard side, which gave them lots of trouble from flooding.

One day they picked up a gray-haired, long-white-bearded old, old, man coming down the river in a bullboat. He had a tub on his head for a hat. He said his name was Noah and he was headed for the Ohio River. He was a marine engineer off a boat in retirement that was built out of wood. Capt. Chick gave him the berth on the starboard side, and they had no more trouble with their Jonestown boilers.

On the port side of this lugger, they had 26 small-tube, high pressure boilers. They kept 13 fired up and 13 cooled down to put in new tubes, as they were continually crowding this old hussy and her tube boilers would not stand up. When the Cackler's steam pipe burst, the boats running on the Missouri River at that time had to lay up three days for the fog and steam to clear up from the explosion. The shells fell all over central Missouri for several days.

This boat had two monster sternwheels and six propellers operating off windmills between the sternwheels. She was very fast when the wind was right but almost helpless on a calm day. One day a sea lawyer came up from the port of New Orleans. He bent the exhaust pipes so they would exhaust the waste steam from the mammoth high-pressure engines against the fans of the windmills. After that, their troubles were over, and the Cackler was a fast boat, indeed.

The extreme hot weather and low water of 1834 almost broke up Capt. Chick. He only made one trip that season, and it got so hot that all the eggs hatched on deck. When he finally arrived at Happy Jack Hollow, he had 9,000 dozen roosters and a lot of hens. When they congratulated him on his foresight, he said that was nothing to crow about.

In some countries they do not raise any chickens; in China, many. One can buy a chicken there with feathers for 10 cents; without, $3.95 and up.

In 1835 Capt. Chick started to buy ducks and geese, but the decksweepers union, which was very strong at that time, threatened to strike, and he went back to eggs and chickens.

The Cackler did a big and profitable business for many years, but in the flood of 1844, the pilots tried to turn her around at the mouth of Grand River and disaster came. Up to this time they had always backed down the river, as there was not room enough to turn around. They

CHAPTER 7 ≈ WHOPPERS

backed her stern away up in the Grand River between two bluffs. The swift current caught her head in the Missouri, and the stern jammed between the bluffs up the smaller stream and fouled the boat, which caused her to break square off in front of the boilers and the big steam pipe.

They sawed off both ends of this boat by clever work, in which a deckhand by the name of Rabbit proved a hero and Rhode Island Red, the first mate, did wonders with his crew of frightened roustabouts. In saving both ends of this boat in these raging rivers, they only lost one-half cord of wood, seven dozen eggs and two roosters.

They put a square or box head on the boat and were again ready for business. This was the start of the first barge line on the Missouri. Capt. Chick, after making one trip, had two more barges built like the end of the Cackler. He named his three barges Rino, Hippo and Sorceress. After many trials and tribulations, he lasted four years. His immense fortune was gone, and he was busted for true.

The Hippo hit a hidden obstruction in Prunty Bend and sank with a heavy cargo of eggs in 40 feet of water and was a total loss. In rounding out under Saline City, the chains broke and the Rino got away and drifted way out of the river at the foot of Nigger Bend before they could catch her. A quick fall left her stranded for all time.

Capt. Chick got back to Happy Hollow in the fall of 1848 with a full cargo, mostly eggs. He drove his chickens to St. Louis, but when he got back to his boat almost all of his crew had left for the Black Hills, after stealing the money out of the safe.

Capt. Bill Massie, one of his famed pilots at that time, was one of the last to leave the Cackler, and he is the man who told me this story just as it is related here. In leaving Capt. Chick, Massie said, "Captain Bantam, I hate to leave you, but this had to come. I begged you with tears in my eyes not to start a barge line, as the Missouri River is not a large-line stream and never will be."

Captain Massie shipped out of St. Louis as pilot on the first boat to the mountains in the spring of 1849 with Captain Gates McGarrah as his master. (Many remember Captain Bill McGarrah, his son, the crack Missouri River, St. Louis and Cairo pilot.) In leaving Captain McGarrah at Fort Benton, Captain Massie, at that time a young man, said, "Captain, I am leaving you for the great gold strike in the Black Hills. Call it deserting you may, but I am going, and if virtue, honesty and industry will make a killing, I shall have one whether I find any gold or not."

Captain Chick stayed with his boat. The severe winter of 1848-49 froze all his eggs, the ice sunk the steamboat, and while all his crew was wandering in the Black Hills in search of gold, he died, some say with a broken heart.

What became of the hull of the barge Sorceress no one knows. Up until a few years ago the wreck of the Cackler could still be seen in dead low water along shore out just below Point Royal. Part of her furnaces and part of her stacks still show above Point Royal. For some reason these stacks were taken ashore and still stick out of the ground. On top of the high Point Royal Bluffs just below these smokestacks are some old graves. These Captain Massie said were the graves of Capt. Chick and the few faithful followers who stayed with him to the bitter end.

Games were often in Steamboat Bill's thoughts as he wrote. In "Rival Towns," written in 1938, he waxed eloquent on the subject of baseball.

Almost a half century ago, when Knighthood was in Flower, and when times were good along the mysterious Big Muddy, when a nickel was as big as a wagon wheel, and when a boy or young man would dig a gallon of worms for a dime, we had, and still have, two rival towns on the Missouri River. In these two little burgs at that time lived two bare-footed boys who our rivers made famous, until they now stand high in the Federal Barge Lines. One is a noted master and pilot, and the other a noted marine engineer. Both have "been places" since that time; and now our story starts:

Since all time in America, nothing in the way of sports causes more rivalry among small towns than two good ball teams, and these two places had them. Along towards the tail end of our season, when Mr. and Mrs. Bob White had raised their flock of young and when the leaves were beginning to turn along the picturesque bluffs of this mighty river, each team of these rival towns had won 12 games. And one fine Sunday afternoon, the deciding game was to be played at the little city farthest down the river. The ballpark was out on a sandbar at the lower end of town. Almost everybody in that community was there, excitement was running high, and fist fights were common.

CHAPTER 7 ≈ WHOPPERS

The players wore no uniforms, their equipment of gloves was scarce, masks and protectors none, and they only had two Spaldings to start the game. Both pitchers were being pounded to all corners of the lot. Although the game from the start was a free-hitting contest, through sensational fielding the score stood close and at the end of the fifth inning was tied 3 to 3.

Then both pitchers settled down to work. At the beginning of the sixth, Slugfest Lewis hit a mighty wallop, which went foul by inches. This smash broke the last factory-made bat square in two. After that the players would pick out bats from a nearby rack heap. At the end of the 14th inning, with the score still tied even, driftwood was getting scarce.

With the score 3 to 3 in the last half of the 15th, Big Burr Head Aram, the hardest hitter on either team, came to bat with two men out. It was getting along towards the shank of the evening, and old Sol was going to his daily rest behind some black clouds. Excitement was at fever heat. The fans were yelling for a hit, a home run.

"Hit her out into the river, Burr Head."

All they had left now for a bat was a piece of fence rail. The first ball was a called strike for the groaning multitude, and this started a small riot. The umpire saved his scalp and got out of town all in one piece by catching a passing freight train. Another umpire called the next effort a ball. Again, long Slim Sanders raised his left wing for another ball, again that slow, graceful wind up, and Sanders dished out another ball. Then on the next pitch Burr Head poled out a long hit that went foul by inches and again broke a bat.

With the count three balls and two strikes on Burr Head, 70-year-old Lady Lulu Belle Smackem, with one wooden leg, jumped up off a big drift log that acted for a seat in one of the grandstands. She ran out towards the home plate crying, "Call time, Mr. Umpire." She unbuckled her starboard wooden leg above the knee, handed it to Burr Head and said, "Use this for a bat, you big bum, and get a hit or else strike for home, you big Hussar."

Again, the long lanky arm of Slim Sanders went up and came around in a rainbow curve. But the ball did not break right, and Burr Head hit it smash in the face. At the crack of the bat or wooden leg, Burr Head rounded the bases like the Smoky City Dutchman at his best. Nobody saw where the ball went, and the umpire made a run for his life. Then they picked up Burr Head and carried him across the railroad tracks and up town to celebrate.

The big climax to this famous ball game came the next day when a dyed-in-the-wool lady fan on the opposite side was visiting with Old Lady Lulu Belle Swatfest. This good woman was complaining about her wooden leg. She said, "Sally, my ball bearings in the knee of my wooden leg are sure hurting me today; I can hardly waddle around." She took off the ex-bat, or hollow wooden leg, turned it upside down, and out rolled the baseball—which caused a scandal that never was straightened out up near where Jessie and Frank James used to roam. [Lady Lulu Belle Smackem and Lady Lulu Belle Swatfest are one in the same. Steamboat Bill simply forgot what he had named her.]

Capt. J. S. Hacker had a few things to say about Steamboat's wandering narrative ways.

Bill Heckmann is a man we all admire and read with interest. Everything he writes is good but not always understandable or relevant. What I want to say about Bill is all in good part and not intended to offend. In the issue of August 31, 1930, he writes about trying to get over Pelican Bar in the Missouri River, the river of his youth and his manhood, but let me quote him:

> *Some 10 days back we had three ministers aboard the steamer Eugenia Woods trying to pull up over Pelican Bar in the Missouri River. A white mule stood on the bank watching us, and One Wing, one of our deckhands, said he could see him smiling to himself. They say a river pilot's spirit comes back to earth in a white mule; I bet they have wished for a good drink this summer.*

No explanation is made as to where he got the ministers and if he got them to help pull up over the bar. Just what part did they take in that effort, what relation was there between the ministers and the gray mule that had in him the spirit of a long departed Missouri River pilot and stood on the bank and smiled as he watched their futile efforts?

Who wished for a good drink—drink of what? He says "they," so it must have been both the mule and the spirit—if spirits drink—that he had within him. Or was it the preachers; or did he mean a gentle stab at Prohibition or the scarcity of water in the Missouri River? Evidently,

CHAPTER 7 ≈ WHOPPERS

he meant that drinks were scarce, but drinks of what? He says a "good" drink, so it must have been water he had in mind, unless he referred to the preachers.

His writing is not in sequence and his ideas are frequently sandwiched, but for all that he is the coming Mark Twain of the Missouri River, though at times he is drawing "deep four," particularly when he gets on the subject of religion. I have seen the statement he is writing a book. I know it will be good.

Anything for a laugh: Steamboat Bill referred to this garb as his Greek costume.

CHAPTER 8

U.S. Army Corps of Engineers
The Story He Forgot to Tell

Steamboat Bill wrote about subjects he thought would interest readers of *The Waterways Journal*. Since this was the riverman's magazine, he assumed readers knew what was happening along the Missouri River. One of his oversights was in not telling more about the work of the U.S. Army Corps of Engineers. Throughout most of his long career, Steamboat Bill served on boats commissioned to do Missouri improvement work. But it is doubtful that even he knew the history of the work of the Corps.

The story of just how the Corps came to be in the river control business is a long one. Rudiments of the U.S. Army Corps of Engineers were established long before settlers of the new nation-to-be realized the importance of inland waterways. The day before the Battle of Bunker Hill was fought, the Continental Congress provided General George Washington with a chief engineer and two assistants "in a separate department" to carry out engineering activities. Washington obtained permission to organize a Corps of Engineers. By the end of the Revolutionary War, the need for military engineers ceased. In the ensuing years Congress disbanded and re-established an engineering department several times, with none becoming permanent.

In 1802 President Thomas Jefferson called on Congress to create a "Defense Establishment," and the Corps was permanently established. A Military Academy was created at West Point, New York, where the Corps' first headquarters was established and where virtually all the nation's engineers were trained.

These engineers were soon involved in major projects. Without them there would have been no Erie Canal, which is how the "water" factor entered the work of the Corps. The U.S. Army Corps of Engineers soon would be known as the largest, most diversified engineering organization in the world.

CHAPTER 8 ≈ U.S. ARMY CORPS OF ENGINEERS

The Corps dealt with engineering surveys, expeditions and surveys of routes for transcontinental railroads. It opened the Great Lakes to navigation, developed a successful seagoing hopper dredge capable of deepening Atlantic harbors for larger vessels and improved navigation on major rivers. The hallmark of the 20th-century Corps was its growing involvement in flood control and navigation.

Several divisions for jurisdiction of the Corps were established, as the need for better navigation and flood control became acute in the Ohio, Mississippi, Missouri, Columbia and Sacramento valleys. Because of its location on the lower reaches of the Missouri River, the Kansas City District's history is deeply entwined with the "Big Muddy."

While exploring the Mississippi River in 1673, Father Pere Marquette came across the mouth of the wild and turbulent Missouri River. It was not until Lewis and Clark fought their way upstream in 1804-1805, propelled by long poles, the cordelle and, occasionally, small sails, that any real knowledge of the Missouri River Valley became available.

Beginning at Three Forks, Montana, three rivers—the Gallatin, Jefferson and the Madison—converge to form the Missouri headwaters. Some 2,500 twisted miles later, the Missouri joins the Mississippi River about 18 miles above St. Louis, Missouri. Dreams of a waterway to the West were common, and as soon as steamboats were available, regular trips "to the mountains" were established. Pilots who could maneuver a steamer through the intricate braid of waters to safely deliver a cargo to the upper reaches of the river demanded high salaries—$1,000 to $2,000 per month. Many mountain pilots successfully demanded pay by the trip.

The first steamers on the Missouri were primitive affairs. They required more power than those designed for the more placid Eastern streams. Major Stephen H. Long of the Army Corps of Engineers, who had led expeditions up the Mississippi River, proposed building a steamboat that was strong enough to fight the Missouri's current and that had a draft shallow enough to pass over its sandbars.

Long's orders were to sail from St. Louis to the mouth of the Yellowstone River—a distance of more than 2,000 miles. His small fleet fell far short of its goal. The Thomas Jefferson sank near Cote Sans Dessein, less than 150 miles upriver. The Independence made it well over 200 miles, while the Western Engineer, the boat under Long's direction, ascended all the way to Council Bluffs, Iowa, almost 700 miles. Long never reached the upper reaches

≈ STEAMBOAT TREASURES ≈

Taming the wild Missouri: Willow mats were woven along the banks and then moved into position. Then pilings were set to hold the mats in place.

CHAPTER 8 ≈ U.S. ARMY CORPS OF ENGINEERS

of the river, but he did prove that the Missouri could be navigated with steamboats.

The Corps continued to work on the problem. Major Charles R. Suter, often referred to as the mastermind of Missouri River stabilization, concluded that protection of concave bends by revetment, constriction of the prism width and the removal of snags should create a situation of uniform width, slope and depth. When the 1881 Congress increased the appropriation for Missouri River work to $850,000, it appeared river improvements would accelerate dramatically. The Missouri River Commission was established in 1884 to systematically upgrade the river. Suter, who was one of three Corps of Engineers officers on the five-man board, served as Commission president from its creation until the end of 1895. (It was the old Missouri River Commission that gave Steamboat Bill his first berth on a government boat, the little steamer Arethusa.)

Now the problem was a lack of blueprints on how to conquer a river. Stabilizing a sand bottom required something to hold it in place. Out of this need came the use of the willow mat, which by the mid-1880s had become fairly standard. Willow limbs were woven into a sturdy mat, which was slid onto the bank and weighed down with stones. Sometimes piling was driven through the mats. The willow mattress underwent numerous improvements through the years and proved itself a mainstay of bank stabilization.

Starting in 1903 and continuing for five wet years, there were disastrous floods in the Missouri Valley. The weather pattern was similar to one that hung over the Missouri Valley during 1993-1994. The River and Harbor Act of 1907 authorized $450,000 for maintenance of navigation on the Missouri River and ordered a survey of the river from its mouth to Sioux City, Iowa.

Capt. Edward Schultz, first commander of the Kansas City office, compiled a detailed, comprehensive study of work that had been done and work still needed. This report was not sent to the House of Representatives until December of 1908, too late for an appropriation, and the 1909 appropriations did not even mention the Missouri River. However, the next year $2 million went into the project, with a goal of completing a 6-foot channel from Kansas City to the mouth in 10 years. This proved an impossible task.

World War I shifted the Army's focus from navigation to the war in Europe. At the close of the war, renewed interest in river improvement included flood control, as well as navigation. Dams were proposed, and a question soon arose. Would the purpose of the dams be flood control or a controlled flow of water to maintain a 6-foot channel? Dam sites were chosen at Arlington on the Gasconade River, Chillicothe on the Grand River, Topeka on the Kansas River and Fort Peck on the Missouri River. The Fort Peck dam was the only one built, and, as on essentially every man-made lake, recreational interests soon attempted to override the original goals of the project. The battle continues to this day.

Dam construction by the Army Corps of Engineers fell short of the original goal, but many private dams were constructed, such as Bagnell dam on the Osage River, which was to be a power dam, with flood control as a secondary factor. Little did the builders know that recreational interests would so largely influence the use of the resulting Lake of the Ozarks.

In the early 1970s the Corps of Engineers built Truman dam to aid Bagnell. Reversible turbines can pump water back up into the reservoir during slack periods so more water will be available for power production when demand increases. This more sophisticated technique was made possible because the headwaters of the Lake of the Ozarks extend to the foot of Truman dam. Hydroelectric power is not a major aspect of the Kansas City District; it is another dimension of the overall tasks undertaken by the Corps.

The years between 1907 and 1933 were turbulent for the Kansas City District. The Missouri Valley grew dramatically in population, commerce and industry. Nature's whims alternately overran vast areas with flood waters or baked the land hard with drought. The work of the Corps was expanded to meet these challenges.

When Colonel Lawrence J. Lincoln was assigned District Engineer of the Kansas District in July 1950, he was in charge of flood control and river development work for his district, as well as maintenance and improvement of the Missouri River channel and construction of agricultural levees along both banks from Rulo, Nebraska, to the mouth, a few miles above St. Louis.

At this time the district's flood control activities covered an area of more than 110,000 square miles, including roughly two-thirds of Missouri, the northern half of Kansas, a portion of southwestern Iowa, the southern half of Nebraska and the eastern third of Colorado. In addition, the Kansas City District supervised military construction at numerous facilities, including five large air bases, three large army posts and three ordnance arsenals.

Steamboat Bill lived in hope of seeing the control of floods with the construction of the huge dams on the upper Missouri. Somehow, the idea

CHAPTER 8 ≈ U.S. ARMY CORPS OF ENGINEERS

Snags, fire and ice were all destroyers of steamboats. The Corps of Engineers used big snagboats to pull obstructions from the channel.

was perfect, but the results were not. The Fort Peck Dam was completed and also the Big Bend and Garrison dams. For most of his working life, he was in command of the little steamers that helped in the revetment work. He worked for companies that had contracts for river improvement work—DeWitt and Shoby, the Kansas City Missouri River Bridge Company and, for the last 15 years of his career, Woods Brothers Construction Company. Their little steamers moved people and the quarter boats where the crews were housed and fed, pile drivers, dredges and snag boats and materials—willow mats, pilings and rock.

When World War II came along in 1941, there were dramatic changes on the river. Shipping declined tremendously, new work almost ceased and maintenance received scant attention. Above St. Joseph, the river started to return to an uncontrolled wild state. In contrast, the war brought a sudden frenzy of boatbuilding at the Gasconade Corps of Engineers Boatyard—not for river work, but for the war effort.

The Gasconade Boatyard was established by the Missouri River Commission on November 1, 1892, at the junction of the Missouri and Gasconade rivers. In its early days it was a modest operation with just a few buildings, including a two-story living quarters, an engine and boiler room and a steam-powered saw and planing room. Its location on the Missouri River provided an ideal spot for the marine way, and a spur line from the Missouri Pacific Railroad allowed easy access for heavy supplies.

One of the first boats constructed was the "Office Boat" Margaret. As soon as it was readied, the supervisory staff moved on board, closing the temporary office at Hermann, Missouri. After completing revetment along the Missouri bank, the young installation appeared ready to move forward. It would be difficult to give an accurate count of the many boats that were built at the boatyard and the countless boats that put in there for repairs and maintenance.

The success of the Gasconade Boatyard was evident in the yard's absorption of other boatyards. In 1897 the Ewing's Landing Yard closed; Osage Point Boatyard and Bonnot's Mill Supply Depot followed suit in 1899. Their functions were taken over by Gasconade.

However, the declining use of the river in the 1890s placed even Gasconade in a precarious position. Fortunately, the need for a good winter harbor, as well as confidence in the future of river commerce, led to the purchase in 1910 of land that had been leased. This area, larger than the original yard, included a stretch of the Gasconade River bank where a mooring could be developed that was safe from ice gorges on the Missouri. In the years that followed, activity increased with the expansion of interest in navigation.

Expanded again in 1929 with the purchase of more land, the yard was able to a provide space where large vessels could be removed from the water and repaired. The harbor was expanded and storage space increased. Two little boats, the Patrick Gass and the John Ordway, were built at the yard in record time and became famous for the long and tedious journey they made to Fort Peck, where they were to assist in the construction of the Fort Peck dam. The Ordway remained there for several years, working on the project. This trip was to make a "mountain pilot" out of Steamboat Bill, but his leave ran out, and he had to return to his position with the Woods Brothers Construction Company before reaching that goal.

Despite the long record of achievement, the Gasconade Boatyard's useful life finally ran out. Two factors sealed its fate: the virtual completion of the navigation project on the Missouri and the increased use of contract labor for navigation work. During the summer of 1972, the U.S. Engineers Boatyard became part of Missouri River history, leaving only a winter harboring place at the mouth of the Gasconade.

CHAPTER 8 ≈ U.S. ARMY CORPS OF ENGINEERS

Bound for the mountains: The Patrick Gass and the John Ordway

To the residents of the Gasconade area, the closing meant loss of work. Many a local boy had his start in life working on the river. George Kishmar, for example, started work at age 17 on willow mattress construction. He was operating a pile driver within a year, then motor boat operator at age 19. In May of 1940 he was appointed channel inspector, Boonville to Gasconade, and from 1941 to 1965 he was channel inspector from Gasconade to the mouth of the Missouri.

In his various job capacities, Kishmar handled the willow mats, the pile driver, channel soundings, the placing of the channel markers, the bouys, the lights and the dayboards. In "My Experiences and Years on the Missouri River" he describes the early buoys and lights.

> *Of the two types of buoys, one called a can was 18 inches in diameter and about 4 feet in length. The other buoy was called a Nun, painted red, with 15 inches of its top white, 18 inches at the center, 5 feet in length tapered to 5 inches at the top and about 8 inches at the bottom.*

As channel inspector during World War II, Kishmar patrolled the river for various Navy craft, taking soundings and writing reports. On occasion, he would board a craft and ride in the pilothouse to post the pilot on the channel. There were mail boxes where he left channel reports so they could

Permeable dikes like these near Omaha narrowed the Missouri River channel and created thousands of acres of new land.

Photo courtesy of The Waterways Journal

be picked up to post a new pilot.

Kishmar also was a channel inspector on the upper reaches of the river for boats coming out of the Leavenworth, Kansas, boatyards. On one occasion, he posted the pilot on the Coast Guard Cutter Sumac, commanded by Lt. Commander Edward Heckmann, one of Steamboat Bill's younger brothers. The Sumac is still running today.

Sadly, today the once famous and busy boatyard is mostly in ruins, with just one small building that serves as an office. But in its day it was a major arm of the Kansas City Corps of Engineers, working hard to provide a 6-foot channel, tame the wild and unruly river within designated banks and stabilize farm lands with levees.

Steamboat Bill did not live to see the end of the boatyards and the improvement work on the river. He always believed the age of steam would return, bringing with it the good old days on the river, especially since a controlled river would provide a fine channel for boats.

CHAPTER 9

Missouri River Pilot

*W*hen *Will L. Heckmann Jr. married in 1892, he was working as a pilot for the hometown Hermann Ferry and Packet Company. In 1894 he responded to an offer of employment on the Missouri River Improvement project with the old Missouri River Commission, forerunner of the U.S. Army Corps of Engineers. He wrote copiously about his years working for the government and particularly enjoyed his little steamer, the Arethusa. He worked on a number of other government boats, but after six years the itch to be a boat owner hit him—no doubt, the same itch that afflicted his father. In later years, Steamboat Bill often voiced his regret in leaving government service. But, apparently, the security of a steady paycheck lacked sufficient appeal.*

I left the Arethusa up in Randolph Bend, eight miles below Kansas City, in the fall of 1900 to come down home to organize the St. Louis and Hermann Packet Company. This company purchased the sternwheel steamer W. H. Grapevine and put her in the weekly St. Louis and Rocheport trade. I was the master pilot all the time she ran in that trade. It was about that same time that they pinned the name of Steamboat Bill on me, and it has clung to me ever since.

Watching his father probably made Steamboat Bill want to scratch his boat-owning itch. The senior Heckmann was, to all appearances, rolling in money and giving free reign to his entrepreneurial drive. From the early 1890s until about 1900, things looked great. Papa bought the old Pryor Mill on the Gasconade River and, according to Will Jr., spent $35,000, all borrowed, on improvements.

Papa sold his stock in the Hermann Ferry and Packet Company, according to his wife "got completely out of boats," and began a most impressive cam-

Heckmann's Mill on the Gasconade River

paign to see how fast he could spend money, all with the best of intentions, thinking he had an unbeatable formula for success.

In conjunction with the mill project, he built the Kingfisher, an ingeniously designed boat that was absolutely suited for the Gasconade River. With a draft of only nine inches, it was said she could run on a heavy dew. Young Will called the Kingfisher a lifesaver—a $3,500 boat that financed a $35,000 mill. Will Sr. also bought the steamer Annie Dell, but after a run-in with high water, he rebuilt her into the steamer Jack Rabbit, a boat famous for being slower than molasses in January.

Newspapers eagerly reported Capt. Heckmann's activities at the mill. One ventured the opinion that he could start a town of his own by simply giving each of his 14 children a lot and declaring himself mayor. Another declared he was planning rail service from the mill to Jefferson City. Steamboat Bill had his own description of his father and the St. Louis and Hermann Packet Company.

Capt. Bill Heckmann Sr. soon found himself owning 55 of the outstanding 100 shares of stock of this lucky and successful little steamboat company. And then he tried to set the world on fire. He quit organizing and went out on his own.

"The time is coming," he said, "when the Missouri River will go almost dry like the Rio Grande, and I am going to buy some islands." He homesteaded and bought what was known as the Bluffton Islands, but now known as the Heckmann Island. He built two houses on them and found some good renters. He then bought McGirk's Island from Capt. Henry Wohlt, three miles above Hermann, which is now also known as Heckmann's Island. This island had one big two-story house on it.

Whenever Father had a good, honest and industrious man on our boats who wanted to be a farmer, he would furnish him a piece of land, build him a house and supply him with stock and implements. When he had spent about $30,000 on his farming venture—about the time the mysterious old river was supposed to commence to go dry—the most destructive flood in history occurred in 1903. The corn on 400 acres of land was waist-high, the golden wheat was ready to cut, and he had eight houses on the islands with a group of fine tenants. This flood sanded the Bluffton Islands and washed seven houses, farm equipment and whatnot into the river. When the flood went down, only 50 acres were left of the 700-acre island. One of his houses was cocked up on one side and appeared to be saying, "Ain't it about time, Capt. Bill, for your river to commence to go dry?"

The other island fared no better.

Today these three islands are back again, and they are among the garden spots in the whole state of Missouri. In 1905 and 1907 there were more floods. In 1915 the river went over the low bottom lands six different times, and it was said that more water went down the river to the sea in that year than was ever before recorded. Now we are building dams in the upper Missouri and on side streams, which will stop these disastrous floods.

The 1915 flood also involved a story about Steamboat Bill and his rival, Curly Young, who were both working for the Missouri River Navigation Company. Steamboat was on the Advance and Curly was on the A.M. Scott when the Missouri River played a trick on Camden, Missouri, the "toe" in a 10-mile long horseshoe bend, ripping out a new channel and leaving the town five miles from water.

≈ STEAMBOAT TREASURES ≈

The way Steamboat Bill told the tale, at midnight he turned the watch over to his nephew, Roy Miller, who had just received his pilot's license. Steamboat went to bed. After a while the young pilot noticed that the boat and barge were making remarkably fast time going upstream on flood water, but he did not want to admit that he didn't know what was causing the strange behavior.

I woke up just at the break of dawn and looked out my stateroom window and saw disaster approaching. I ran up on deck in my underpants and grabbed the wheel. I yelled to Roy, "Set her back! You get down on deck! All hell's about to break loose!"

I did not mean to demote my pilot, but I knew he was an A-1 deckhand, and we needed the best right then. About that time, we hit the bank at what seemed like a rate of 10 miles an hour. Cables and lines flew in all directions. The barge broke loose and started down the cutoff, but she was not satisfied, for she went down some 200 yards and came back on a big eddy three different times and seemed to prefer the cataract in the cutoff to the main channel. The third time she came up, she poked her stern in just the right position for me to give her a bump that sent her out of the rapids and into the main channel.

Steamboat Bill had a very nattily attired deckhand, Silk Hat Harry. Harry's brother worked for a haberdashery in St. Louis. Every time the store changed lines of merchandise, the brother got what was left and generously shared with Harry.

An enormous sycamore tree had lodged in the middle of the cutoff, along with about a quarter mile of rack. The barge paused briefly against this sycamore. Silk Hat Harry grabbed a 2-inch line from the prow of the barge and snubbed one end around the tree. But the other two deckhands could not get a turn on the bitts, for the barge was now on her way and was in a hurry. Silk Hat Harry remained on that rack for 36 hours, until some farmer in a skiff took him ashore. He said he never thought there were so many coons, possums, snakes and other assorted wild life as roosted on that rack with him during the night.

To avoid the barge on its upstream trips, we were forced to back the old boat into the bank, where we knocked off the monkey rudder. We now had a barge with three men on board heading at full speed downriver and an old towboat with an 8-inch freeboard that would flip over

CHAPTER 9 ≈ MISSOURI RIVER PILOT

like a turtle if we let her get crosswise. We finally eased her out into the main stream, and away we went around the horn to catch our runaway barge. As we passed Wellington, Missouri, half the town was on the bank and told us the barge had already passed down the river. We caught same, just as she was going down in the head of a snaggy chute in which there had not been a barge or boat for a hundred years.

We finally got to Kansas City, and Silk Hat Harry was waiting. He drew his pay and said, "Captain, I am going so far from the river that the natives do not know what a steamboat smokestack or an oar looks like."

And he kept his word. Several years later one of his buddies met him in a honky-tonk out west. He had worked all season for $15 a month and said, "Come on boys, have another." Come easy, go easy.

Miami, a crew member from the A. M. Scott, told the tale from a somewhat different perspective.

The A.M. Scott now was making its turn into the Camden Bend, and Henry Thomas was busy in the pilothouse. The searchlight swept about, throwing its beams into the bend and upon Globe Point to the right.

Now above the thunder of the river, I heard another sound. It was a deep, tearing "boom," seemingly coming from the left along the bluffs by Wellington. It was sinister and rending. I had never heard anything like it in my experience on the river. The searchlight clung to the river, never once veering toward the bank. As we turned to pass Globe Point, a giant sycamore apparently 150 feet in length swept past, raking the barge. I dropped flat onto the deck as the heavy branches brushed over me.

We came into the head of the bend in the gray light of early dawn, and the waterscape looked peculiar. I looked to our right, and I was surprised to see our sister towboat, the Advance, standing in the river with her big barge in tow. She seemed to be anchored there. Her master, Steamboat Bill Heckmann, was standing on her roof and looking toward the A. M. Scott.

To the left, I saw the source of the deafening roar—something few men have ever seen. After hundreds of years of running the great bend, the Missouri had now changed its course! Abandoning its orthodox turn, the river had formed a new and mighty channel running straight down the bluffs. It was chewing the silt in a raging broadening millrace, and at the head of the new chute, there was a sort of waterfall—at least a 10-foot drop in the first 100 feet of water. Just downstream from this were several great eddies, with the brown waters whirling like the funnels of tornadoes.

To understand what happened next, you must first understand the long-time rivalry between Capt. Young and Capt. Heckmann. Capt. Heckmann had been a Missouri river pilot when Curly Young was born. Despite this, Capt. Young's admirers were sure that he, as an all-round pilot and river man, stood head and shoulders above Heckmann.

Heckmann's outfit now stood in the river, out of the channel and well away from the deadly cutoff. Below the head of the vortex, the A.M. Scott likewise treaded water, as Henry Thomas looked over the situation and wondered what could be done. Then Heckmann himself raised his megaphone and shouted to Curly, "You'll never make it. We nearly turned turtle!"

Now, at the Camden cutoff, the two captains were at loggerheads again and again in a risky situation. Capt. Young yelled at Heckmann through his megaphone. "Watch Scott, Steamboat Bill, and learn something!"

We were driving out of the bend passing Napoleon. We later learned that Captain Bill had gone far off channel and brought his tow through a Camden cornfield.

After making up another tow at Kansas City, Curly Young decided he would be the first to take a boat through the new chute. Miami's tale continues:

The river was six inches higher and still rising when we started down. The A.M. Scott was making train time. We approached the deadly chute at 35 miles an hour. Curly was on the roof and yelled down to me, "Miami, get out on the head of the barge and see if you can locate the bottom of the river!"

The chute had cut narrow, but deep, and was not much wider than the boat and the big Epsilon ahead of our tow blocks. Up in the pilothouse, Capt. Thomas aimed the barge as if he were aiming a rifle. He stopped the engines when we reached the waterfall. For a moment the Epsilon hovered on the brink, straining; two of the chain ratchets parted with reports like shotgun blasts, but the five-inch lines from bitts to

CHAPTER 9 ≈ MISSOURI RIVER PILOT

timberhead held steady, and we dropped into the chute. We came out of the chute and passed Wellington as if fired from a cannon.

About 20 years before this adventure, Steamboat Bill's father had decided to leave the river. Will Heckmann Sr., according to the local papers, had acquired more than 2,000 acres of prime farmland on the islands. The mill site itself added another 300 acres. Always the avid sportsman, Will Sr. was going to satisfy his far-flung friends by providing them with a hunting and fishing Utopia.

He built a spacious clubhouse on the "island" between the mill race and the river proper. Nonetheless, he still took his long hunting trips with his city friends. As usual, he was on one of these trips when his last child was born in December of 1894 at the family home at the mill. Two days after the birth, Papa arrived home for his first glimpse of his latest offspring—a boy, named Norman Colman for his mother's editor at Colman's Rural World and his father's bosom hunting and fishing companion.

After the mill went into production, it was soon apparent that the beautiful scenario Will Sr. had envisioned was not working out. Farmers did not ship their wheat to the mill on Heckmann boats and receive the flour by return boat, as he had imagined. Flour from the mill did not sell. By the time Steamboat Bill quit his job with the government, the handwriting was on the wall. The Heckmann family returned to live in the house in Hermann; the Jack Rabbit was exchanged for stock in the Hermann Ferry and Packet Company; the Kingfisher was sold down south for ready cash. The mill was offered for sale, but there were no buyers. When the Heckmann family moved back to Hermann, the Advertiser-Courier gleefully reported, "Captain Heckmann is back in the steamboat business....We told you so when he left."

Steamboat Bill doesn't say just how Will Sr. became a working partner in the new St. Louis and Hermann Packet Company. The mystery deepens, considering the father had already used the steamer Jack Rabbit to buy back into the Hermann Ferry and Packet Company.

Also baffling is just how Will Sr. borrowed $5,000 from his oldest son. Young Will had built a new house and started a new company, two projects that took a lot of money. The fact that he had $5,000 to lend is probably a credit to Annie's money management skills. But Annie required some security for the loan—the Heckmann family home in Hermann. Whatever the financial arrangements between father and son, the new company prospered. Steamboat Bill wrote about the steamer Grapevine.

Roustabouts load the Steamer W. H. Grapevine, circa 1900.

It should be easy for me to write about the last days of this "old lugger" on our rivers. As you will see, she was the last boat to come in to St. Louis with her spars and rigging hung for use on short notice. She was the last spoonbill packet, and she was the last real steamboat in the once famous and profitable St. Louis and Rocheport packet trade. She was also about the last in any steamboat race.

A railroad started to build an incline into Cairo, Illinois, about the time the Grapevine entered the Ohio River on her trial trip. Some wit said she was so slow that the incline beat her into Cairo. She did not have much power, but she got there just the same and, for her size, was one of the most remarkable boats on any man's river. For our needs she suited very well, but she was not enough boat for the trade. The engineers were ordered to set the throttle at 4-1/2 miles per hour, whether the rivers were high or low, and even if the headwinds were blowing on her upstream trips.

During the season of 1901, she was the most regular boat that ever ran on the Missouri. The boat cleared 28 percent on our investment. In

CHAPTER 9 ≈ MISSOURI RIVER PILOT

making 39 round trips in this trade, loaded flat both ways, she never wet a spar and never failed to leave St. Louis every Saturday night. When early Friday morning, fellow boatmen came down over the levee or the watchmen on the old wharfboats looked up above the Eads Bridge, they were disappointed if they did not see the Grapevine lying at the foot of Franklin Avenue.

The St. Louis and Herman Packet Company bought this boat from an excursion company in Kansas City in the fall of 1900. We made three round trips in the St. Louis and Rocheport trade that fall. In the season of 1901, we made 39 round trips in this trade. In 1902 we had another good season, but our boat was by far too small for this trade, and we commenced to lose freight because we could not accommodate all the loyal shippers.

The 1903 flood not only broke my father, but it gave us unexpected work. While father was out with the steamer Kennedy moving other people's property, his own islands were washed away. After working night and day for about three weeks in rescue work, father came back to inspect his own property. He found 30 acres of one island left, with one house on it turned over and leaning crazily against a big cottonwood tree.

The steamer Kennedy was a 200-ton boat, sternwheel, roomy, light and fast—in fact, the fastest boat that ever was operated on the Missouri River. Father was in charge of this boat all through the flood, and it was his last big steamboating. It was typical of this great-hearted man that he should be rendering a last tribute of help to his many friends along the river, even while he himself was suffering a property loss so great that recovery was impossible to a man of his age.

When the river was nearing the crest, an urgent telegram for help came from St. Charles, Missouri. The big body of land between the Mississippi and the Missouri, known as "Missouri Point" and the home of St. Charles White Corn, was under water and crying for help. Things above and below Hermann were pretty well in hand, and the fast Kennedy lost no time in getting underway "far down Ole Man River."

The steamer W. H. Grapevine, in my charge, had been above New Haven, Missouri, for two days and nights moving people and their property out of Pinkney Bottom. Just about dark the Kennedy came alongside, and father asked for a pilot, as he had been without sleep for several days and needed help very badly. I loaned him Capt. Roy Coulter, a famous river pilot.

It was dark when they backed away from the Grapevine—8:30 p.m. to be exact—and at 10:30 p.m. they landed at St. Charles, 61 miles down the river, having made one landing to pick up Jim Murdock. The Kennedy was burning coal and cordwood. The old Dutch engineer had thrown the cutoffs on the engine away, and they were working her to the last ditch as the old boat went down the river that night. When they passed Pinckney Point that boat was flying, and big sparks with pieces of wood were soaring high out of her smokestacks. When she passed Washington, Missouri, lots of people thought that a comet was sailing by the town. This downstream trip of 61 miles in less than two hours was the fastest time ever made by a steamboat on any river in America. At and below St. Charles, the Kennedy worked for three days and three nights taking people off housetops and out of trees and moving livestock up to dry land. They cut telegraph wires and ran boats over the M.K.&T. railroad tracks that were miles from the main river—so wide had the flood spread.

On the trip down to St. Charles, I mentioned that there had been one stop to pick up Jim Murdock. In steamboating days the Murdocks were prominent men and river shippers and boosters. They lived across the river from St. Albans in the big river bottom out from Matson's.

In 1903 Jim Murdock owned a fine, big farm on the banks of the river he loved so well. On the way down on this eventful trip, the steamer Kennedy landed alongside Murdock's house, and father found his old friend sitting up in the second story of his big house. The water was already halfway up to the second story, and it was hard to make Murdock believe that it would come any higher or that it was time to move. When invitations and coaxing did not convince him, they shanghaied him and went on down the river.

When they came back up the river, near old Howell's Landing in St. Louis County, they saw a big white house lodged against some willows and cottonwoods. Dad said, "Look, Jim, there's your house." Murdock merely snorted at so preposterous a statement, but when they ran the Kennedy close, this proved to be the case. They landed, went inside, picked up the things of most value and went on up the river where the house was supposed to be anchored. Not only was the house gone, but most of the land was washed away. And what seemed to hurt Murdock most, two beautiful black stallions were lost someplace in the swirling waters.

My charge, the steamer W. H. Grapevine, had been running as a passenger and freight boat between St. Louis and Rocheport, Missouri, a weekly packet with a 210-mile run. The river commenced to swell—and when we reached the mouth of the Missouri, 17 miles above St. Louis, just before dark, the saddest sight ever to stir my eyes on our rivers was before us.

It was impossible to run this stretch after dark on account of the "drift" and everything imaginable coming out of the Big Muddy. We could see houses, whole trees—roots and all, tumbling into the Mississippi. Hogs, horses and cows were swimming for their lives. Chickens, rabbits and such small stock were drifting along on anything afloat. What a gamble of death for these innocent creatures!

All the way up to New Haven, we moved people and whatever they could salvage onto higher ground. Just above New Haven, we were hailed into Pinkney Bottom where we worked three days and three nights doing real rescue work in this vicinity. The Grapevine was the largest boat operating out of the port of Hermann, Missouri, and my crew were mostly young men, and I could still act young in those days.

We waded, swam, pulled and tugged with men and beasts, bringing scared, helpless humans and their belongings out of the swollen river for some two weeks. We knew our business on the river was ruined for the year, but we fought a young man's fight in the faith that the river would one day come back to its own. We also expected loyalty from those we rescued, but they simply went back to shipping by rail when the flood water receded. In retrospect, we were all too loyal and liberal to our patrons and friends after the flood.

And the Grapevine, the old boat lay down like an overloaded camel. The after end of her boilers burned out, her doctor pump went on a rampage with nobody in the engine room, and when the steam was shut off, we looked for pieces all over the engine room.

Coincidentally, at that time the steamer Sprague was lying at the foot of Carr Street having her big engines set up by the St. Louis Iron and Machine Company. We were laid up a week to build a new wheel and make other repairs. During this week the Terminal Railroad had a collision on the levee, and one car rolled down the levee, straddled a spar and knocked the old boat out in the river. It almost destroyed Aunt Susan's cookhouse. On top of that, "Crazy Charley" Price, a colored rouster, wrecked a saloon on Franklin Avenue. We had other mishaps as well, both profitable and costly.

We then went to work and again made our regular trips through a country that was desolate from the flood, and there was no freight. The stockholders, not rivermen like myself, could not see through all this. They got disgusted and sold the old boat out from under the broken-hearted Steamboat Bill to some folks around Cincinnati way, and the owners again converted her into an excursion boat. She was sunk by the ice either in the winter of 1905 or 1906 while lying alongside the Coney Island wharfboat. Her owners sued the Coney Island people, and old Steamboat was called over to Cincinnati as a witness in this case.

The Grapevine made friends enough for us to continue in the St. Louis and Rocheport trade until 1910, with boats like the Kennedy, Lora, India Givens and Julius F. Silber, but fate or ignorance was against us, for we never had sense enough to build a large boat suitable for this trade.

The W. H. Grapevine made some 90 round trips in her trade, not one without the writer on the roof or in the pilothouse. The other pilots on her were: Capts. John Massie, "Billie" Wild, George Young, E. M. Baldwin, Tom La Barge, Bill Earp, Bill Hall, Arthur Thompson, Leroy Coulter and Fred Heckmann. The engineers were Frank Blaske, Fred Heckmann, Leroy and Bert Coulter, Ed Roehrig and S. S. Clifford. Hummel, Adkins, Kuhn and Zibelin were the clerks, and Huey McGuire, mate. All were loyal to the core, mostly because they saw daylight begin to dawn on the horizon in a trade that had been dead for years.

•

Before and After Harvest

Before my time on the river, the downstream cargoes on the Big Muddy were mainly furs, hemp and tobacco. Then, in the early '70s, wheat became king, and the dull season in the St. Louis and Kansas City trade was during corn planting time and the harvesting of wheat. Any boat that went through that period with a good wheat harvest

CHAPTER 9 ≈ MISSOURI RIVER PILOT

coming on had a good chance to finish a profitable season.

The steamer Dacotah loaded 12,000 sacks of wheat at one landing in Malta Bend and came out of the Missouri with over 16,000 sacks of wheat. The little steamer Helena put 160,000 sacks of wheat in the old St. Louis elevator at the foot of Carr Street in one season. The big sidewheeler David R. Powell made the mouth of the Missouri River with 19,000 sacks of wheat on the boat and two barges, but in coming out of the river, the Powell hit bottom, and her tow was broken up. In picking up her tow she rammed and sank one barge with 8,000 sacks of wheat, so this record-breaking trip was a failure. These and many other stories could be told as to what the golden grain of the West meant to our old boats.

Now let me give you an account of a trip before and after harvest on the steamer Grapevine in the year of our Lord 1902. Both our up- and downstream trips had been heavy all spring on the old boat until the last one before harvest, a voyage that tried our souls. If ever you owned a packet boat, or even was master of one where your berth depended on her success, you will fully appreciate the first part of this account. We were at the foot of Franklin Avenue, St. Louis, one Saturday morning at the end of June, all cleaned up to receive our upstream cargo.

First came Roy Parker with the Susie Hazard and a coal bill to pay. Next came a dray load of empty baskets. (We had a flat rate to Jefferson City with the Goddard Grocery, and this trip it was all baskets.) Then down over the hill came Bill Arste of The Waterways Journal with some blank bills of lading and with some freight bills to deliver and collect for. With the barkeeper from uptown, there then arrived a week's supply of whiskey, which the clerk had to pay for; then a load of empty egg cases going back upstream gratis.

Along about noon the old sidewheel Grey Eagle, came along, and they decided to land alongside to unload some lumber on the upper levee. In the pilothouse Capt. George Keith was on watch, and with an on-shore wind and with all his skill, the big heavy boat came in so hard that she tripped our spars and shoved us up on the levee. Capt. Keith, in apology, said, "Boys, you all know I did not do this on purpose. It looks like you are going to have a light trip, but you are putting up a good fight, and with a big harvest in prospect, I wish you all the luck in the world."

The afternoon was just as dull, but a drunken roustabout caused some excitement by taking two shots with a big bulldog pistol at a captain of the watch. More bills were sent down to be paid, and with the engineers and supplies aboard, we got away for once right on time. However, at Bissel's Point, we had to land and back two little roustabouts off the stage who, with their razors, had chased all the other roustabouts upstairs. These were two tough men, and the other roustabouts said, "Dem's ginnies from New Orleans, and dey's bad."

During all this trip we had all kinds of trouble. But when coming downstream, about halfway back to St. Louis, the cry went up that a sack pile was in sight. That meant new wheat and new hopes. We loaded a small shipment of wheat and with an almost empty boat arrived all OK in St. Louis. On Friday evening, with the old lugger ready to receive freight the next day, some six members of the crew and passengers went uptown to celebrate. One, a farmer, said, "Boys, I do not believe in strong liquor, but if you will partake, I will spend a few nickels for soda pop."

Then we all went to the old Columbia Theatre and for 25 cents apiece saw acting never surpassed in Hollywood. After the show, we went up to Two John's stand, bought a big 5-cent pig's foot apiece, along with a schooner of real beer, and sat on the curbing. After this feast we went back to the boat, only to be in dreamland before 11 o'clock. We slept without the aid of Tums and were ready for the harvest.

The next trip all went well. We got out of St. Louis with the good boat down low in the water, and we delivered our cargo on time. When we turned our head downstream, we were hardly ever out of sight of a sack pile. The little old boat plowed and puffed, loaded flat both ways, and yet for several months, it looked like we had not made a hole in those immense piles of sacks of golden grain piled along the banks of the lower river.

But when fall came, all was cleaned, and we went into winter quarters at the mouth of the Gasconade River. By then the Grapevine had established the unbelievable fact for 1902 that a boat could operate on the Missouri at a fine profit. What is more, the St. Louis and Hermann Packet Company had plans made to build a brand-new and much larger boat for Steamboat Bill. In fact, the stockholders were willing to put up any amount of money for any kind of boat my heart desired.

CHAPTER 9 ≈ MISSOURI RIVER PILOT

Just then my father took a big railroad contract for freighting on upper White River. We bought the brand-new steamer Kennedy and took the steamer Buck Elk out of a very profitable trade on the Gasconade River. Both these outfits went to the upper White, and Dad said for me to get along another season with the Grapevine and that the two boats on White River "will make enough to buy any kind of a boat you want."

We lost $25,000 on the White River, the 1903 flood came on the Missouri and with no harvest, and in 1904 the old Grapevine went haywire. Our stockholders became discouraged and sold the Grapevine. By 1910 they sold the Kennedy, Buck Elk, Columbia, barges, warehouses all for a song. Why, we even lost the little Napoleon, Andy Franz, as a clerk who would have saved us some of our loss.

•

We left for White River with the steamer Kennedy in January ice. George Keith took us out to Memphis, and the king bee of White River pilots, Ed Warner, took us to the upper reaches of that stream. Andy Franz came aboard at St. Louis to ask for a clerkship, but found four Heckmanns headed for Arkansas and to see the upper White. He said it looked too much like a family boat, and he did not ask to be employed; while, at the same time, we were looking for a clerk.

You all, I hope, will pardon me if we again open up the book of memories to say we did not only lose our all but that Steamboat Bill also lost his one ambition in life, which was to build a suitable boat for the lower Missouri River trade. Thus my claim still stands that if they had given me a proper boat at that time I would still be doing business at the old stand, despite railroads, trucks or aircraft.

By 1903 all of the Hermann boats were back home from the White River, just in time to run some remarkable rescue missions during the flood.

We had seven fine steamboats running out of Hermann, of which the W. H. Grapevine was the flagship. These boats saved a number of lives and some $2 million worth of property. We charged less for our services than the other Missouri River boats doing relief work, thinking we would be paid back by grateful customers. But we figured wrong.

When the Grapevine left, the Kennedy took over the packet trade.

The Steamer Kennedy at Hermann during the 1903 flood

E. B. Trail, the father of our noted Missouri River historian, once said to me when we landed at New Haven, Missouri, "Well, Captain, I have been around this burg for many a long year, but you are the first man that ever ran a packet boat on time past this man's town."

Now let's see what we had to do to keep on time.

Our regular downstream time at New Haven was Wednesday night. One trip, we landed late with the steamer Kennedy at the foot of Pinkney Bend to load 600 sacks of wheat. At that time the crossing from the foot of the bend to the New Haven bluffs was infested with snags and sawyers. One had to go down between two very large snags about 150 feet apart with some dozen bad snags all around. Dark caught us there in what proved to be a pitch-black night. We debated how to get down to New Haven.

The old boat was flattened out, and my brother Fred, always more daring than Steamboat Bill, said, "Let's light up this old stream and get down to Zip's town on time." (Henry, "Zip" Zibelin was our second clerk and lived at New Haven, at the time—later, in St. Louis.)

It was so dark we could not see the snags, but by rowing out in a skiff, we could locate them by the noise made by the current running against them. In that way we located 13 snags and hung a lighted lantern on each snag, and on the two big snags we hung the signal lights. This made things as plain as day and was perhaps the first time anybody had any luck running a boat between two signal lights. We left brother Fred and a deck hand to pick up our markers, went on down to New Haven, loaded our chickens and eggs there and left at daylight to arrive on time at St. Louis, Thursday evening.

Steamboat Bill frequently interspersed personal opinions in his writings.

A properly built hull of a steamboat or barge, with a square knuckle, when aground and kept square with the current, will soon wash down over a crossing on the Missouri. A boat or barge hull with a round knuckle will squat down, stay put and will either have to be pulled or dredged off. When we figure out many of the peculiarities of this stream, then and then only will we be able to tame it.

•

Here is another thing which I believe never took place on any river but the Missouri—and that is the way the old mountain boats in the Dakotas and Montana secured ice in mid summer. The severe winters at times made ice more than 3-feet thick. In the spring breakup it would pile up on the banks, on the heads of islands and on large sandbars. With a mighty crash and roar it would push ice everywhere, even down into the sandbars and out of sight. When these boatmen were not fighting Indians, cutting wood or hunting game, they would send a yawl out to the head of some big sandbar, dig down into the sand and get all the ice they wanted.

Ice was the scourge of riverboats and the constant wintertime worry of every steamboatman. Steamboat Bill wrote of this danger in February of 1930.

The lines of The steamer Phil Chappell's hull were the finest I ever saw for a Missouri river freighter, and the boat was built unusually strong but was not very fast, being light of power. She never was very successful and had a checkered career. They loaded her flat with ties on the Osage River while lying over a flat-gravel bar. During the night the river fell, and before they could unload ties next morning, she was left high and dry on a flat-gravel bar, and there she stayed a long, long time waiting for another rise in the river. Next we hear of her caught in the ice near St. Aubert, Missouri. Spring came, and the ice broke up with a big rise before the crew could raise steam or get the boat cut out of the ice.

In Captain Kay's words, "We tore loose just at dark, and it was as black a night as you ever saw." The ice would move a mile or two and then gorge. At times we were clean up out of water, and I would not have given 10 cents for the boat or our lives. The hull and cabin would hump and crack; the ice would let go with a roar and pile up hundreds of feet high on the head of the high bars; we were knocked around like a cork going over Niagara Falls. At Portland, Missouri, we went in behind McGirk's Island, down through a chute where a boat had not run for years. We went hell bent for election over the worst bunch of snags on the whole Missouri River. We could not get any work out of the rousters, white or black. From the captain on down, all were scared hopeless as far as work was concerned.

Some years later, this same boat got caught in the ice and laid all winter here at the wharf in Hermann, Missouri. In the spring the ice again went out with a rise before they could cut this boat loose or raise steam. When the ice moved, the lines began to pop, the ring bolts and hitching posts flew up in the air, and the crew hopped off that old craft on shore like bees out of a plowed-up bumble bees' nest. Two men stayed aboard and went on out in the river with the boat. They were both tanked up with good liquor, which made them brave. The ice moved about a mile and gorged, leaving an open space to shore. Some men went out to the boat in a skiff and ran a line ashore, and when the ice again moved, the boat drifted into shore and was saved.

•

The steamer Kennedy, in my opinion, was the fastest small boat that ever ran on the Missouri River. We on the Kennedy were chartered to the contractors that were building the St. Charles Electric Bridge at that time. Capt. Joe McCullough was the watch when the Gage started to cut didoes and capers on our dark-brown river. They had waited too long to call for help. They were supposed to have knocked a small hole in her head while landing on the St. Charles side of the river. The upper seams were dried out and wide open, and when the ferry filled up

CHAPTER 9 ≈ MISSOURI RIVER PILOT

to those open seams, she rapidly went down. When we got to her, men like Capt. William C. ("Billy") Lepper and diver Delps were the type who were needed.

A man on the bank, perhaps the one who took the picture, cried out to Capt. McCullough, "Take her down to the bone yard, Captain, and pile her up on the other two fine big ferryboats that lay there." The bone yard was under a big cinder point that lies out in the river below the Electric Bridge.

The Gage had made two round trips across the river with that hole in her hull before they found out someone had blundered.

•

The little Julius Silber was busy before the St. Louis and Hermann Packet Company stockholders sold all their boats.

Some time ago a man with an operator's license, a man that never was in the channel of the Missouri River unless he was crossing same on a ferryboat said, "Well, Bill, I see where you have the steamer Julius F. Silber listed in your book as a troubleshooter. Why that boat never done nothing and had to land to blow a landing whistle."

He did not buy my book but borrowed one and then opened up his trap. What Steamboat Bill said to him would not be fit for print. So let's see, now, why we said this little boat was a troubleshooter.

Along about 1909 the big sidewheel snagboat Missouri ran aground one year going over the last crossing on the Missouri River before going out into the mighty Mississippi. Her two stem heads were about 30 feet over a bluff reef. They ran two, 2-1/2-inch hawsers out to the bank and got a good strain on them before dark caught them. The captain said, "Knock off, and we will pull her off in the morning."

That night the river fell about one foot, and the next morning they could not budge her. The river kept falling, and they broke all their spars. The sternwheel steamer King came up from St. Louis. This boat was about the most powerful that ever operated out of the U. S. Arsenal. She broke a lot of lines and pulled off some fastenings and never moved the snagboat any, if at all. They then sent one of the light tenders up to help. They fooled around some time and, again, left the old snagboat hard aground. The tender, too, went back home.

Then they got a shipment of empty sacks, got a lot of willows and tried to build a dike that would throw the water over and wash the old

The Kennedy was on hand to lend assistance when the Steamer J. P. Gage sank at St. Charles.

lugger off. Her wheels were sanding in, and she was surely a "sanded in" and grounded boat. The Silber was running in the St. Louis and Rocheport trade. We were loading out for our weekly trip, and a Mr. DeWitt called up "Steamboat Bill" and said, "What do you think about the Missouri?" My reply was, "It is a simple matter just to get her afloat."

Mr. DeWitt replied, "Well, Bill, I have lots of confidence in you, but you sure have lots of confidence in yourself. We have the finest crew of old-time steamboatmen on the Missouri River on the snagboat. We have had any help we wanted from the Mississippi River Commission, and still the old boat does not move, and they say she never will until the river rises."

Still, I said it would be a simple matter to put her afloat.

"Well, if you are so smart, go up and get her afloat." My reply was that we would be back the next Thursday and would then put her afloat.

Mr. DeWitt said, "Well, if she is there, go ahead and make your own price."

CHAPTER 9 ≈ MISSOURI RIVER PILOT

We made our trip in a hurry, and Thursday evening we landed alongside of the snagboat, and the veteran captain said, "What do you want here with that rattle trap?"

"We are going to put you afloat." His reply was, "Well, go ahead, but remember you are not fooling with one of them Hermann pinochle boats."

Everything was in our favor. We ran up above the snagboat, heaved out an anchor and dropped down to within a foot of her big wide stern. We ran a line to each corner of her stern and to the Silber. We started our sternwheel ahead and kept her running for 35 hours without stopping. We could have had the boat afloat in 24 hours, but the crew offered no help with their big sidewheels and never made a pull on their lines. Finally, when the boat was practically afloat, a dredge boat was passing the mouth of the Missouri River. They called her in, and with one little pull the snagboat was afloat. This was only done to take the honor away from the little Silber. The tender that came to help was a better boat than the Silber, but the fact of the matter was all the brains on the snagboat, dredge and tender did not know what to do. About the only one I remember who can vouch for this statement is Capt. Frank Ingrum, who was the chief engineer on the Silber at that time.

•

When Teddy Roosevelt went from St. Louis to New Orleans, the Silber was in the St. Louis and Chesley Island garbage trade. When Bill Heckmann drew the last pay, the good man in charge of the garbage contract said, "Well, Bill, I hate to see you go. The Silber, the smallest boat that ever handled the garbage, gave us by far the best service; you never missed a trip."

Now about the big whistle—When this boat was running night and day in the packet trade, when on time (and she always was) on Thursday evening, she blew the landing whistle coming downstream for Hermann. Capt. Hugh C. Blaske, sitting on his ferryboat at Washington, could plainly hear our whistle. Washington is 29 miles from Hermann as the crow flies, and no doubt Capt. Blaske will verify this statement.

We could go on for hours telling about this little craft. She had a big Scotch marine boiler that allowed 210 pounds of steam. She always had plenty of steam for everything, and no sternwheel boat of like size ever did more work on the western rivers than the steamer Julius F. Silber.

She was a real boat until The Woods Brothers Construction Company bought her. They put a full cabin on her, and then she was a sailboat.

The whistle on the Silber was one of the few good things rescued from the Heckmann's White River debacle.

Whistle Melody

One day we were traveling up along the once-famous stream, with the present-day dean of White River pilots, Capt. Ed Warner, on watch at the wheel. Away up the river a steamboat blew for a landing, and some 10 minutes later when the echoes had died away from among those White River hills, my brother Fred said, "What in the world is that?"

Capt. Warner replied, "That is the steamer Joe Wheeler blowing a landing whistle. She is not much of a boat, but she has the finest nickel-plated whistle on top of her pilothouse that ever steam went through."

We tried in every way we knew to get the whistle, but the fine old southern gentleman who owned the Wheeler would not part with it. When leaving there in the spring, my last request to brother Fred was to get that whistle one way or another, but to be as easy on the old captain as possible. (You know how us Missourians make these requests about oil, whistles, etc.)

The old Wheeler loaded up a big, dangerous trip of powder and baled hay, and when about halfway up to where she was going, they had a serious breakdown and had to go to the bank. The railroad needed this blasting powder badly and was pushing and begging for its delivery. About this time the Kennedy came steaming along, faster than any boat that ever ran on the White River. The captain hailed her in and said, "Fred, you old Yankee, you have always traded square with us, and if you will tow us up to our destination, I will pay you anything within reason."

Fred said, "In this case you cannot hire the Kennedy for money, but that whistle talks. We will trade whistles, then tow you up where you want to go and then tow you back down empty to where you can get repairs."

The old captain mourned. "I have had many ups and down in my day, and in my last days this sorrow has to come upon me. I have lost some fine boats by burning and sinking, but nothing has hurt me like this. Take the whistle, son; the South is used to giving up to the North, and I knew that when that new, fast-stepping boat came down here, it boded no good for the Ozark Queen, the Joe Wheeler or even the Quickstep."

When the Kennedy came back from the White River, she blew the landing signal for Hermann, Missouri, with that big whistle. It was heard in Washington some 29 miles away. When we sold the Kennedy to Col. Parker, the whistle went on the steamer Lora. When we sold the Lora to Sam Gregory and Billy Mills, the whistle was moved over to the Julius F. Silber. When Steamboat Bill took charge of the steamer Chester in 1912, this piece of machinery went on that craft.

The Chester was one of the first, if not the first, tunnel propeller boats on western rivers. Figuring that the owners of the Chester had used the whistle three years gratis and it was time to make a change, the old horse trader, Steamboat Bill, sold the melodious monster to Mr. Dresser at Leavenworth. The whistle then went on the little towboat Leavenworth.

Along about that time, Capt. Hugo Blaske and Bill Heckmann went around to Peoria and tried to buy one of the Swain oscillating sidewheelers for an excursion boat on the Missouri River. We offered Mr. Dresser $50 for the whistle, then $60. But "no ducks." Then $75, and still no results. Then one night when we were considering offering him 100 bucks for the whistle, the steamer Leavenworth was laid up for the night outside of two barges at Napoleon, Missouri. A big storm came up, and she turned over on her side and sank in 50 feet of water. We passed down the next morning with the steamer Advance, and there was only a small riffle on top of the water where the Leavenworth went down, and a few days later there was no sign of the little towboat and her big whistle. All went down to Davey Jones' locker, and we might as well have tried to find a bird of paradise as that musical trumpet.

When this whistle went down in the brown-colored deep, my interest in an excursion boat faded away, for we had lost our biggest advertisement.

≈ STEAMBOAT TREASURES ≈

The landing whistle was not the same on every river. In "Missouri River Notes," written in 1952, Steamboat Bill says the Missouri River landing whistle—one long, two short, one long and two short—originated with his father and his then partner, Archie Bryan. Writing in The Waterways Journal in 1943, A.F. Winn described the sounds of an old-time steamboat.

The era of the packets is nearing a fadeout, and the last of the old steamers may be the last of the time. Though the light and romance of packet boating faded along with the freight and vanishing affluence of the river, there is still some demand for that class of travel, as attested by the patronage of these remaining packets. Steamboats may come and go, but the beauty and charm of the river stand fast.

Before these last survivors of a brilliant epoch of transportation pass into history, there should be recorded the sounds in the engine rooms and the throb of engines in perfect cadence with the rocket-like roar through the smokestacks. Like a measured beat in a symphony, the sound goes on and on in the same tempo while the boat is underway, restful as the sigh of a summer breeze.

A rendition by the iron orchestra in the engine room is all the more impressive when accompanied by the clear, silvery ringing of the old-type engine bells. There was something indefinable put in the tones of those bells; they are unforgettable. Of the many times that the writer had heard engine bells, the best effect was to hear from the shore when the boat was coming in to a landing and when the far-off tinkle of those bells came like a song over the water—the slow bell—the stopping bell—according to conditions of landing.

Much has been written of notable whistles on famous boats and how the manufacturers excelled in putting beautiful tonal qualities in whistles' chimes and their combination. Melodious steamboat whistles have cast their spells upon the hearers during all their time on the river. Whether the whistle was near and loud or distant and mellow in tone, it was a quickening and realistic thing. As in the days of sail, when the pungent odor of tar and hemp and the various smells of cargo about the docks and the ships beckoned the youth to mysterious places beyond the seas, the steamboat whistle was an imperious call to the river.

Some years ago when the writer was in a railroad office in St. Louis, steamboat whistles were not infrequently heard; they always cast their spell and had a devastating effect upon the business at hand! As a youthful passenger, the writer remembers well the landing signal of the Anchor Line—one long, two short and one long. Those musical tones trailing off and re-echoing in the distant shores. There was also the Memphis and Cincinnati White Collar Line signal, two long blasts and one short. There was something eloquent about the silence that came after that final short blast had rumbled away in the distant shore. What was it? Mere words are inadequate to do justice to steamboat whistles. There should be a recording! [*The Sons and Daughters of Pioneer Rivermen did make such recordings at the "Tootenanny," held in Marietta, Ohio.*]

The swishing and the deep beat of paddle wheels on the water is another unforgettable sound, whether from aboard the boat or from a vantage point ashore. Standing on shore, I have known that sound made by the sidewheel boat to carry so far ahead that it could be heard before the boat would come into view from around a bend. Within the range of sound, the more distant the boat the deeper the beat of the wheels on the water. An impressive thing, the beating of the paddles of a sidewheeler full steam ahead!

There should also be recorded the sounding of the channel, an operation now practically confined to towboating. With navigation conditions as they are and are to be, heaving the lead will just about pass away along with other notable things about a steamboat. It would be good to hear again some deep-voiced Negro leadsman call "Q-u-a-h-t-a-h—l-e-s s—T-W-A-I-N!" and the other readings on the lead line while the boat glides along quietly under slow engine; and but for the plumb of the lead in the water, the call of the leadsman to the hurricane deck and the relay call in the pilothouse, there is a hush about the boat as though some sacred and mysterious rite of the river were being performed—when finally the ceremony ends with "N-o-o—b-o-t-t-o-m; H-a-l-f—T-W-A-I-N!" or some other call satisfactory to the pilot, and the quiet is shattered by an explosion of the big bell on the hurricane deck—the 'scape roars and the engines pounding again in "full speed" tempo.

It has been some years since the writer has been a listener with other passengers standing transfixed at the rail during a sounding rite. In earlier times there was a technique of voice and pride and dignity in the calling of the channel depths. It was almost like a song.

Perhaps there may not be so many now who are interested in the bygone things of the river. The crowd may not be very large, but it is good company.

The famed packets that graced the river in an earlier day, the radiant personalities who staged the great river show, the engines, the whistles, the bells, the songs of the roustabouts, the calls of the leadsmen and other memorable things that cast their brightness upon the scene are all and forever at one with the great river that gave them their color and their being "Q-u-a-h-t-a-h-h—T-W-A-I-N!"

For the crews of the little Missouri River boats, a landing in St. Louis must have been quite an enjoyable experience. The shows the big palatial steamers put on when landing and leaving the dock were quite spectacular. Capt. J. S. Hacker gave a good description of such a departure in "A Letter to Steamboat Bill," published in October 1941.

Those were the days when steamboatmen took special pride in jack staffs, bells and whistles. A story is told that when the bell for the Robert E. Lee was cast, Capt. Cannon threw 100 silver dollars into the metal to improve the tone. Capt. Harry Crane, a long time in the Tennessee River Packet Company, owned a bell of deep agreeable tone, which he carried with him aboard boats of which he was master. The last I knew of that bell it was on the Dick Fowler.

Returning to the city of Alton at the wharf, as the rousters realized they were near the end of their task, shouts of song were heard along the line. She had a noble jack staff. On top was a gilded weathervane—an Indian with a bow and arrow taking aim. Forward of her gallows frame was a spear, with a black bull carved from wood. In fact, the nickname of the city of Alton was "Bull of the Woods." The Union Jack flew from the jack staff, and from a high flag staff amidships floated a streamer with the boat's name. From a flagpole at her port wheel house floated a streamer with the name "St. Louis" on it, while from her starboard wheel house floated a streamer with "New Orleans" on it, while the American flag fluttered nobly from a high staff at her stern.

The Captain struck his bell three strokes. Every man took his place, the gangway plank was taken in, the clerks came aboard with the billing, and the Captain struck his bell one stroke, and every line was cast off, hauled in and coiled. A big Negro, the finest specimen of physical manhood I ever saw, clothed in a red shirt, black pants and a disreputable cap,

CHAPTER 9 ≈ MISSOURI RIVER PILOT

The elder Heckmanns at their Second Street home in Hermann. After Will Sr. died, Annie demanded possession of the house, which had been used as collateral on a loan.

with a black snake whip in his hand, took a position on the bitts, and the rousters stood around him on the deck. The mate, stevedores and deck sweepers stood on the bottom step of the grand stairway. As the boat rounded out into the stream, the man with the whip cracked the black bull whip and sang out in a roaring voice, "The Bull of the Woods is bound for New Orleans, where the Captain git some money in his jeans."

Then the rousters sang out in chorus, "Row Mollie, row gal, I'll see my girl in New Orleans and feed her up on turnip greens; row, Mollie, row gal; steam boatman have no home, he make a living on his shoulder bone; row, Mollie, row gal."

When the boat had straightened downstream, the Captain struck one stroke of the big bell, and down came every flag simultaneously. The "Bull of the Woods" was on her way.

In 1907, shortly after the White River debacle, Capt. William L. Heckmann Sr. made his last port of call. He died broken in finances and spirit. Never again would his eldest son have to abide by his edicts where steamboats were concerned.

CHAPTER 10

Adventures in Piloting

Old pilots never quit, they just go fishing.

*I wonder why the time goes by so fast
when the trip is slow.* —John Hartford

Steamboat Bill wrote and wrote and wrote about piloting. There was no chronological sequence—he wrote whatever popped into his head when the muse struck. This made the task of selecting piloting stories particularly difficult. It was impossible to avoid some overlap of subjects. This random selection is meant to give the reader a glimpse of life on the Missouri River and what the government was trying to achieve with the river improvement program. When the St. Louis and Hermann Packet Co. finally closed its books, Steamboat Bill said, "With all our bad luck, I want to state that none of it was due to navigating conditions on what is supposed to be the most treacherous river of all."

Steamboat Bill returned to the steamer John R. Wells, working for DeWitte and Shobe. He was always a staunch supporter of any boat he commanded—with the exception of tunnel boats!

Up until 1910, before the company sold us out, we operated the Julius F. Silber, India Givens, Lora, Peerless and Royal in the St. Louis-Rocheport trade. But the fight against the iron horse was a losing battle, and the St. Louis and Hermann Packet Company was finally forced to close its books. With all our bad luck, I want to state that none of it was due to navigating conditions on what is supposed to be the most treacherous river to navigate.

The Hermann Ferry company bought the Julius F. Silber and placed

CHAPTER 10 ≈ ADVENTURES IN PILOTING

her in the same trade, St. Louis to Rocheport, and for three seasons this boat paid for herself every year. She was eventually sold to Capt. Jesse B. Neil, of Arrow Rock, Missouri, and he, in turn, sold her to some Ohio River people.

Towing on the Big Muddy
January 3, 1920

I will now give your paper a statement of work done this season by the steamer J. R. Wells, built 21 years ago on the Osage River by Capt. P. F. Hauenstein.

She is not a modern steamer. She has several unsound ribs, her pecan bottom is thin in places, her cabin is some twisted, and it leans toward Reinhardts. The smoke, at least some of it, leaves her stack before it goes out of the top; her possum bellies leak, but the contractors never had to wait on the Old Lady, and she was always as ready to go as an old maid is to get married.

Some three years ago, a new engineer just off one of the Navigation Company's boats, took unto himself the job on this boat. He looked her over and said to the owner, "We will have to have some packing and some work done on the boilers." The owner said, "It is strange that this boat has run 18 years without any repairs to her engines and, when you get aboard, the first thing you want to do is to spend money."

Anyway, I promised to tell what the Old Lugger done this season and want to say before going to press that she run over nine months on the Missouri River over some of the worst river and over the shoalest water we have had on this stream since boating commenced here 100 years back. We never grounded boat or barge. One hundred dollars will put this boat in shape for another season's work. The engineer, Ed Roehrig, never made a mistake and answered over 20,000 bells over the old antique method of jingle, which goes to show that the Missouri River is not physically unfit for proper boats, and there is yet no reason for an old timer to change his views or feel himself slipping.

She towed 27,267 concrete blocks from Gasconade to Pelican Bend, distance 100 miles, 2,454 tons; handled 46 barges of brush, 800 tons; 135 barges of rock, 9,500 tons; miscellaneous freight, 1,000 tons; burned 15,200 bushels coal; handled 3,358 total pieces; run 7,626 total miles.

≈ STEAMBOAT TREASURES ≈

By 1912 Steamboat Bill had signed up to work for Kansas City Missouri River Navigation Company, a $1 million company.

Unfortunately, they did not build a new boat to suit the trade but instead bought or built a number of unsuitable boats and barges. In the fall of 1918 these misfits were sold to the then new Federal Barge Line. The mammoth motor vessel Chester was retained. After completing three years in the St. Louis-Kansas City trade, she was placed in the excursion business out of Kansas City. I was the master for the three years. The Chester was a passenger and freight boat between St. Louis and Kansas City—and she was the last boat of her kind to operate in that trade.

•

In the year 1911 the sensational, powerful, light-draft, triple-screw fine passenger and packet steamer Chester entered into the St. Louis and Kansas City trade in charge of the noted river captain, S. T. (Trim) Wadlington. Capt. Trim was not very successful with this boat, but neither was the writer. In fact, I hope to live to see the day and a boatman that could make a success with a boat of this kind. In the spring of 1912 the Kansas City-Missouri River Navigation Company put Yours Truly in charge of this mighty craft, and one of the first things I observed onboard was a big curly-haired, blond giant deckhand by the name of Tobe Zung. And old Steamboat Bill said to himself, "There is a boy that will go far on our rivers if given a chance." And most boatmen know how well this inner thought came true.

On the Chester at this time, we had as our mate the historic character Alex Shay. We grounded near Arrow Rock, and there we performed the last act of old-time sparring of a boat off a Missouri River sandbar. Mr. Shay was the favorite mate of Capts. Billy Balls and George G. Keith; a better mate never walked aboard any man's boat. This exhibition of sparring was some of—if not the last—work of the fine old man on his beloved river.

Zung became Captain Zung and remained with the navigation company until it was sold out to the Federal Barge Line. Some years later, we find him as a pilot in this same line, and then we find him as a master pilot on the sure-enough big tunnel boats. And before he retired to his farm near DeWitt, Missouri, he was known by many to be one of the best master pilots in the whole line.

CHAPTER 10 ≈ ADVENTURES IN PILOTING

Steamboat Bill atop the Chester, after she had been rebuilt as a tunnel boat, an "improvement" about which he had serious reservations.

Steamboat Bill was never sold on the virtues of the Chester, or any other tunnel boat. He did, however, occasionally enumerate some of their finer attributes while holding forth on another subject. "Music in the Engine Room," written in 1951, is one example.

Talk about music in the engine room—why those boys I knew made it sound like a 100-piece brass band! I can remember well the symphonies they conducted—but instead of a baton, they employed an oil can or a crescent wrench.

The best engine room music that I ever listened to came from the bells of the U. S. sternwheeler Minnetonka; the most musical exhaust that ever reached my flappy ears emitted from the sternwheel packet Gus Fowler.

The Gus had ample boiler power and blew a fine exhaust all the time. And she didn't do it through pressure bellies in her big smokestacks either. At times she let go with notes that equaled anything Harry James ever tooted on a trumpet. It was a real thrill for a man to just sit back and listen.

Also, where is the man who would not pay a pretty penny if only again he could cock his ears and listen, his heart pounding, to the exhaust music of the sternwheeler Louis Houck? Her engines came off that big, lightning fast, sidewheel floating palace of all riverdom, the Will S. Hays. She could blare forth with such a variety of noises that she often rivaled an orchestra.

Then again, where in the whole wide world would one go to find a man who wouldn't want to establish residence in an engine room merely to watch a doctor pump in action? No piece of machinery in any corner of the globe ever equaled the gracefulness of this one. I never saw the day that I couldn't stay in an engine room hotter than Hades and watch a doctor strut its stuff without frills or Hadacol. *[Steamboat Bill was a great believer in patent medicines, which accounts for the occasional reference to whatever he happened to be taking at the moment.]*

The most perfect working doctor was on the old sternwheeler Chester. The story is told that Sam Critchfield, who used to chew a pound of 'bacco a day while racing this steamer in the St. Louis-Chester trade, had his doctor working so well that at times he was tempted to jump ship and turn the boat over to its command. It had a way of supplying water to the boilers that is just unimaginable. I don't think a more faithful servant ever turned a flywheel.

The good people of Kansas City put their money in the Navigation Co. in good faith and besides furnished more freight than the unsuitable outfits could handle. Did they get a square deal? I, for one, say no. I suppose the new owners will make some changes on this good old hulk. For their benefit, I want to say that she will stand hitched and has gone through lots of changes.

In an earlier story, "September Notes," written in 1924 when memory was still fresh from the time that Steamboat himself was on the Chester, he offered this observation.

In 1913 a man plowed right by the modern super triple-screw steamer

CHAPTER 10 ≈ ADVENTURES IN PILOTING

Chester. She was upstream bound, and the farmer not having to shove very hard on the lines to win the race.... It would take a good pilot to run a boat that drew six feet loaded with 150 tons on a river that quite often got down to 3-1/2 feet in the main channel.

In 1920 he wrote "The last of the Chester on the Missouri" for his hometown newspaper, the Advertiser-Courier.

Along about 4 o'clock, with a fair wind from the east, the supermodern steamer Chester passed down by Hermann, Missouri—they say bound for Cuba.

Since this freak quit the excursion business in Kansas City several years ago, many sparrows have been raised in her cabin of modern architecture built by hatchet carpenters.

When this ark passed down by this burg, memory took me back some nine years ago to the promises made and the predictions scattered to the four winds by the four-flushers of what this pioneer was going to do on the Missouri River. This ship was to out-push the Sprague and take two barges to Kansas City, or a total cargo of 2,300 tons.

The largest trip she ever took to Kansas City was less than 300 tons, and a crippled mallard hen swam past her going up Hill's Bend when she was at her best and doing all old Sam Critchfield could do to her, and he was the best engineer that ever rode this old lugger, either when she was a "bear cat" with her stern wheel or when she was a "tortoise" as a tunnel boat. They say history repeats itself, but I hope the next flock of emancipators will practice on some other river besides the Missouri.

My figures may be wrong, but this misfit and the other experimental hulks that followed her have set the Missouri back some 50 years and done more harm than the millions of dollars spent by our railroads to run the old boats off the Missouri River.

Capt. J. S. Hacker often replied to Steamboat Bill's comments and opinions. He was still trying to persuade Steamboat on the virtues of the tunnel boats when he wrote "Greets Steamboat Bill, Would Like to Meet Him," Nov. 3, 1923.

I hope Capt. Heckmann has had an opportunity to see the tunnel boat Memphis turn Cairo Point and walk up against a rise in the Mississippi with four loaded barges, which she has done lately.

It seems to be an even break as to upkeep between the tunnel boats and sternwheelers....

If Capt. Heckmann has seen these boats and these performances about here, in comparison, I think he will have a better opinion of the tunnel boats.

Steamboat Bill remained with the Missouri River Navigation Company for the next seven years before the itch to own a big steamer hit him again.

In 1918 I put in another season on the John R. Wells for Hauton and Jones, of Leavenworth, Kansas. The Wells had a peculiar hull made of pecan wood, and she was equipped with a big Mississippi-type boiler from John Rohan and Sons, of St. Louis, that had cost $500. The elder Rohan made that price because he said that times were hard and he wanted to keep his men at work.

Several Heckmann sons worked on the river during World War I, exempt from active service because of moving strategic materials. Other Heckmann sons served overseas. The youngest, Norman, ran a barge on the Seine in France, to his great delight.

Tall and lanky, Norman was a great southpaw pitcher—he had been recruited by Branch Rickey of the St. Louis Browns when Uncle Sam tapped him on the shoulder. Norman never forgave the government for ruining his chance at a career as a professional ball player. The French made amends by arranging for him to play in many games. His letters to the hometown paper were literary works of art.

Cousin Roy Miller, son of Justina Heckmann Miller and Robert Miller, also served in France, where he distinguished himself in a great act of bravery, according to the January 24, 1920, edition of the Advertiser-Courier. The book of Company B, 57th Engineers, A.E.F., has the following to say:

Miller, Roy A., 2550274
Pilot, Steersman and Bargeman, of Bluffton, Missouri

Roy showed up well before we left Laurel and kept his stride straight through; he has more to his credit than any other man in the company,

CHAPTER 10 ≈ ADVENTURES IN PILOTING

so far as grabbing off the honors in the war goes. He was a clean man, mentally and physically, and when he pulled off the burning-gasoline-barge stunt in Paris, no one was greatly surprised. He wears the British Meritoria Medal and has a Croix de Guerre coming and has an American citation for bravery. He was recommended for a commission in the towboat service and richly deserved it, but it went the same way that so many of our recommended promotions did—they didn't come through, due to no fault of the man recommended. Miller knows the Seine, and after a turn on the barges and the "Trio Fille," he was master of the U.S. Tug 12 and also on a British tug for awhile. At Nantes he was a ship boss and was requisitioned to do a commissioned officer's work on a tugboat at St. Nazaire and returned to the States from there.

Norman Heckmann ran a barge in France during World War I.

Generations of Millers had regularly used the Missouri River as a swimming pool. Being an accomplished and fearless swimmer came in handy for Roy during the war.

For distinguished conduct and courage displayed on the River Seine at Paris on the night of August 22, 1918, Sgt. Miller, in charge of Barge EU-3 at Quai Javel, was awakened by a heavy explosion and hurrying ashore found a British barge, loaded with naptha, on fire at a nearby dock. The drums of naptha were exploding, threatening considerable property.

After assisting in cutting loose the barge, Sgt. Miller swam out and attempted to fasten a line to the barge from which the guiding lines had been burnt and which was drifting into another dangerous position, threatening life and property. Unsuccessful in his first effort, Sgt. Miller made a second attempt, despite the intense heat and constant explosions, and succeeded in securing the rope which was almost immediately burnt.

Undaunted, Sgt. Miller swam to a British yacht, secured a small boat and another line, and, with the assistance of two American comrades, fastened this line to the barge, which he succeeded in towing out of the danger zone. He then further risked his life by boarding the barge and placing chains on it in order to hold it securely in place.

Captain Miller is a Missouri River pilot and has served as master of the Steamer J. R. Wells three seasons and has piloted on the Advance, U.S. Golden Rod, Vernie Mae and a number of smaller boats on the Missouri. He served one year with the 57th Engineers in France. While in France, he was pilot and master of Tug No. 12 on the Seine, running between LaHarve and Grigny. He has been up to the head of navigation for steam tugs on the Seine—up so far they have no more river, just canal. After leaving the Seine, he was ship boss at Nantes for a short time and then sent, or transferred, to St. Nazaire where he was pilot and master of tugs Gwalia, Cadmus and No. 21 of the Army Transport Service. These tugs are ocean-going tugs and are about 400 ton.

Since Roy has been home, he has been in the construction business, and he has just recently purchased an eighth interest in the Hermann Ferry and Packet Co., at Hermann, Missouri.

Steamboat Bill seldom mentioned the younger members of his family, who were left destitute when the father died. His mother died in 1909 while on a train en route from St. Louis to Hermann to visit her soon-to-be daughter-in-law, Alice Bock. His sister, Mary, married Robert Doerges after her mother's death. Ed finally extricated himself from the burden of supporting the family and married Alice Bock in 1911. Sister Lottie, who also had helped support the family, married Herman Hundhausen shortly thereafter. Brother John married Annie Kuhn in 1913.

Sister Lizzie never married, and sister Martha, widowed, continued to scratch out a living for herself and her little daughter, Harriett. Somehow she managed voice lessons for Harriett, who went on to sing with the New York Metropolitan Opera.

Brother George married Helen Fallis. Brother John died an untimely death at 29 from complications of yet another bout of typhoid fever. The older boys were married, as was sister Annie. Norman was in the Army. Bob defected from the family work on the river; he went railroading and married Myrtle Lapham.

CHAPTER 10 ≈ ADVENTURES IN PILOTING

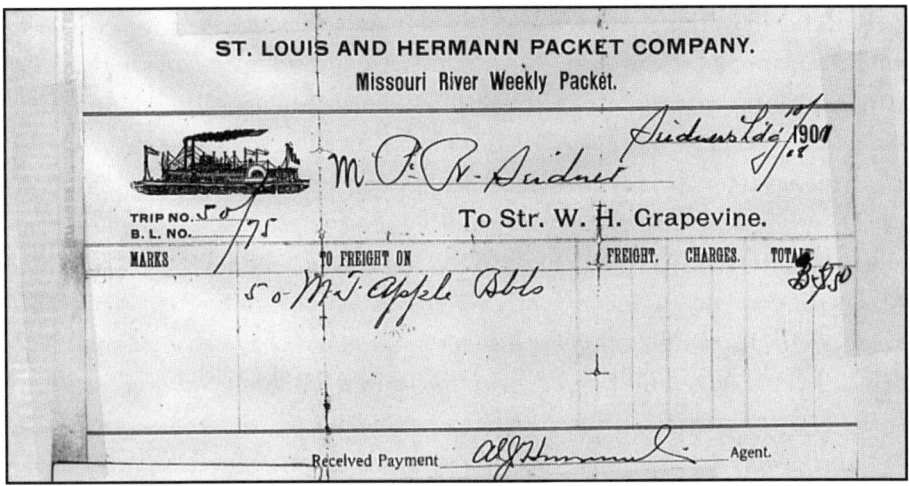

During 1920-21, I was president of the old Hermann Ferry and Packet Company and was faced with insurmountable difficulties. A big bar formed in front of Hermann, which prevented us from being able to land at that port during most of the season. Trucks, too, were coming in and grabbing off the business. At the annual meeting in 1921, our little secretary sat on a big high stool and said, "We are only able to declare a 6 percent interest this season. Your father was a great steamboat man, but you are not worth a dime. The rest of our stockholders are saying this behind your back, but I am saying it to your face." This latter statement is all that kept him from being slapped off that stool into a corner of the room.

Thus ends the saga of Steamboat Bill and the hometown business. What he fails to mention is that he had just attempted to start a rival venture, the Big Muddy Steamboat Company. A more improbable endeavor could not have been imagined. Nonetheless, Steamboat Bill wanted a big boat so he could prove that the freight business on the Missouri River would pay.

World War I had devastated the little town of Hermann, splitting the German community. Brothers found themselves fighting brothers in Germany, cousins against cousins—the situation was tragic. In addition, the Volstead Act (the 18th Amendment, better known as Prohibition) closed down the wineries. Wonderful vineyards on the hills were left to go to weeds; the coopers were unemployed, since barrels were no longer needed, and the town's main source of income was gone.

Building in Hermann had come to a halt during the war. Now there was no money to build anything new. The frugal Germans made do and repaired and patched. Quite by accident, this resulted in preservation of the original German architecture. Today the little German village is a tourist attraction.

In the midst of this economic debacle came not one, not two, but three Heckmann brothers and one cousin peddling stock in proposed steamboat companies. To add to the confusion, the Hermann Ferry and Packet Company also was raising money for a new boat. Steamboat stock had a good track record locally—the Ferry Company had always made money and declared good dividends. People were looking for a sure thing in a world of chaos. Steamboat Bill, in partnership with his cousin Oscar Heckmann, had organized the Big Muddy Steamboat Company. The newspapers of 1918 carried stories about the endeavor.

Several local people bought stock in the Big Muddy Navigation Company being promoted by Capts. William L. and Oscar Heckmann of Hermann, Missouri, two experienced rivermen. H. J. Wallaw will in all probability build a warehouse as soon as the new company begins operating. A tunnel under the Missouri Pacific track from the river to one of the streets is also contemplated.

Messrs. Heckmann explained the purposes of the company and its intention to a large meeting at the Commercial Club headquarters. Capt. Heckmann explained how the company expected to reduce freight rates for local merchants. He stated that the boat line would carry freight at 20 percent less than the railroads.

A big 400-ton boat is to be purchased at a cost of approximately $30,000. Captain Heckmann explained that the boat would carry only freight and that it would ply regularly for at least nine months of the year between Rocheport and St. Louis. "The river," Capt. Bill Heckmann said, "is in 25 percent better condition now than it was years ago when a packet line was operated between a point above here and St. Louis. It would require two and a half days for the boat to make the trip from Rocheport to St. Louis."

He handed out a fancy dark green prospectus, neatly bound and looking very professional.

The Heckmanns have been at Washington, Hermann, New Haven and Berger, and quite a number of people interested themselves financially in the proposed company. There is little doubt but that the $40,000

CHAPTER 10 ≈ ADVENTURES IN PILOTING

necessary will be subscribed in a short time.

The Central Missouri Trust Co. purchased $500 worth of stock at $50 a share, R. Dallmeyer took $400 worth of stock, the Produce Company $100, and H. J. Wallaw $200, and Julius Beck, $50. Many others have expressed a willingness to invest in the company and give it the necessary impetus.

Captain Heckmann has been a riverman for 40 years, and his cousin, Oscar Heckmann, for the past 20 years. They are among the best-known rivermen in the state and have every confidence that the boat line will prove a success.

But, once more, Steamboat Bill was doomed to failure. The Big Muddy Steamboat Company never got off the drawing board, and Steamboat Bill's dream of a big boat, one, in his estimation, large enough to adequately handle the freight, died a'borning.

Our reason for not getting a boat was we were unable to subscribe the required amount to get a first-class boat and without which this the enterprise would fail.

In the meantime, Steamboat Bill's next-youngest brother, Sam (known as Greeley or Cy) Heckmann was selling stock in the Gasconade River Farmer's Steamboat Company. He raised enough money to build the trim, beautiful little steamer Cinderella and her barge, the Golden Slipper. Success would have been assured if the wheat crop along the Gasconade River had been bountiful that year. But the wheat crop failed, and the company was forced to sell the little steamboat.

Captain Ed Heckmann, 15 years younger than Steamboat Bill, lost out on the benefits the older boys had enjoyed with their father in his heyday. No longer did Papa provide a boat for his sons when they were ready for the river. Unable to find work at home, Ed took off for Alaska, where he put in four seasons steamboating on the Yukon River and its tributaries. He might have had money for a boat of his own, if his mother and younger siblings had not needed every cent he could make.

In addition, Ed wanted to get married, and his itch to get into steamboating had to be postponed, since his bride-to-be was emphatic that she did not want to marry a steamboatman. After the marriage, however, his efforts to earn a living on dry land soon convinced her that steamboating was better than starving.

Ed's early ventures with the little steamer Myrtle proved so remunerative that he, too, gave in to the compulsion to build a big boat. This was what he was peddling—stock in a really big boat, the largest ever built on the Missouri River with private funds. He succeeded where his older brother had failed. In theory, at least, Ed's boat was exactly what Steamboat Bill had dreamed about for so many years, just the sort of boat he would have purchased had his stock-selling scheme not failed.

Ed sold $25,000 worth of stock and built the John Heckmann, named in memory of his recently deceased younger brother. Ed quickly proved it was impossible to make a living carrying freight on the Missouri River. Within a year, he converted the John Heckmann to an excursion boat, with more stock, this time to the tune of $50,000. This venture also failed to make money. The steamer John Heckmann was advertised for sale, but there were no buyers. It was too much, too late. Not even Steamboat Bill would purchase his long dreamed of big boat.

The Ferry and Packet Company also succeeded in selling enough stock to build a new boat. This little company had continued to pay dividends when every other Hermann business was in dire straits. The ferry company was a good business up until the completion of the bridge across the river in 1930. The company struggled along with a little trip work for the little steamer Hermann until 1935 when everything was sold to Bilhorn, Bower and Peters, and the company was dissolved.

Not surprisingly, Steamboat Bill had parted company with the Hermann Ferry and Packet Company long before the company expired.

In the winter of 1921, my application went in to the Woods Brothers Construction Company, at Lincoln, Nebraska, for a berth as a pilot on one of their steamboats. In a short while, a letter came from Wayne Pringle, their river manager at that time, saying, "Your reputation as a pilot has come to us as being the best, or at least one of the best, on the Missouri River. We shall be glad to have you report in the spring." At the opening of the season of 1922, they sent for me to go as pilot on the old Castalia at Omaha, Nebraska. The Castalia was later renamed Eugenia Woods. This same boat later became both Mr. Pringle's and my own favorite for many years.

When arriving at Omaha, the Castalia was still out on the bank, and all was hustle and bustle. In a few days we moved down the river some 15 miles and were not at work there long when Mr. Pringle said, "Say, Cap, we want you to go down to St. Louis and bring our new purchase,

CHAPTER 10 ≈ ADVENTURES IN PILOTING

the Kennett Dillman, up to Waverly, Missouri. This is Tuesday; how long will this trip take?" My reply was that "the Dillman will be at Waverly next Tuesday at 10 o'clock in the morning."

We had to slow up 20 minutes in Waverly Bend to arrive at Waverly at exactly 10 o'clock that particular Tuesday morning. From then on my reputation was made with the finest man I ever worked for or associated with on any man's river.

Time rolled on, and in 15 years my services were required on every one of their one dozen steamboats. I have, in fact, been in charge of four different boats in this Line in one season. On these boats, at times, we accomplished things that seemed and were very unreasonable and impossible. Capt. Davie (Crockett) Walters and myself left Omaha on December 2 one winter with the Eliza Woods and two partly loaded barges bound for Waverly, Missouri. The river was dead low, and this outfit was drawing every inch of water there was in it. Winter caught us in the head of Bartlett Bend, where we grounded on the head of a big sandbar. The weather was bitter cold, and the river falling and full of floating ice. This ice would cut our manila lines as fast as we could lay them.

Darkness and a snowstorm were coming on, and Davie said, "Cap, we are ruined; we will be stranded on the head of that bar by morning and not even be able to get ashore."

One of the barges was loaded with cable, some of it over 1-inch thick. One big spool that weighed about three tons lay out on the head of the barge. We fastened two big cables to this spool, fastened them to each corner of our barges, rolled the big spool in the river for an anchor and went to bed.

The next morning we were afloat, so we laid a cable to the bank, cut loose from the spool and drifted in behind a retard. In several days the weather turned warmer, and by hard work, we made Waverly. The loss of the spool of cable was never reported to the company. It was my idea to use it—not to report the loss.

On the old Kennett Dillman, later renamed the George Woods, we left Kansas City one late summer day with five loaded barges for Isabelle, Missouri, some 240 miles down the river. They gave us five days to make this trip, but we ran wild and got lost; and in two days we were landed two miles below Isabelle. One of the men the company had keeping track of this boat asked a government employee near Hodge, Missouri, if he had seen the Dillman pass. "Yes," he said, "she passed here yesterday afternoon, and if she kept on going like she passed here, she is down to New Orleans by this time."

We made many record-breaking trips with these boats and some slow ones. The old Castalia was 31 days going from Alton Slough to Lexington, Missouri, on a high-water trip, and nothing was said. This was when "knighthood was in flower" with the company. Several years later than this, the steamer George Woods, [formerly the Dillman] was on an upriver trip, and when we got to Bee Creek Bend, we found the river shut off with dikes. A government boat, with all the power in the world and drawing less that the Dillman, was over two days getting up past these dikes. After consulting with Bob Vivian, a sure enough river foreman, we decided to put the Dillman through a big dry bar that laid under the end of a dike and was near deep water. In less than 12 hours, with the help of one of Ross Wogan's little diesel boats, the Dillman, with her tow of five pieces, was on her way up the river, having practically washed her way over dry land.

My work on these boats was mostly on the Castalia. In one season the little Castalia, with Johnny McMillan as boat foreman, made more money for its company than any boat of the same size ever made on any man's river within the extent of my knowledge. The side-wheel steamer Wm. J. Lewis was paid for with a profit of $65,000; but the Eugenia Woods [as the Castalia was later renamed] was instrumental in paying for herself 12 times over in one season's work for this construction company.

In all the long time this boat was in my charge, we never put a scratch on her of any kind except to knock off a few rudders, and that was only after rudder bumpers had been done away with and soft wood used for rudder stocks.

When the government had trouble making a new river in front of Dundee, for months at a time, there was only one boat, the little steamer Hermann, that could pass through about two miles of river at that place. Along about the worst time in this territory, Mr. Pringle ordered me to take the Mary Frances down to St. Charles, which meant going through this place.

My brother, Cy Heckmann, was in charge of the Hermann and felt

CHAPTER 10 ≈ ADVENTURES IN PILOTING

like he owned this piece of river, two miles with less than two feet of water in many places. The Mary Frances drew four feet of water. Capt. Cy and men with river reputations like Charlie Martin and, in fact, all said the boat could not be taken through this place.

When this was reported to Mr. Pringle, he said his man "will find a way or make one. Tell him to go ahead." This was enough for me. We put the old boat down in this chute stern first and in less than four days had washed our way through the shallow water.

•

In these 15 years this good company sent me over a lot of territory going to and from their boats. On one occasion they sent me to Washington, D.C., to appear before a river board there. Cleveland A. Newton, then in Congress, said afterwards many a time that Heckmann told that board more about the Missouri River in 10 minutes than all the rest of the many men told all together.

While writing about a big pop rise on the Missouri above St. Joseph, Missouri, Steamboat Bill told of the trials and tribulations of currents and mud.

In looking at the boats with big power pushing around the swift places, their wheels threw up almost pure mud, and they looked like the tailings of a pipeline on a big dredge working full power.

In cleaning the Mark Woods' boilers after less than three days run, we found balls of pure gumbo the size of hens eggs, and it had not hailed gumbo either. Some of the boats just quit, some double tripped, and three of the best kept right on about their business and had all they wanted at that.

To give an idea about what is being moved, we'll say that the Massman Construction Company had something like 76 pieces of river equipment tied up at one time lately at St. Joe, Missouri. Woods Brothers are moving about that many pieces up river, and the Kansas City Bridge Company has an immense fleet at St. Joe and a big lot underway.... All are on their way to the glorious West.

In the big, long and cutting bend below the little town of Nodaway, Missouri, last Sunday, the boats were still numerous and busy on Sunday, September 17. [1933] With the government and Bilhorn, Bower and Peters starting new jobs, it looked like Barnum and Bailey's circus had come to town that Sunday afternoon at Nodaway. The banks were lined with visitors watching the boats come and go and the new work starting. It seemed the ladies were the most interested—rosy-faced, lovely big mothers with their boys and girls, beautiful girls, as innocent as the cutting banks were destructive.

This report by an unidentified writer rather succinctly sums up the work that was being done to improve the Missouri River.

Missouri River Work By One Who Helped
July 19, 1930

The Missouri River, the swift, dark, unruly stream that gives the boys who live on its banks a thrill when they read in the geography that, with its lower end, the Mississippi, it is almost the longest river in the world. I have lived in sight of its bluffs and bottoms so long that I feel a certain friendly personal interest, a sort of pride in its extreme vagaries.

A short trip anywhere east of Kansas City will give one an opportunity to see what has been and is being done. The observer is apt to take a pessimistic view of the project unless he takes more time and looks more carefully into details than the average observer is apt to. He will see long rows of piling with gaps in them where the ice has taken some of them out, and the river will look just as wide, the sandbars just as large and numerous as ever, and the water at the crossing is still thin.

But talk to someone who has an intimate knowledge of the locality. He will call your attention to a large acreage of young willows, the result of a bit of river work done last year. He will show you cornfields made by work done 10 years ago. While the "river rats," as Uncle Sam's workmen call themselves, lose sometimes, I think a general balance will show they are winning.

But it is a work not to be done in a limited time, as our river is not accustomed to restraint, nor will it yield readily. Indeed, I think our Uncle Sam is busy with a project that presents difficulties as great as the Suez Canal, and while the benefits will be purely local, they will be very much worthwhile. He is putting forests upside down along the river banks, and his workmen are weaving miles of fabric, which might be described as open work, the woof and warp of which is pine lumber and iron.

CHAPTER 10 ≈ ADVENTURES IN PILOTING

And when the workmen have fashioned it and it is properly fitted to its piling, barges loaded with rock are floated over, and it is weighted to the bottom. The banks are sloped and paved. Should you visit the place next year, you would probably find a new sandbar, and maybe in a few years the willows will give way to corn, and the channel will be narrower and deeper.

The army doing this work is made up of units. Each unit consists of a quarterboat, or a flatboat with a full-length, double-deck cabin. The lower floor has a kitchen, mess hall, pumping plant, lighting unit and a small ice machine. The upper floor is a bunk room and an office for the men in charge.

There may be another bunk boat, also a supply boat. There will be a barge to weave mats on, also a boat and maybe a land driver, which is a pile driver on wheels, and numerous barges, motor- and rowboats. There will be a steamboat—a floating battery of machinery built to move heavily laden barges against wind and current. She is mother to her fleet or fleets, bringing as she does the piles of lumber, the mountains of stone and the miles of iron cable, providing for the needs of her lusty broods.

There will be a fleet of motorboats (yawl is the word in the terminology of the rivermen). They are the big sisters of the fleet, hurrying here and there, fussing with a great overgrown barge, suggesting a very little girl with a very large baby or herding lots of piling to their proper places. Maybe it's a roll of cable that the mat boat is crying for or a load of men to be delivered some place where they are needed. They go night and day, fair weather or foul, always busy and always efficient.

The personnel is surprisingly youthful. Most of them are boys who have left the horses and cows, the plow and the harrow, to find excitement and an outlet for their energy on the brown water. Uncle Sam treats them well enough, and they are satisfied with conditions for which only an exuberance of optimism could find a balm, for in winter they spend their days drenched with icy water while the north wind and the driven sand tear at their very vitals. And the reflected sun of summer burns by day, while the night is a battle for life with countless millions of mosquitoes. I am told the mosquitoes are equipped with chrome steel piping and heavy duty pumps. A hard-boiled top sergeant would feel perfectly at home in one of Uncle Sam's quarterboats.

And still the drivers thump and pile, and the mat workers fashion their fabric of timber and iron while the river rushes on its way, foaming and fretting among these new impediments. If one will look, he will notice slackwater below the rows of piling, which means to the riverman sandbars, willow-covered, and a narrower, deeper channel in which boats may move the merchandise of the world.

All his life Steamboat Bill had written glowingly of the mountain pilots. Finally, rather late in life, he had an opportunity to be one himself, thanks to construction on the first big dam on the Missouri River at Fork Peck. James V. Swift gave the background to the story in the April 30, 1983, issue of The Waterways Journal:

...This was also the year that the Missouri River Division was begun. It was separated from the upper Mississippi Valley Division, with three districts at Fort Peck, Omaha and Kansas City. Missouri River work in the past had been handled by the Missouri River Commission, the Northwest Division with headquarters in Sioux City, Iowa ,and a number of other U.S. Engineers organizations.

Brig. Gen. Mark J. Sisinyak of the Missouri River Division recalled the beginning of the Fort Peck project.

In less than two years the government payroll on the project would exceed 10,000 persons. As one Fort Peck veteran put it, "Another 10,000 came up here to live off that first 10,000." They came from every part of a hungry nation, and they traveled anyway they could. They hoboed by boxcar. They came in jalopies. They walked hundreds of miles. They lived in shacks built over a weekend. They lived in tents. They lived in packing cases.... Literally true, and this was during some of Montana's severest winters.

To serve this new project, the engineers built two new boats, the John Ordway and the Patrick Gass, at Gasconade, Missouri, named for Army sergeants on the Lewis and Clark expedition. These were diesel-powered boats, which was a little unusual for that period. The voyage up the Missouri caused quite a stir, according to J. Mack Gamble in the December 29, 1934, issue of *The Waterways Journal*.

It is hard to tell just how long it has been since any sternwheel riverboats had left on such a mountain trip, 2,000 miles in length, quite

CHAPTER 10 ≈ ADVENTURES IN PILOTING

common back in the 1870s and 1880s. These two towboats did not complete their long trip this season but were beached for the winter far up in the Dakotas. They did penetrate to a point almost unknown so far as present day navigation is concerned, and Capt. William L. "Steamboat Bill" Heckmann, who piloted one of the craft, brought back pictures of Indians and buffalo.

Steamboat Bill wrote about some of the characters he encountered en route.

On our trip up towards Fort Peck with the diesel towboats, John Ordway and the Patrick Gass, we met many interesting people. But the most interesting character we met on all this trip was a 12-year-old Indian boy up in North Dakota. He swam out in midstream to the Patrick Gass, and we pulled him aboard by the nape of the neck. Within the next hour he told us all about North Dakota in a way that held us spellbound. We finally asked him how far up the river he wanted to go. He replied, "Do not pay any attention to me; I will swim back home."

After looking the whole boat over, he bid us all good-bye, jumped in the water, and swam on down toward his home some six miles down the river.

The upper Missouri River was not in the best condition for boats when the Gass and the Ordway attempted their trip to the head of navigation. Steamboat offered his own descriptions and explanations, some of which were written before he himself headed for the mountains.

From where the Missouri River tumbles over the great falls above Fort Benton, Montana, is about 1,600 miles. When able to steamboat there, you are known as a "Mountain Pilot," and there is no other stretch of river of this length in the known world where as much skill is needed to get a boat up and down the river as there is right here.

This river will change its channel while you are eating breakfast. When you go up the river with a boat, you cannot come back down over the same course. You will start out on a long, flat crossing drawing four feet scant; you squint your eyes and look ahead to see a long, flat, slick, swift stretch of river ahead. You start sounding; the bottom of the river will be as flat as a table; the man sounding water will cry out, "four feet," and he will continue to do this until up in the pilothouse you get the jim jams and pray for daylight and deep water. The government is now going to make this river navigable. They should leave it as it is and use it for a pilot's school to make some more good pilots so badly needed on our rivers. Anyone who can pilot a boat successfully here can qualify as a first-class pilot on any river in the world.

When our government first issued licenses to pilot to the mountains, they gave each successful applicant ammunition and a gun. This equipment was for Indian attacks and for shooting buffaloes and wild meat for the table. Later, a law was made to exclude the ladies from the pilothouse while underway, but offered no protection for them when the boat is tied to the bank, when a pilot really had time for devilment. This law was not necessary on the upper river, as a pilot cannot leave the wheel long enough to get a chew of tobacco, much less to take time to fondle a woman....

There is no place where romance likes better to tarry than in the pilothouse of a mountain steamboat. The very air is filled with life that one cannot feel anywhere else in the world....

Few now remember the old-time pilots. I will mention at this time when we had over 300 of these pathfinders; and about each and every one a little story could be told. These men were sturdy, true, resourceful, intelligent and had a never-failing memory. All had their way with the ladies when they desired to meet the feminine gender halfway, before the time of permanent waves, manufactured faces and women politicians.

It meant something to be a river captain in them days. You left St. Louis with 250 tons of freight, that many passengers and their baggage, and you knew you had to spar over sandbars, warp up over the rapids, cut your own fuel, look out for Indians and protect your women and children from men weaker or meaner than yourself. These great men did this all with honor, and history has never given them the credit due them.

The 1934 Log of the John Ordway and the Patrick Gass describes the scene.

On July 2, 1934, the brand-new diesel towboats John Ordway and the Patrick Gass of the U. S. Engineer Department nosed their way into the muddy water of the Missouri River at Gasconade, Missouri, and started on an 1,875-mile journey to Fort Peck, Montana. The two boats, built at the Gasconade boatyard of the U.S. Engineer Department, are

CHAPTER 10 ≈ ADVENTURES IN PILOTING

destined to act as prime movers for the four electrically operated, non-propelled, suction-head dredges now being completed for use on the 230-foot earth dam across the Missouri River in Montana. The expedition was commanded by the veteran master and pilot, Capt. W. I. (Tobe) Maulding, recently retired from active duty to the job of Lockmaster at the picturesque Lock and Dam No. 1 on the Osage River in Missouri. Captain Maulding had active charge of the towboat John Ordway during the trip. The Patrick Gass was captained by the veteran pilot, Captain William L. (Steamboat Bill) Heckmann, who is normally employed as a master and pilot by the Woods Brothers Construction Company of Lincoln, Nebraska.

The crew of the John Ordway, composed: Capt. Walter I. Maulding, master and pilot; Gilbert Kirchner, pilot; Charles Nichols, chief engineer; George Heckmann, assistant engineer; Clinton McMillan, cook; Leonard Thompson, head deckhand; Ray Patterson, deckhand; and Russell Stephenson, shipkeeper.

The crew of the Patrick Gass composed: Capt. William L. Heckmann, master; Joseph Leach, pilot; Walter Ray, engineer; Robert Hilger, striker; William Jeffries, cook; Kermit Baecker, head deckhand; Adolph Wolff, deckhand; and Carl Jackson, shipkeeper.

During the journey the boats were serviced by a government truck driven by Raymond Simms and dispatched by William Gardner. This truck contacted the boats at points along the river and delivered mail, provisions and emergency lubricants.

The two towboats are sternwheelers, each powered by a 210 hp Fairbanks-Morse diesel engine. All major pieces of machinery on the boats, including the electric starting apparatus and the electric capstans, were furnished by the Fairbanks-Morse Company. The boats have steel hulls, wooden superstructures, chain drives, and have the following dimensions: length molded, 90 feet; length overall, 107 feet; breadth overall, 22 feet, 7 inches; depth molded, 5 feet; displacement, 3 feet.

The boats were laid out and assembled at the Gasconade Boatyard of the U.S. Engineer Department in less than four months, having been started on or about March 12, 1934. George Streeter and James J. Hurd, supervisor of the boatyard and master mechanic respectively, were in active charge of the construction.

Operating at reduced speed in order to thoroughly break in the engines, the two boats reached Jefferson City the first night, having covered 40 miles; the second day, Boonville, 54 miles; third day, Miami Station, 69 miles; fourth day, Missouri City, 88 miles....The 280-mile stretch of river between Gasconade and Kansas City was navigated with comparative ease, despite the unusually low water that prevailed at that season of the year. Commenting on the condition of the lower Missouri, Capt. Maulding remarked, "We didn't have a sounding pole down on the entire trip to Kansas City."

The first delay due to bad water was experienced a few miles above St. Joseph, Missouri, where the War Department was just beginning to develop a navigable channel.... From Sioux City, Iowa, the boats turned westward through the Dakotas.... Approximately 2,500 people were on hand at Pierre, South Dakota, to examine the Ordway and Gass. At that point a railroad bridge draw span was opened for the first time in many years....

Although numerous delays were experienced beyond this point due to the extreme shoal water during one of the driest seasons of record, the longest delay occurred at Artichoke Creek, 75 miles above Pierre, South Dakota. Beginning August 22, the boats spent five days washing over a 8,900-foot crossing. The longest continuous stretch of shoal water, a 1,000-foot crossing, was encountered just below Chamberlain, South Dakota....

Through an agreement with the Woods Brothers Construction Company, Capt. "Bill" Heckmann left the boats shortly before they reached Mobridge, South Dakota, in order to take up his duties as a pilot for that company on the lower river. The command of the Patrick Gass was given to Pilot Joseph R. Leach. The expedition continued on at a snail's pace through extremely bad water to Mobridge, arriving at that city on September 17, 1934. The approach of winter caused the district engineer, Kansas City district, who had been charged with the delivery of the boats to Montana, to order the boats pulled out on to the banks until travel could be resumed safely in the spring.

One of the crew members commented about the lack of water and the fact that it was impossible to wash a channel through rock. At one particularly trying time when the boats had been stuck quite a while, an Indian came down to the river and dipped a bucket of water. One wit on board called out, "Pour

CHAPTER 10 ≈ ADVENTURES IN PILOTING

that back! We need every drop." Reportedly, the Indian went right ahead and called back, "Need water. Squaw having baby."

Capt. Joseph Leach has been left with a crew of two men at Mobridge to guard and maintain the two towboats through the long Dakota winter. Early in the spring of 1935, Capt. Maulding is expecting to return to Mobridge to resume command of the expedition and complete the remaining 641 miles of the journey to Fort Peck, Montana. With a normal winter of snow in the Rocky Mountains and the usual spring thaw in the upper river, no difficulty is expected during the final leg of this historic waterway expedition.

Steamboat Bill often wrote with great admiration of Capt. Wm. Massie, one of the mountain pilots—the very best, according to Steamboat. He also mentioned the unique license held by Massie—Fort Peck to the mouth of the Mississippi.

But he never mentioned that his brother, Edward Heckmann, had Massie beat. Ed's license covered everything from Fort Peck to the mouth of the Mississippi, plus the Ohio, Tennessee, Cumberland and Illinois rivers, plus the Yukon and its tributaries—all vessels, all tons. Apparently, a little sibling rivalry precluded admitting this in print.

Steamboat simply did not write about things that did not agree with his reasoning. He was not in favor of a barge line on the Missouri River, so while lengthy accounts of the first barge line appeared in print in 1932, he remained closemouthed. Nonetheless, when Secretary of War, Patrick J. Hurley came to inspect the river, Steamboat Bill felt left out. He was not included in the party aboard the Mark Twain, Hurley's conveyance, an oversight he himself quickly remedied.

Drawing alongside the Mark Twain in his hand-powered skiff—rather the worse for wear—and looking like a bum himself, he produced a huge channel catfish—variously reported at 45 or 35 pounds. This he presented to Hurley. He was invited aboard to join the party. He refused, requesting that he be allowed to join the party upriver the next day. It was a request that could not be refused, so Steamboat Bill got aboard as a guest for the remainder of the trip. It took a Kansas City reporter to tell this story from firsthand observation for a good insight into the character called Steamboat Bill.

Steamboat Bill made the trip to the mountains—or almost there—when he was 65. He continued to work for Woods Brothers until 1937.

Now, folks, at the age of 67 years, I am shifting for myself, and if anyone wants to hire or raise an old man that is handy around the pilothouse next spring, then this old man is ready to go on any man's boat that has a cookhouse on it. My services are for sale.

When Steamboat Bill "retired" he had no long wait in the unemployment line. He wrote of numerous brief encounters with assorted boats.

Tripwork for Steamboat Bill
October, 1939

I had the pleasure of making a trip from Hickman, Kentucky, to Kansas City, Missouri, on the motor towboat G. F. Maitland, a fine little diesel boat named in honor of a fine man. Getting back on one of these little towboats with the Kansas City Bridge Company touched a tender spot in my heart. Alexander Maitland Sr. was a dear friend of the Heckmann boys. Capt. J. Fred Heckmann worked many years for this company, and both he and Capt. Johnnie Heckmann died while employed as pilots for the bridge company.

To catch this boat, Engineer Ralston and myself went from Jefferson City to the foot of Island No. 8 by auto with one of the bridge company's superintendents. This trip was a pleasant one except that I left my best coat, a fine pair of glasses and a lot of other junk hanging on a stump in old Kentucky, and if it had not been for the courtesy and honesty of some good people down there, this garment would never have seen the "Show Me" state again.

On a later trip, Steamboat piloted the showboat Dixie Queen from Gasconade to St. Louis.

This fine new showboat was built at Kansas City by Mr. and Mrs. A.E. Cooper. Both of these good people are old troupers and are swell actors. Their son, too, is destined some day to follow in their footsteps. All the actors on this boat were wonderful. They put on a fine show and deserve every success in life's hard battle. This showboat is being towed by the little towboat Abbigale, recently converted from a steam sternwheeler into a gas boat. This is the first showboat I ever piloted, and the Abbigale is the first gas boat ever in my charge. Fortune may

CHAPTER 10 ≈ ADVENTURES IN PILOTING

again see me on another showboat, but, ladies and gentlemen, this is my first and last adventure on a gas boat.

Leaving Hermann we had bad luck by breaking the wheel shaft, and at Washington, Missouri, we could not land without taking a big chance on account of shallow water and rock. When Uncle Sam took the river out of Hellbush Bend, he almost put Washington, Missouri, off our river map. On a number of crossings between Gasconade and the mouth of the river, we only found three feet of water. This old mysterious river has got them all guessing, even Steamboat Bill. My guess is that the big dredges on the Missouri River are to blame for our shallow river; they have loosened up what heretofore was packed sand, which makes it easier for each rise to wash this loose sand downstream, and this same sand is not only lodging on our crossings but is filling up all our deep river. Therefore, if this practice is not stopped, we will have no river at all in low water stages.

Bill and Annie Heckmann with their granddaughter, Mary Ann

The showboat Dixie Queen made a long home stand at the foot of Holmes Street, Kansas City, after which Capt. Floyd Dean took her from Kansas City to St. Joseph, Missouri, and then back to Kansas City. From Kansas City to Gasconade, Capt. Bill Fegans was the skipper, and as mentioned before, Bill Heckmann from Gasconade to St. Louis.

Anyone getting a chance should visit this showboat for it deserves every success in the whole wide world, and as they make their way southward along the mighty Mississippi, even the ducks and geese will wonder why the public sidesteps real action for pictures.

Retirement was not all work and no play. Hunting and fishing had long been part of life for most Heckmann men, and Steamboat Bill was no exception. While his hunting was sporadic, his fishing was continuous—so much so that the family worried about him out on the river all alone. He continued to spurn anything run by gas—no outboard motors for him. So he rowed his johnboat across the swift and treacherous Missouri to go fishing in the Loutre River. If the weather was bad or the river was flooded, he walked three miles, crossing a narrow bridge with no pedestrian walk and cars going both directions, just to go fishing.

In later years, when his health was failing and after he had spent time in the Marine Hospital, he took to walking out from town a mile or two, even on the most scorching days, to fish in some holes in tiny Frene Creek. Neither he nor his brother Ed ever declared enough of a truce with the internal combustion engine to own or drive a car. To their dying days, they walked. By 1949 he was complaining about his physical restrictions.

Talking about fishing, it is quite a come down for Yours Truly, who for the last four years has been used to catching some 200 pounds of fine fish per day, to have to confine himself to creek fishing around this burg. Capt. Delmar Ruediger and Steamboat Bill are organizing an Invalid's Fishing Corporation here. In order to buy stock in this company, you have to spend at least one month in a Marine Hospital. We are offering for sale 1,000 shares of common because it will be a very common company. We will not offer any preferred since we do not want any of the "400" or preferred people mixed up with us. If Capt. G. Lolson, Clarence Friemonth, Gilbert Kirchner or Paul Smith want to help along these lines, when they make their fishing trips and have any bait left over, we hope they send it along to us. We will take anything from a bull calf to a horsefly. Same invitation to Capt. C. C. Wallaw.

In 1947 he made fishing news with an illustrated write up in the June issue of The Missouri Conservationist. The article said that for years Steamboat had been tracking down reports of big fish taken from the Missouri River. The

CHAPTER 10 ≈ ADVENTURES IN PILOTING

largest catfish was a 315 pounder landed near Morrison in about 1870 by a youth named Struttman, who had help from Capt. Heckmann's father. The fish was said to be caught on a special hook hammered out by the local blacksmith and baited with half a spoiled ham.

Some of Steamboat's fishing escapades made local news. One chilly day, during high water, he walked across the Missouri River bridge to his favorite fishing spot on the Loutre River. He set out a trot line, tying one end to a bridge girder and weighing the other with a large rock. Soon he noticed he had a big fish in about the center of the line. But when he tried to pull the fish up, the weight was too much for him.

Capts. Greeley, Bill and Ed Heckmann proudly display their catch of the day.

After giving the situation some thought, he took off his clothes and hung them on a bridge girder. Into the flood water he went, right up to his neck, hanging onto the bridge frame to keep from being washed away by the flood waters. He had almost reached the fish when he stepped on one of the hooks on the trot line, running it through his foot.

Now he really had a problem. He could not let go of the bridge to reach down to his foot, and the tied line with the big fish and rock gave him no slack. So there he stood, in the water up to his neck, for nearly two hours.

The fish was the first to win—he pulled loose. After a long struggle, the fisherman finally got enough slack in the line to reach for his pants and get his pocketknife—no easy task since he still could not let go of the bridge for fear of being swept away. Holding the knife in his mouth, he used his free hand to drag enough slack in the line so he could finally sever it. The exhausted fisherman then dragged himself out of the water, got into his clothes and cut the fish hook out of his foot. Then he walked three miles back home with a very sore foot. He was 86 at the time.

The big catfish and channel buffaloes say Hermann is the most dangerous place between St. Louis and Fort Benton to swim by, either up or downstream, without being caught, on the whole darn river.

•

We caught a 50-pound channel cat. One of our men had the head cleaned and fixed up to suit his taste. He ate the whole outfit, about three pounds, for supper. What I mean is supper—not what society people call dinner. Next morning he got up and said, "I rolled and was storm-tossed all night and dreamed that the catfish head I ate was swimming downstream and was singing, 'I ain't got no body!'"

•

Lon Wilson and I had our picture taken with an 80-pound flathead catfish we caught. This is a sample of the fish caught in the Missouri River by men that drink only "Coke," "Seven-up" and root beer and take their sorrows, griefs, faith, hope and charity straight to Simon Peter's teacher.

Even before retirement, any chance to go fishing was welcome. He jumped at an invitation to explore Charette Creek, sometimes called a river. He was told, "If you arrange to get to the mouth of Wigglie Wigglie about 3 o'clock, you will get to see the big carp as they are floating now."

Let us see if we can describe this fish, for see him we did. We landed some 50 yards above the described place, got on the bank, sneaked down; and lo and behold, there laid the old lugger floating on his side in water as clear as crystal. He was a battle-scarred veteran of many wars. How much he weighed none could tell as his scales were all gone years ago and he was as naked as a jay bird after a hail storm. On the side next to us, along about the seventh rib, someone had put a gig in him that had left an ugly scar. His mouth was torn and rotten from the many hooks that failed to hold. His dorsal fin looked like a battered battleship ready to strike her colors, and even his mighty tail had been in battle, as the lower half was gone. In breathless wonder we gazed at this monster, not knowing what to do. We finally retreated and held a council of war.

Bickel wished to go for his high-powered rifle; for myself, I said, "You have been popping off all morning saying what you were going to do with these fish up here. You have not showed anything yet. Take this rail and knock him for a home run." This he did and with all his might, but he hit him along about the cook house, too far aft, and Mr. Carp made one splash of his tail and was gone, leaving us in a shower of spray, wet and wiser in a way.

The loss of this fish was a blow to me, and I did not fail to tell Bickel so. He 'lowed I could not have done any better, but take it from a modest man, if ever I get a crack like that at this bird, his side will be caved in and another Heckmann will be famous! We quarreled all the way home about this fish. Along toward evening the shadows commenced to lengthen, and we got off our course to run full tilt into a mulberry tree. We hit this so hard that we knocked four fox squirrels in the river, and a big bull snake fell across the head of our boat. His hurry in getting back into the water saved us the trouble and made us forget the big carp.

Steamboat loved a good fish story, even if it was about the Mississippi River.

Credit this one to Capt. Jim Phillips, a noted pilot and master on all our western rivers.

When he was a young man, he and his father caught many fine catfish on the upper Mississippi. Most of their largest fish were caught jug fishing. One day they started out on a jugging trip with a bunch of bullfrogs for bait. The river was dead low; the surface looked like a big mirror.

Jim had said they ought to snare some big ones that trip. They pulled out in the channel of the river, threw out their jugs, drifted back about 300 yards behind them and waited for results. They floated about 10 miles and never got a bite. The elder Mr. Phillips said, "There is something wrong here, but I cannot figure things out."

About that time they were floating under one of the upper river bridges. The bridge tender hollered out and said, "Mr. Phillips, are you catching any today?"

"Not a thing."

The bridge tender hollered back and said, "No, and you won't catch anything until you chase them bullfrogs from the top of them jugs."

There was no weight on their stagins,' and in investigation they found a bullfrog on every jug, floating down the scenic upper Mississippi, enjoying the scenery.

Flies, mosquitoes and yellow jackets were among the many pests that added to the difficulty of life on the river.

We met opposition by a heat wave, swarms of mosquitoes, a new species of fly, also a tough guy who owned a private road out to civilization, if we still have anything like that.

Getting back to the new kind of a fly—they were so thick that the deckhands could hardly tie the boat up to the bank. I wish some bug scientist would study this new pest that is some smaller than a horsefly, and when they light on you, they stay put until you kill them, immovable, detestable and dishonorable creatures, ugly and bold. They have red stripes around their bodies from amidships clean back to their monkey rudders. They have both hair and feathers all over their bodies, and they are jet-black where the stripes do not predominate, and around their snoots they have a big yellow ring. Facing you, they look 100 percent the pest they are. We saw a few of these farther down the river, but at the mouth of the Missouri, there was an epidemic of these creatures.

•

Things have not been breaking all right for Steamboat Bill lately. Some three months ago he slipped down the river bank, landed in his beloved river and, when back on shore, he found he had sprained his starboard ankle. After hobbling around for some two months, one evening when the sun was ending its daily task in the west, he decided to pull up some grass and clean up a terrace about 15 feet back of his home. He slipped and poked his unlucky foot into a yellow jacket nest. They disputed his presence on his own terrace, and before the inside of the house was reached, the ornery critters stung him eight times. One of the little rats followed clear into the house and lit on the curtain alongside the favorite rocking chair where he was consoling himself and licking his wounds. Mrs. Heckmann, who has been hobbling around on a crutch for almost four years now, brought her favorite weapon, a fly swatter, and made a pass at him (or her) and missed. She handed me the swatter and said, "You kill him. You started this flight and fight."

The first swat I missed him, but on the next swat he fell, crippled, to the floor, but not until he made a final shot at my left eye on which blindness had already taken place. Here we might say, "Et To Brute."

At this point my brother, Capt. Ed Heckmann, an ex-warrior on flying varmints, offered his assistance. He damaged our winter snow shovel when swatting at the nest. Finally we poured two pints of coal oil into the nest and burned up two Globe Democrats, one a Sunday edition. Two days after that some of these truly home-loving creatures were still flying around that nest.

Each colony, according to their species, has from eight to 20 home guards who gather no honey but stay at home to protect same. These home guards routed me without calling out any of their regulars or reserves. They had neither military training nor five-star generals, and, when you come to think of it, here is one man who says our next war will be won in the air.

•

More About the Yellow Boys
March 28, 1953

Loutre Island lies across the river from Hermann, Missouri. It is 6 miles long and from one-half to 2 miles wide, the largest island on the lower Missouri River. A slough runs all the way around it and is, or was, some 50 to 150 feet wide.

In the early '80s, we used to go up this slough with our Hermann boats for wheat, ties and cordwood, and in the days when the boats still burned wood, it was nothing to find a yellow jacket nest or two in a woodpile in the summertime.

A hornet, about 20 times as large as a yellow jacket, will come buzzing along about 40 miles an hour, hit you smack center in the forehead, knock you flat on your back and go buzzing along about his business. Several hundred yellow jackets will hop on you and, if you have no way of escaping, will come nearer killing you than the Big Boy; and for this reason, Old Steamboat will lay his money on the yellow boys.

One day in the year of 1882, the steamer Hope went around in the Loutre Slough for a load of wheat. A Mr. Heck had threshed some 800 sacks of wheat, and we landed there to load same. A monster-big straw pile lay just back of the pile of wheat. The river had been up but had fallen, and we had to put out two lengths of stage plank over a mud wallow or mud hole. We loaded the wheat, and Dad said we would load four cords of wood, or in steamboat terms, make a woodpile.

We had a mixed crew of white and black roustabouts of about 30 men. Among this number was a fresh German immigrant from the banks of the Rhine River. Soon after starting to load this wood, a rouster by the name of Rastus saw a yellow jacket's nest, and soon all the rousters were toting wood from the other end of the pile. The old German, who had never seen one of these critters, said, "Das macht nix," and kept on carrying from the wrong end of the pile until the wood, nest and all, rolled down.

Then, folks, the battle was on! Everybody moved except our German who put up a mighty battle, which in a few minutes was over and our hero a wreck. Our unfortunate colored roustabout fell off the stage plank into the mud hole, and on him the general in charge ordered an attack. Rousters ran in every direction, a lot to refuge in the hull of the Hope. Dad Heckmann and his one-eyed pilot had reached and barred the pilothouse in advance. Young Will Heckmann ran into the haystack clean out of sight; others ran up and down the slough.

About the only thing that saved us was our fireman. Dad said he was always so full of liquor that he was immune from a sting of flying critters. This "Big Bull," our fireman, carried the German aboard and pulled the unfortunate rouster out of the mud hole, and we were ready to sail. Big George, the head rouster said, "What shall I do with the stage planks?"

"Leave then here for some other time. Cut that head line loose, and let's get away from here," said Dad. He hollered to four rousters up the slough and said, "Come a-running boys, we are ready to leave."

One of them answered back and said, "We're as near that bad hole as we ever expect to get. We will walk up to Hermann, six miles away, and catch you there. Rastus is in pretty bad shape, and we may stop at Mr. Whiteside's overnight for first aid."

To the men down the slough, he said, "Henry, you boys walk down to Rueff's Landing where we will load some more wheat."

Christian Henry Mason, about the only man living Old Rough Head Heckmann was afraid of, answered back, "We will get aboard at Rueff's Landing, but there will be no more wheat loaded on the good steamer Hope today. You're going to take these two men to the doctor, or my name ain't Henry Mason."

We did not load any wheat, for Big Christian Henry Mason practiced the Golden Rule, and Old Rough Head Heckmann at times had a hard time running the Hope in a way to suit him. Besides, Mason was not bashful about telling him how to run a boat. Later, on the steamer

CHAPTER 10 ≈ ADVENTURES IN PILOTING

Gasconade, this good man did many favors for me in keeping my unruly men from mutiny.

After picking up these men, we hightailed it out of that slough and went on our way home after a delay of several hours.

When out in the open river, the one-eyed pilot said, "Take the boat, Capt. Bill. Them damn yellow jackets have stung me on my good eye. They just as well have stung me in my glass eye. As it is, those Dutch pardners of yours will want to fire me, and God knows where I will find another berth." But Old Rough Head stood by him until we sold the old Hope down South....

When we got the two men to Hermann, the doctor said that if it had not been for Aunt Mary (our cook), it is doubtful if they would have gotten well again. Aunt Mary, it seemed, had doused them with homemade molasses and flour.

Some two weeks later the old German came back to work. On his very first trip we were running up Straub's Bend, and part of the bank had slipped in the river, or down about six feet, taking a big black skunk, or polecat along. This animal could not get back up onto the mainland. Our German friend came running out on the forecastle and hollered up to the pilothouse and said, "Stop, Bill. Ich hole him," or "I'll get him!"

I slowed the old lugger down, and Dad said, "What are you going to do now?

"Old Buck wants to catch that skunk."

"Let her go on up the river; that will be worse than a hornet's nest."

Young Bill obeyed orders, thinking to himself, "it seems like Dad does not want to Americanize that Dutchman." A polecat does not sting, but his liquid out of his deadly tail is more sickening than a yellow jacket sting. We will let it go at that.

Two-legged pests also came in for comment. Steamboat Bill was an avid card player and a good craps shooter. He also excelled at more elite card games.

This good lady was my partner last season in an important bridge game. She held the ace, king, queen, ten, nine, eight, five, four, three and deuce of diamonds, the king and queen of spades and the king of clubs, and she did not make a bid on this hand. That she is still hale and hearty speaks well for the steamboat fraternity.

≈ STEAMBOAT TREASURES ≈

Usually Steamboat Bill spoke in defense of a good craps game, but even he could tie a moral to a story about these games. He told of a friend who hit him up for a loan of $10.

Jim takes the 10, plays the races and wins 160 bucks. Two strong-arm men see him win this money and lay plans to hold him up. It is not yet time to go in for the day, and Jim looks up a craps game where he loses the $160 and what he has left of Bill's 10 dollars. He reaches his hotel about dark, and as he starts up the steps to go to his room, the two toughs hold him up, hurt his back and take his coat and vest, his watch and chain, his pocketknife and his rabbit's foot.

The moral of which is not to put too much faith in a rabbit's foot!

Occasionally, others took delight in writing about Steamboat Bill, as in this piece published in 1928.

There are two famous "Bills" on the Missouri River—W. L. Heckmann of Hermann and W. L. (Wild Bill) Thompson of Bonnott's Mill. At various times Steamboat Bill has retailed a number of stories at the expense of Wild Bill, at present, master of the towboat Alert. And that recalls to the latter how Bloody Island in the Osage River derived its bloody name.

Once upon a time, the two Bills, who are friends but rivals, went up the Osage one winter to this then-unknown island on a deer hunting trip, accompanied by Steamboat Bill's brother, Greeley, and Wild Bill's brother, Arthur, the latter being master at the present time of the towboat Richard Roe. On looking out of their tent the first morning, it was noticed that a deer was crouched down under a bluff across the river.

Both Bills shot at the same time. Steamboat Bill called, "I got him!" Wild Bill said, "No, I got him." But Steamboat Bill countered with, "No, I saw his tail drop when I shot." So the two Bills argued until they decided to fight it out, the best man to get the deer. They fought backward and forward until the whole island was covered with blood.

Meantime, brothers Greeley and Arthur rowed over to get the deer, but soon hollered back, "Quit fighting; this deer's been dead a month." And sure enough, the deer had evidently fallen over the bluff, had broken its neck and had been devoured by scavengers, all except the hide and horns.

CHAPTER 10 ≈ ADVENTURES IN PILOTING

In 1942 Steamboat Bill wrote to the Waterways Journal:

Have been on the Idlewild since July 10 as pilot on the Missouri River and roof watchman on other rivers. Have been to St. Joseph, Missouri, Joliet and Nashville, seeing a lot, learning a lot and hearing plenty....Will try to see you on the way home some time in October.

In 1943 he was back on the Idlewild, enjoying every minute.

You will put on your glad rags and go down to the river for a moonlight ride on the excursion steamer Idlewild. The calliope plays, the big whistle blows, the stars twinkle and shine, the electric lights flicker in the night's darkness, and soon you are on your way to see a full moon coming over the mountain with the devil in it instead of a man.

Steamboat wrote five long installments about this unforgettable experience. He was 73 years old, and this was to be some of his last big river work. When Capt. Frederick Way published his book, the Log of the Betsy Ann, Steamboat Bill caught the writing urge to write a book on steamboating.

Mrs. Heckmann read my copy of Frederick Way's book from cover to cover. She handed it back to me and said, "That is a mighty fine book, and you could write one like that from your experience in the packet business." One would have to live with a woman like Mrs. Heckmann some 40 years, like I have, to know just how fine a compliment this is to a young author. She was pal enough not to mention what we went through during the 10 years from 1900 to 1910 in the packet business, and at that she never knew all that hubby went through, and it was h— at times to make both ends meet; yet I made thousands of friends and rendered help in times of disaster, inasmuch as we had four big floods on the Missouri during those 10 years. As we look back at the 10 years, they stand away out as the most useful of my long life on the river.

By 1931 Steamboat was getting discouraged. He had written his book, and it went from publisher to publisher, friend to friend, and yet there was no light at the end of the tunnel as to when the book might be published. At the time J. Mack Gamble, then still a young man, was typing, correcting and proofreading Steamboat's stories, all written in his Spencerian longhand. The story Gamble picked as the best, so far, for the book was a tale of Capt. Will L. Heckmann Sr.

Right after the Civil War my father was a contractor in houses and bridges. He made two large fortunes in contracting and steamboating and spent three in sawmilling, farming and grain milling. In the year 1867, he was building a bridge near Chamois, Missouri, and one Saturday noon he wanted to go see his intended wife, my dear mother, who lived down the Big Muddy at Bluffton, Missouri, nine miles down the stream.

He nailed some dry cottonwood logs together, put an empty nail keg on for a seat and started floating down Old Man River. When about one-half way on his journey of courtship, he was passing Portland, Missouri. The dry logs, none too large, had become water-soaked and had sunk below the surface of the water—but still holding his weight. He was sitting on his nail keg, reading a newspaper, when an old colored woman out on the bank at Portland, hollered to him, "Before Gawd, man, whar am you goin'?"

"I am going to St. Louis."

"Oh, you is, is you? All I got to say is you will never get there on that nail keg."

Even with the help of friends and relatives, the book continued to bounce about. Steamboat was downright jealous of others whose book did get published.

If hard times keep knocking at the door and the worst becomes worser, ye editor of *The Waterways Journal*, as an act of charity, will publish all of my stories in his paper. We will then have it set in type and can print our own book. To this there is the objection that my *Waterways Journal* friends will read my stories gratis and my best market for the book will be shot full of holes.

Finally, in 1950, when Steamboat was 81, the book was published by the Burton Publishing Co. of Kansas City. "Steamboating Sixty-five Years on Missouri's Rivers" enjoyed modest sales. For the next several years, Steamboat continued to give the book a plug at any given opportunity. His friends got into the act and also tried to help, including Robert D. Burnett, who wrote for The Chillicothe Bulletin.

CHAPTER 10 ≈ ADVENTURES IN PILOTING

This 1935 photograph, taken aboard the Steamer George Woods, was on the cover of Steamboat Bill's book.

Speaking of books we like to re-read, we must not neglect that all-time old favorite, "Steamboating Sixty-Five Years On Missouri's Rivers," by Capt. William L. Heckmann. Capt. Bill is 87 years young and first went on the river shortly after his 12th birthday. There were 15 children in Bill's family, and of the eight boys, seven of them became rivermen. We think Bill is safe in defying anyone to break that record.

The Missouri River is his stamping ground, and few men know it so well. His book is full of old river legends and personal experiences that out rival most legends. For anyone to write a history of the Missouri River and leave out the name Heckmann would be as ridiculous as writing about Christmas without mentioning Santa Claus....We ordered our first copy of Bill's book several months before it was published, and about a year after we received it, we had to order another because the original was dog-eared from re-reading and lending it to others to read.

For anyone who really likes the river and likes to read what a real riverman has to say about it, there is a possibility that a letter addressed to Capt. W. L. Heckmann, Hermann, Missouri, will turn up, for perhaps as little as $5, an extra copy.

CHAPTER 11

Eulogies

Whatever else Steamboat Bill wrote about, he never missed a chance to eulogize his friends and acquaintances. Death brought on most of his eloquent tributes, but they sometimes came while the recipients were still living. He deplored the fact that so few are recognized for their achievements in life. Flowers after death are rather useless, he said, because they so soon fade away.

Of all mysteries in this mysterious world, the greatest mystery is death. When we die, loving relatives and friends cover our coffin with flowers that in their freshness show the difference between life and death, but these same flowers too soon will wither and die. Then, when we visit our loved one's grave, it seems desolation has now really settled down over the beloved being still covered with withered flowers and yellow clay.

While still in life, we also receive bouquets in the way of letters, telegrams and in face-to-face compliments. These bouquets are lifeless but will not wither and are highly appreciated.

Steamboat did his best to praise and comment at any opportunity. He wrote many eulogies honoring his father, many praising his crew members and the roustabouts. He also wrote a number of stories about himself that could easily be described as eulogies. Upon occasion, he even produced an entire composite praise of boats and crews. He took particular delight in praising the deckhands and roustabouts. In 1933 he wrote a tribute to Herman Kaiser, a deckhand and sometimes fireman, for the hometown newspaper, the Advertiser-Courier:

When my father took me out of public school 41 years ago, Herman Kaiser had left the farm and was working on the river. Along about 1884, the Wohlt Bros. built the Str. Royal and put this boat in opposi-

CHAPTER 11 ≈ EULOGIES

tion to the Hermann Ferry & Packet Co., owned then by Heckmann and Talbot.

After less than 2 years of bitter opposition, the Wohlt's again combined forces with the old company that survives to this day. During this bitter struggle, Hermann Kaiser remained loyal to the Wohlts, and the shippers on the Gasconade enjoyed the best service they ever had on this river while opposition lasted. The boats ran almost night and day; they came and went, freight or no freight. More than one trip the boats came back to Hermann without a pound of freight.

The old company made something like one hundred percent during this time. The Royal and the Wohlts did not do so well and would have fared worse without the service of Mr. Kaiser; he was always their ace in the hole. After opposition ceased, it was my pleasure to make many a trip with this good man right down on deck as a fellow worker, and often he and I carried every pound of freight on and off a boat on a round trip.

If you could have seen two men carrying 900 sacks of wheat out of the warehouses or off the high banks of the Gasconade in less than a day, or sometimes after night, in rain or shine, you could say you saw men at work.

Kaiser never complained. He was a devout Catholic, but duty came first with this good man. He seldom used a curse word, was always ready to work and always in the lead. In my long time on the river, if any praise or honor has come to me, to this man belongs part of the credit.

Capt. Hal Dodd, the Missouri's most noted character, a man who had owned his own boats, who had made many a trip up the Big Muddy to the mountains and who had worked many thousands of men, after he had worked here one season on the ferry boat, said that Kaiser was the most dependable, most industrious man he ever saw on our western rivers.

He held duty sacred. It was Dodd who gave him the nickname "Old War Horse," and this same Dodd was the most stingy man with his praise we ever had. In my presence Kaiser is the only man he ever praised, and this alone would make this good man an outstanding character.

For over 40 years he was on the different ferryboats here, and in all that time he was never late. You told him when you wanted to be ready to go, and you could bet your last dollar Kaiser would have everything ready to go when you got there. The people across the river trusted and honored him, and the ferry service here, the best they had anywhere on the Missouri, would not have been what it was without this good man.

Late one fall, after the last ferry trip, we went up into the Gasconade to tow a raft of ties to Gore. We made up our tow to the raft and had everything ready for an early morning start. My two oldest daughters, Monica and Hazel, school girls at that time, volunteered to go along as cooks for the trip. Kaiser was the fireman and deckhand. I was the pilot.

It turned bitter cold during the night, and in the land-locked harbor of the Gasconade, we did not notice the wind so much. When we got out into the Missouri, the wind was blowing a gale that soon developed into a storm. One of the two lines to the raft parted, and the "Old War Horse" got out on the raft to replace it. The other line parted and left Mr. Kaiser out alone on the raft. In maneuvering the boat to keep it from getting crossways in the storm, the raft drifted away. The wind was throwing the waves over this frail construction and up against the old navigator, who stood there foursquare to the wind. He looked and acted the part of the Ancient Mariner.

The old boat was now in the trough of the storm, shaking and cracking in every joint; the two seasick cooks were no help, neither the pilot nor engineer could leave his post. A boy by the name of "Bad Eye" had gone along as a kind of stowaway, to spark the cooks it is supposed. Mr. Kaiser called to him to throw some coal in the furnace, but "Bad Eye" had a death grip on the bull railing and was too scared to move.

Finally the wind blew the old lugger against the raft. Kaiser crawled aboard with a line. The wind ceased some, and when the steam came back, we managed to land boat and raft at the Hermann wharf. When we had landed, the two cooks lost no time in getting reassigned, and away they ran for home. "Bad Eye" was not long in hitting the bank, and he, too, hiked to sounder foundations.

Kaiser, in his days, worked for almost every captain who ever steamboated out of Hermann, and no doubt every one could tell a story of this kind about this good man. If space would permit, it would not

CHAPTER 11 ≈ EULOGIES

be hard for me to tell of many such experiences. He lived to be over 81 years old and raised a large and useful family.

Only one of his four boys, Theo Kaiser, followed him on the river; he is a steamboat engineer. In these times when graft runs rampant, when every thing is wrong in this topsy-turvy world, one wonders what a paradise our stay on earth would be if all of us could follow in the footsteps of a splendid man like Kaiser.

Friend Kaiser lies buried in St. George's Cemetery, overlooking the old river he loved and the across-the-river territory he served so well. He was a friend to everybody; he had no enemies. In my conclusion, and in a borrowed way to do justice to a departed friend, I will quote from Walter Savage Landor.

> *Leaf after leaf drops off,*
> *Flower after flower.*
> *Some in the chill, some in the warmer hour;*
> *Alive they flourish, and alive they fall,*
> *And Earth who nourished them received them all.*
> *Should we, her wiser sons, be less content*
> *To sink into her lap when life is spent?*

When Captain August Wohlt and Captain Gustave Wohlt passed away, Steamboat Bill wrote a veritable history of steamboating out of Hermann, Missouri, crediting these two men and their father with the vision and courage to start a river business that had meant so much to the development of the surrounding land. The Hermann Ferry and Packet Company flourished for more than 50 years. In January 1936, the death of that successful company was finally recorded.

Hermann Ferry Company Quit on December 31, 1935

The Hermann Ferry and Packet Company recently sold all its warehouses and its last boat to the Schoellhorn-Albrecht Machine Company of St. Louis. It was the ferryboat Hermann. The company, on December 31, 1935, dissolved after doing business since 1872. Henry Wohlt and Son began the business with the little steamer Stem. In 1874 the Light Western was built at Hermann, which was succeeded by the Fawn, Vienna, Royal, Pin Oak and a host of other light steamers.

In 1890 the Hermann Ferry and Packet Company was organized and incorporated with Capt. William L. Heckmann Sr., president; August Wohlt, treasurer; Fred Lang, secretary; and August and Gustave Wohlt and Fred Lang, directors. If the packet, ferry and transport business had continued to April 27, 1936, Fred Lang could have celebrated his golden jubilee of active service in the river transportation business.

Besides the steamboats named, the now dissolved ferry company, in the course of years, built the Mill Boy, Gasconade, Peerless, Henry Wohlt, August Wohlt, Wm. L. Heckmann and the Hermann, also several barges, the Katherin, Flora and Kaiser, as well as 10 open-hull barges.

When death claimed one of the Hermann pilots, a tribute by Steamboat Bill appeared in short order.

The Life of Captain Frank Blaske
Nov. 20, 1929

Again it becomes my sad duty to pay a last tribute to a departed steamboatman, the late Capt. Frank Blaske, who died at Hermann, Missouri.

He was born at Fredericksburg, Missouri, 75 years ago, and his boyhood days were spent at Washington, Missouri. In 1877 he married Miss Louise Stemma, and to this union were born nine children. Two sons and one daughter preceded him in death. His first wife, a truly great woman, died in the year 1900.

His children now living are: Mrs. Edward Hibbeler, Mrs. George Wolff Jr., Mrs. Eugene Pfautsch, Capt. Hugo C. Blaske, Mrs. Henry Meyer, Mrs. R. Williams, Mrs. Walter Jutz and Mrs. Herbert Williams. The last two named being the daughters of his second wife, Mrs. Louise Vogelsang, who he married in 1902, another true helpmate who is left to mourn his death. All of his children are happily married, three of his daughters married marine engineers, and his only living son, Capt. Hugo C. Blaske, is a crack Missouri and Mississippi river pilot and owns the busy boatyard at Alton, Illinois, where of late years, he has been building equipment for our western rivers.

Capt. Frank Blaske's first berth was as water carrier to the train crews that hauled and loaded cordwood, as that was all they burned at that time. Later he became a brakeman on the Missouri Pacific Railroad. If memory serves me right, his first work on the river was on the Tilda Clara, a horse ferry operating at New Haven, Missouri.

CHAPTER 11 ≈ EULOGIES

In the middle '80s, he, with Capt. Henry Struttman, bought the steamer Vienna from the Hermann Ferry and Packet Company. This boat sank coming out of the head of the old Emily Bend with a load of flour and wheat. This was one of the first, if not the first, boat he stood a watch on as an engineer.

Next we find him running out of Jefferson City as engineer of the fast steamer Edna, in charge of that peerless Capt. Alex Stewart. Again back to New Haven, where he owned an interest in the steamer Dauntless and built the trim little steamer C. H. Hugo. He owned this boat outright and practically built her himself, being a ship's carpenter besides his other trades. He sold this boat South, and it was the writer who piloted her out to St. Louis in the wintertime when the river was ragged and dead low. He paid me double the amount of our agreement, saying, "Will, you did a fine piece of work. Some day my boy will be as good a pilot as you are."

In 1901 Capt. Blaske and my brother Fred were the engineers of the steamer W. H. Grapevine on weekly trips between St. Louis and Rocheport, Missouri. The Grapevine made 35 round trips that season, loaded to the nosing both ways, and these good men did more than their share toward what was perhaps the most successful season a steamboat had on the Missouri River.

Brother Fred died five years ago, just when he began to enjoy life and was most needed on our old river. His partner on this boat lived to be 75 years old.

For several years this good man was a very successful farmer, then we find him back on the river with an interest in the steamer Mill Boy. He owned stock in the Hermann Ferry and Packet Company and stock in the St. Louis and Hermann Packet Company. He bought and sold the steamer Cinderella and the Ashby No. 2.

In all his real estate dealings, he was shrewd and successful, but some of his boat dealings did not prove profitable. But on him who deals in Missouri River property, some rain will always fall, and here we find he carried on to the end, industrious, liberal and true to his calling. While he spent most of his time in the engine room, he was also a skillful master and pilot of late years. When he had retired to a well earned rest, he was called again and again to fill some temporary position on a Missouri river boat, because licensed men became scarce and he was always ready and willing to serve.

Of late years, he was the chief engineer of the steamer John Heckmann, and Capt. Ed Heckmann was his favorite among the river boys. Less than a week before Capt. Blaske died, brother Ed called to see him. He said, "Are you after me Capt. Ed? I'll get ready and go." This was not to be, as he was then fighting a losing and desperate battle with death, but still he was ready to lend a helping hand.

Capt. Blaske was always proud to answer bells for his son Hugh. For Capt. Hugh and for all the Hermann boatmen, the elder Blaske has opened his last throttle and answered the last bell, and he has gone to dwell with those that never come back.

Where, we do not know, which blends sorrow and sadness here below.

At times Steamboat Bill waxed eloquent while the subject of his eulogy was still alive. One such story was about Capt. Bob Marshall.

At Tuscumbia, Missouri, on a picturesque hillside overlooking the Osage River, lives Capt. Bob Marshall and his wife. This loving couple have now wandered down life's golden pathway for some 59 years, and around their beautiful home lingers much history of the Osage and Missouri rivers.

Before her marriage, Mrs. Marshall was a Hauenstine, which no doubt helped Capt. Bob in his water career, inasmuch as her folks were noted Osage River boatmen. Capt. Bob is Scotch, which perhaps helped him be one of the few boatmen who ever left the river with money enough in his pockets to become a banker, property man and mill owner.

In 1882 Capt. Marshall owned the Osage River steamer Hulbert and then joined with Capt. Henry Castrup in ownership of the steamer Frederick. These two boats did a big business for years in connection with the Missouri Pacific Railroad at Osage City and were very successful. Later, they bought the long, lanky packet steamer John R. Hugo and, with the larger boat, branched out on the Missouri River, using her as a packet and towboat.

In the latter '80s, we find the John R. Hugo towing for the Missouri River Commission up near Florence, Nebraska, and Council Bluffs, Iowa, in charge of Capt. Bob Marshall and with one of the Missouri

CHAPTER 11 ≈ EULOGIES

River's most noted pilots, Bill Thompson, in the pilothouse. In 1899 the Hugo lost all her upper works by fire at Florence. Some time later the hull of this boat was floated with nothing but raft oars from Florence, Nebraska, to Osage City, Missouri, by the Thompson brothers, Bill and Hal, which, in itself, was a noted achievement only made possible by good rivermen.

In 1899 Capt. Bob sold out his interest in the Frederick and Hugo to Castrup and Shannon, who put the Hugo's machinery on a brand-new boat named Osage that was built by ship carpenter Ben Knagie at Osage City. This boat ran a short time on the Osage and Missouri and was then sold down south. Soon after the sale the river business began fading away on the Osage. By 1920 the shadows had darkened the horizon of river activity on this little Ozark stream after lasting almost a hundred years.

Capt. Tom Dodd always claimed the steamer Last Chance took 8,000 barrels of salt from the Ohio River to the usual head of navigation at Warsaw, Missouri, on the Osage. One of the last new boats built for the Osage River was the Homer C. Wright, named in honor of Capt. Wright, present manager of the Tuscumbia Milling Company.

Capt. Henry Castrup died in 1930 in his country home near Horseshoe Lake in Cambridge Bend, in sight of the Missouri River.

Capt. William D. Earp did his first boating for Marshall and Castrup, as did also Charlie Jenkins, a retired U.S. marine engineer living at Eugene, Missouri.

Time marches on. Capt. Bob and his good wife are traveling along foursquare to the wind with Time, and may they have many more happy days together before the bell rings for them to go on watch in that unknown world where they have melodious whistles on all steamboats and no railroads at all! At least this is the wish of Capt. Kermit Baecker, Adolph Wolf, Steamboat Bill, and Brother and Cookie Jeffries, who lately had a pleasant visit with Capt. Marshall and his wife.

A Tribute to Our Departed Friends
October 22, 1932

In life we neglect our old friends, in death we try to atone for our shortcomings by writing of their long and useful lives, and it is to the credit of *The Waterways Journal* that we are able to do this.

When the Heckmann family moved from Bluffton to Hermann, Missouri, 55 years ago, as a boy, I first met Capt. Henry Zibelin who died some two months ago and was buried in St. Louis. He was a 110-pound bantam weight of a man, full of energy and pluck, honest, sturdy and industrious to a degree seldom found in a man. He had then already served some time as a brakeman on the Missouri Pacific Railroad, which meant something in old-time railroading. He had made a trip to the "Mountains" on the steamer Yellow Stone and had been one of the pilots on the old May Bryan at Washington, Missouri, for Capts. Hoelscher and Roehrig.

When I was 10 years old, he was the night watchman on the good towboat Hope for my sainted father, and for over 50 years no one was closer to Dad and Capt. August Wohlt than Henry Zibelin. At that time the Missouri River was still full of fish. On a jugging trip with him from Portland to Hermann, a distance of 16 miles, we caught seven blue channel catfish that weighed in the aggregate 280 pounds.

At our home he met, courted and married Annie Melius. With this good woman he lived over 50 years, and she preceded him in death about three months before he passed on. Annie Melius sometimes helped my mother when the Heckmann kids were a nuisance and very numerous. As a buxom, brown-eyed, pretty, good-natured, lovable girl, I choose to remember this good woman who, through all her life, never spoke one harsh word to the old codger who is writing this.

This worthy couple was blessed with three children. Mrs. Sophia Marvin was the girl of the family and the oldest child, who is now living at Eldon, Missouri. Harry Zibelin, a dutiful son, passed to the Great Beyond some five years ago, and August, the youngest son, is left to mourn the loss of his dear ones.

Capt. Zibelin had a host of river friends, and perhaps he and his partner, the old Irish mate, Huey McQuire, were the two best known men in the lower Missouri River trade. They worked together on many different boats in this trade, and if one could see all the freight Huey sent "up the hill" and Henry checked, your eyes would open wide indeed.

Capt. Henry had charge of different ferryboats in his time at St. Charles, Washington, New Haven, Hermann, and Lexington, Missouri. He was second clerk on the Helena in the early '80s when this trim

CHAPTER 11 ≈ EULOGIES

little packet unloaded 160,000 sacks of wheat in the old St. Louis Elevator at the foot of Carr Street in one season. There may have been second clerks who could check freight faster than Henry, but none who looked after the welfare of the boat owner and shipper any better. He was on the old Benton with Huey when this boat cleared $1,700 on a round trip to Rocheport. This was after she was worn out in the "Mountain" trade and when opposition was at its worst from the railroads, transfer boats and other packets.

In the year of the big cyclone, 1896, he was at the foot of Franklin Avenue checking freight on the old Libbie Conger. It was near "leaving time," and they had just started to load a big 5,000-gallon wine cask for the Augusta Wine Cellars when this disaster hit St. Louis and the riverfront. When the wind eased up some, the boat, cask and all on the levee were blown away except Henry and a pile of wheat that had been unloaded on the levee. An old man with a big gray horse had been loading some of this wheat to haul it to the mill. Henry had told him, "Uncle, we are going to have a storm; you had better get up town."

The wind picked up man, horse and wagon and blew them into the river. A big, wild-eyed roustabout, hatless and bleeding from cuts on his head, came running down the levee. Henry, always looking after the interest of the shipper, yelled to him and said, "Partner, help me pull this tarpaulin over this wheat." The roustabout said, "Damn you and your tarpaulin," and ran just as straight into the river as fast as his legs could carry him, to disappear in the rain and the mighty Mississippi.

Henry was with me the 10 years we were in the lower Missouri River packet trade on the W. H. Grapevine, Kennedy, Lora, India Givens and Julius F. Silber. He went through the 1903 flood on the Grapevine, an experience hard to forget. He was on the Advance of the Kansas City Missouri River Navigation Company with me in 1915, the banner year of this company. Both the A. M. Scott and the Advance made 28 round trips to Kansas City that season. In 1916, he was with Captain Hugo C. Blaske on this boat, and with the help of this good man, he secured the night watchman's berth at the Navigation Company's East St. Louis warehouse. This place he held down for several years, and after a few years at watchman on sand dredges in the St. Louis harbor, Henry returned to his home in St. Louis. "Well done, thou good and faithful servant."

Ring the bell, Huey, Henry has checked his last cargo, we have put him off at Everlasting Landing, the old Grapevine must get up the river. Doug Giles will be waiting for her at the end of the route.

Keep the home fires burning, Henry. We'll be along pretty soon.

Even a transient came up for praise. This piece was written for the Hermann Independent, March 6, 1942, and reprinted in The Waterways Journal, April 3, 1943.

Tale of a Salt Water Sailor
Who Came at Last to Rest in a Sweet Water Port

In the early '90s the new steamer Arethusa was launched at the Gasconade U.S. Boatyard. Uncle Sam put Steamboat Bill in charge of the craft, and at that time I met Christian Clausen, a robust and strong man, who worked on a chartered boat, name now forgotten, as a deckhand. He was at that time about 30 years old and had already sailed the seven seas on his father's trading boat and many other ships of all descriptions. How he got this far inland we do not know, but he did not serve long as a sweet water sailor and soon went back to his first love, the briny deep. Then, almost 50 years later, we again meet Christian Clausen on the streets of Hermann, Missouri.

He said, "I have now entered my last port, Capt. Heckmann, and if they let me keep what I have saved, I can live to be a real old man in your good little old town."

Among other things he said, "I have sailed every sea and entered every port where fighting is now going on around Singapore and the Philippines and know that country, Captain, like you do the Missouri River. I have seen cities, towns and hamlets by the thousands all over the known wide world in the last 70 years, but Hermann appealed to me most, and here I have come to stay. The United States is my favorite country, but it is not what it used to be."

"My folks taught me to work, and when 12 years old, I was already a full-fledged sailor. Whenever the people think they can get along without honest work, they are due for a fall."

When this good man first came to town, one of his first visits was to see Rev. Kasmann, and his pastor advised him to go to an old-folks' home. This advice was taken but did not stick long, and soon he was

CHAPTER 11 ≈ EULOGIES

back in Hermann again. His ambition and hopes were to live to be 90. But fate so ordained that this should not be so, and he died suddenly at the age of 80 in the little city of his choice.

He died before the flowers bloom in the spring; February snows were still with us. Spring will come, and someone will plant a flower on his grave. Then all will be forgotten, and the old sailor's memories will lie buried in the yellow clay.

Sometime before he died, he said to me, "Captain, as you know, I am a sailor and a sinner, but I have always put my trust in God, and many a time in storm and disaster, sometimes away up in the storm-tossed rigging, I have prayed to my God, and I fully believe this is the reason I am still here. How I would like to live to see all nations at peace. All the world with all their sins can live in peace if they repent and do as I have done in my declining years."

What a man, what a wanderer, and what tales he could tell. That this man picked our town to live in from the whole world's surface should be an honor to us all. But, here again, we come to one of the great mysteries of death, and here, too, is another mystery to me. In preaching his services Rev. Kasmann gave a masterful sermon for the old sailor to almost an empty room. If some broken down Hollywood actor or some actress seeking her second or third divorce, had been stranded, died and buried here, this same chapel would not have held the people, and half the town would have followed to the grave.

Just about 100 years ago this summer, the steamer Big Hatchie blew up at the Hermann wharf. This boat had a full list of passengers, mostly German immigrants, on their way west to seek new homes. Many were killed and injured, and some 38 of these unfortunate people lay buried in our Hermann Cemetery in unmarked graves. So you see, folks, Clausen is not alone among the tombs.

In one of Shakespeare's plays we find this quotation which, in a way, covers our Sailor's life. "Will Heaven forgive him, and forgive us all. Some rise by sin, and some by virtue fall. Some run through brakes of vice and answer none; and some condemned for a fault alone."

The Waterways Journal, April 20, 1935, carried a long story about the steamer J. R. Wells, built by the Anchor Milling Company. In the wake of this detailed account came a eulogy by Steamboat Bill.

The Anchor Milling Company at Tuscumbia, Missouri, requests that we write a few lines about their good little steamer J. R. Wells.

From 1898, when this boat went into service, until the winter of 1920 when she was put out of commission by an ice gorge, many things and much history could be traced to this boat. Built as a very successful Osage River packet, she later drifted out into the Missouri River as a towboat on construction work. In these 22 years this great little craft went through and saw the last efforts at the packet boat game on the Osage River.

Business being scarce, and pilots' berths the same, this little sternwheeler saw a host of Missouri River crack pilots enter her pilothouse. On the Osage River, Capts. Phil F. Hauenstein and John W. Adcock did most of the piloting. When out on the Missouri River, she was piloted in turn by Capts. William L. Thompson, William D. Earp, Arthur Thompson, Hal Thompson and Roy A. Miller. To pick a better bunch of pilots during the dying days on the Big Muddy would be a hard matter.

In 1911 Steamboat Bill was in charge of this boat for contractors DeWitt and Shobe, and in 1919 he was again in charge for contractors Stanton and Jones, the last owners of the boat. He was the man who during the winter of 1919 obeyed orders under protest and took this boat out of what he said was a safe ice harbor, down the river four miles into a harbor at the boot of Pelican Bend. The river was full of heavy, slow floating ice. We knew it was blocking somewhere down the river, but we pulled out just the same. When we got within one-half mile of our so-called safe harbor, the river blocked tight, and this is perhaps the only boat that froze in that way and washed its way one-half mile down the river through a solid river of ice.

The weather was very cold, the newly made ice was tough, and mighty few crews would have stayed to finish up a job like that. We tied her up to the liking of one of the owners and kissed her good-bye, feeling sure we would never see the old boat again, one that held a soft spot in every man's heart that ever worked on her. In the spring breakup of 1920, she went to Davy Jones' Locker, and at that time U. S. Inspector Gibbs wrote the following appropriate poem of this river disaster.

CHAPTER 11 ≈ EULOGIES

Friendship

Time is marked in many ways,
By friends, lives, and by days,
The time of this or the time of that, we oft-times say,
When recalling the friends or pleasures of a bygone day.
Around each epoch of time in life's shifting career,
Linger memories of friends and times we hold dear.
This picture marks the passing of time my memory dwells,
On friends and days of the steamer J. R. Wells

Eulogies flowed freely from the pen of Steamboat Bill, but all were heartfelt and sincere. None compared with his agony when a member of his own family died. This obituary was published in the The Waterways Journal, Jan. 10, 1942. The Vogel family, Alex and Hazel and later their daughters, Ruth and Mary Ann, had always lived with Steamboat Bill and Annie. Both parents worked in their store six days a week, so Grandma Annie usually was in control of the children. After Alex died, Steamboat Bill became father to the girls.

Christmas came to us as usual with sickness in our home, and as the old year was coming to its end, death, with all its sorrow and mysteries, also entered into our home. In the Deaconess Hospital at St. Louis, Friday evening, December the 26th, our beloved son-in-law Alex A. Vogel, 40, died from a cerebral inflammation.

Alex A. Vogel was united in marriage to our daughter Hazel in the year 1923. They were blessed with two children, Ruth Margaret, now 15 years old, and Mary Anne, 12 years old. Ever since their marriage, they have lived with us in our home here at Hermann, Missouri, and to Mother Heckmann, Alex was more than a son. Her every wish was a command. One can also turn this statement around because there was nothing Mrs. Heckmann would not do to help her son-in-law fight the battles of life.

Alex was not a riverman, yet no one was more fond of what little success I have had on our rivers in late years than Alex Vogel. This past fall his morning greeting was generally, "Dad, are you going squirrel hunting this morning?" Or, "Dad, are you going duck hunting?"

He did not seem to get the same kick out of my fishing as he did in what game I bagged. His sole ambition and life work was in the dry goods and grocery business, in which he was an expert in both buying and selling.

Starting as a very young man in the old Helmers general store at Hermann, his only work has been storekeeping. Soon after his marriage, he started from scratch, and at his death he owned one of the finest dry goods and grocery stores in Hermann. His honesty and friendliness to all, his love of family and of the community and his willingness to work made him a citizen any town could not afford to lose at middle life.

One of his last spoken words while lying near death was, "Aren't the flowers nice from the Lion's Club?"

One of his last requests was to keep the store.

To this his 12-year-old daughter said, "Sure, we will keep the store, and we will show them a real store, too,"—a spirit that is commendable in the times that lie ahead of us all.

May his pilgrimage and his stay in his everlasting home be as useful as he has been here on Earth is the wish of his loved ones, Ma and Pa Heckmann.

Eulogies occasionally came in a package. Apparently he felt the need to laud the engineers. This piece was written in May of 1934.

To Engineer H. A. Sheets:

Being as you saw fit, Mr. Sheets, to pay me such a wonderful compliment in the personal columns of *The Waterways Journal* of April 28, I will retaliate and write something about our marine engineers. Let's go back and ask how many men now steamboating remember Billie Alfred, the engineer Capt. George G. Keith put most of his trust in and never ran a boat long without.

I have counted up, Mr. Sheets, and find that in my time on the river, I have stood watch with over 300 engineers. When a boy, my father's best engineer was my uncle, Julius F. Silber. There is no better judge of a man than a 10-year-old boy, and to me Uncle Julius was a man in every sense of the word. He was too good to live long and died before he was 40 years old. Later my father made an engineer out of John Haberstock, the strong man, and the only man besides one who steamboated for the Heckmanns that could carry 27 sticks of cordwood on his starboard shoulder; the other man totes his load on the port

CHAPTER 11 ≈ EULOGIES

side. *[Modesty was never one of Steamboat Bill's long suits—he was the other man!]*

Bill Lalk was an old-time engineer who knocked the man-head in on the old steamer Dora's big boiler with a rail when he still had five pounds of steam and lived to tell the tale. Buford Jett, some kin to this fine old man, who was killed by an assassin's bullet at Mount Sterling, Missouri, is a crack Missouri River engineer at this time. We will pass up the many other engineers I worked with in the old Hermann Ferry and Packet Company while learning the river under my father and Captain Wohlt.

In my seven years on government steamers for Capt. S. Waters Fox, it was my pride and pleasure to be in company with Al and Harry Danberry, who came around from the Ohio River to show us how to carry them hot, and, believe me, we carried the crack little towboat Arethusa that way. No boat ever passed her while the Danberrys were on her, not even the pride of them all, the three-boiler towboat Alert.

While with Uncle Sam, among some 25 different engineers I worked with, those that stand out in front are: S. S. Clifford, Bob Powell, Frank Liliker Silbernickle, Al Emerson, Rudy Schrok and Frank Glaser.

Perren Kay, the great father of Fred R. Kay, was on the Arethusa one season with us as our engineer. No pen of mine can write a fit compliment for such a man. He could build a boat complete, take charge of any berth on her and fill it with distinction. Nobody that ever steamboated with him could part with him and not be a better man; they lost the mold when Perren Kay was born.

Next my footsteps followed the packet trade for 10 years. In 1902 the steamer W. H. Grapevine made 36 weekly round trips from St. Louis to Rocheport, Missouri. She never missed leaving St. Louis every Saturday night during the boating season, a record never equaled by any man's boat on the Missouri. Fred J. Heckmann and Frank Blaske were our engineers, both gone but not forgotten. While in this trade, we had seven different packet boats and some 20 different engineers. Among this number were Frank Ingrum, Roy and Bert Coulter and, again, S. S. Clifford.

Next, back in the old ferry company for several years, and one year on the John R. Wells with Ed Roehrig as my partner. Then seven years with the Kansas City-Missouri River Navigation Company. Here fortune put me in touch with such men as Sam Critchfield, George E. Berry, Fred R. Kay, Horace Armstrong and Louis A. ("Lonnie") Galatas. Among them and the many others, Critchfield and Berry especially impressed. Both were and are my good friends, friends to be proud of indeed.

Then again back in the ferry company for two years where the engineers, Captain Bill and all, were failures, they say. Then with the Woods Brothers Construction Company for the last 12 years. Fresh in my memory here are engineers Walter Walkenhauer, Louis Kendrick, Ed Stratton, Ollie Brown, C. M. Jenkins and others too numerous to mention as my story is getting too long now; still some of my good engineer friends will feel hurt. However, my memory is slipping, folks, even if my heart means well.

No story on the Missouri would be complete though without mentioning Bill and Fred Dierking, Capt. Archie Bryan's crack engineers, born and raised at Dierking's Landing where many a big buck deer jumped in the Missouri River to swim to the other side and head for Pilots Knob to outwit a pack of hounds. Then we might mention such men as Shackelford, Sibottom, Grant and Garret, engineers that took their boat from St. Louis to Fort Benton and back knowing they would not see a machine shop until they got back to the Mound City.

If I had a million-dollar boat in the St. Louis and Kansas City trade, she would not be a deaf and dumb boat; you could hear her cough for 20 miles. Neither would she be adorned with any kind of a propeller, not even as an ornament. Engineers Koehler and F. Van Den Heurk, please notice, but let's not start another argument; this is only some more of that sentimental stuff. My engineers on this boat would be Louis Hoelscher and George Williams, good enough for any man's boat and men it is an honor to have steamboated with.

Who said Charlie Wichern, whose good work has helped make the screw boats famous? I even almost forgot brother George Heckmann, who almost made the Inco No. 1 famous; my friend Snodgrass, the Cliftons, my nephew Harvey Heckmann, who has helped many a boxcar, on the railroad transport boats; then the baby boy of the family, Normam J. Heckmann, the ex-engineer and ball player, who is now selling packing for Crandall in Ohio; and I almost forgot Sam Simon, who I never boated with but always wanted to.

CHAPTER 11 ≈ EULOGIES

So now, with God's blessing, let's quit, or my story will never end. Nobody is prouder, Mr. Sheets, than myself of the pilots I have helped make; we have none better on our western rivers. As for myself, I am like Uncle Joe Cannon—standing on my record and still going strong.

In 1941, when Steamboat Bill was 72, old age was the topic occupying his thoughts.

The Blessing of Seasoned Timbers

Milo, perhaps the greatest athlete of all time—in his old age while witnessing a prize fight—looked at his once mighty arms and wistfully said, "Alas, but these are now dead."

One of his feats was carrying a full-grown live ox across the Arena on his back at the annual games in Rome. This was some 250 years B.C. Foolish Old Man! Did he not know that no one can compete with Father Time?"

Now, folks, this is as far as necessary to go in the Classics, and from here on this is my own philosophy of old age.

To me it seems at times that old age, when your faculties are not all intact, is like an old dusty garret. What one finds there among the dust and cobwebs of time no one knows until fully explored.

Youth, in all its strength, ambitions and hopes, cannot write with wisdom on this subject. Only oldsters, in their thoughts alone, can enjoy the blessings of writing about themselves. When one is able, as I am, to look back and see the harbor and levee at St. Louis in the year 1875, he should be entitled to some consideration on what to say about being old.

These, too, are thoughts you can take to bed with you, even though they will not bring the pleasure of your first night's honeymoon.

Sometimes articles appeared "about" rather than "by" Steamboat Bill. In April of 1934 Ottmar Stark of St. Louis wrote a letter to Steamboat Bill's hometown paper, the Advertiser-Courier.

Now appears Commodore "Steamboat Bill" Heckmann in these columns and refers to some of my previous articles. Good old Bill; he is a friend of mine. I do not want to get into any discussion with him. My simple answer to his article is, "Bill is a first-class riverman."

≈ STEAMBOAT TREASURES ≈

It was with fond recollection that I let my thoughts go back 35 years to the days when Capt. Bill and I were business associates; more precisely, we were both directors of the then St. Louis and Hermann Packet Company. There were 11 directors in all, including Bill and his father; my father and I; good-natured George Kraettly, Frank Bruens and John Ochsner. I do not remember the other four.

Bill is amiable and tactful, is considerate and mindful of the rights of others. He is a man easy to get along with, and I have never had cause to find fault with him. It is a rare pleasure to know such a man and to possess his friendship, which friendship is real and not affected, as he is not deceitful.

One day, about 1900, Bill told me that he would like to organize a packet company with steamboats plying the Missouri, Gasconade and Osage rivers. I promised to help him, and at a meeting of potential investors, enough capital was subscribed in full to incorporate the St. Louis and Hermann Packet Company.

A day or two later, Bill's father, the old Capt. Bill, George Kraettly and I went to Kansas City and there bought the steamboat W. H. Grapevine. Other boats were acquired until we had a fleet of them plying the Missouri, Gasconade and Osage rivers; the large ones on the Missouri River and the small boats on the tributaries as feeders for the large boats.

Old Capt. Bill was superintendent of the fleet. Steamboat Bill and his brothers were captains of the respective boats. Regularly scheduled trips were maintained between St. Louis and Jefferson City and points west. Agents and warehouses were located at the principal river ports. The large boats on the Big Muddy had double crews and ran day and night.

On one of the periodical trips of auditing the boats' books, George Kraettly and I were on the Grapevine commanded by Steamboat Bill. On the way back from St. Louis, the pilot discovered a flock of wild geese on a sandbar. Throwing the powerful searchlight upon them and sounding the boat's siren, he caused the geese to take flight. The searchlight blinded them; they flew towards the light, became entangled in the cables and wires until the upper deck was full of geese. One flew against my chest and bowled me over. Every man on deck scrambled to get his goose. All got at least one, and several got two geese. It was great sport.

CHAPTER 11 ≈ EULOGIES

To ply the treacherous and ever-changing Missouri River in those days required real skill and ability as a navigator. Bill was fully able to master the river and never had any mishap. He would be equally well able to master the Amazon, Congo and Yangtse rivers, although the latter requires shooting of rapids. All rivers look alike to him; they are his home.

Anyone who knows me well knows also that I am not in the habit of praising people; nor do I belong to any Mutual Admiration Society. I am more apt to tell a fellow to go to the devil. Therefore, when I do praise Steamboat Bill, I am prompted by having good reasons to do so.

Time took its inevitable toll on Steamboat Bill. He survived several bouts of major surgery, one for a burst appendix, another for cancer of the mouth, which cost him most of his lower lip. His heart began to fail, and he truly did grow old.

Capt. Bill made his last landing on August 21, 1957. He walked out to his garden, and five minutes later his wife found him there dead. Tributes poured into the Waterways Journal for several weeks. Now The Waterways Journal had the privilege of providing a eulogy for Steamboat Bill, a contributor for more than 50 years. James V. Swift wrote:

… For many years, pilots of towboats passing Hermann blew Capt. Bill a salute as they passed below "his bluff." He would be pleased to know that two of them passed the day of his funeral; Sioux City and New Orleans Barge Line, Inc., was downbound just an hour before the funeral; the Federal Barge Lines' Helena, was upbound that morning.

Capt. Donald Wright, editor of The Waterways Journal, and James V. Swift drove up from St. Louis to Hermann to attend the funeral.

Upon arriving last Saturday at Hermann, Missouri, two hours before 2 o'clock, the time for the funeral of Capt. William L. Heckmann—Steamboat Bill—the automobile was parked at the Heckmann residence and respects paid to Mrs. Heckmann. Ready in her hand was the last article her husband had written for *The Waterways Journal*. He had begun it on Tuesday and completed it the morning of the next day, August 21, the day on which he died, suddenly, about 3:50 p.m.…

In St. Louis, the man who has edited Steamboat Bill's articles since back in the 1890 issues reported that two years ago Steamboat sent 13 articles in one mail, nearly half a dozen of which are still unpublished. One of these, "Our Colored Roustabouts," is already in type and may appear as early as next week. Another, an extra-long and good one, is a biography of Capt. William, L. Heckmann Sr., Steamboat Bill's father. This last article, "Personal Paragraphs," one finished by the scant margin of four hours before the Last Crossing, is believed to have been inspired by a picture in the July 20 issue of *The Waterways Journal*.

Steamboat Bill was no poet, but he liked to collect gems of poetry that appealed to him because of their preciseness of thought and word. One was written by Colonel Will S. Hays.

> *Mate, be ready down on deck,*
> *I'm heading for the shore;*
> *I'll ring the bell, for I must land*
> *This boat forever more.*
> *Say, Pilot, can you see that light—*
> *I do—where angels stand?*
> *Well, hold her jackstaff hard on that,*
> *For there I'm going to land.*
> *That looks like Death that's hailing me,*
> *So ghastly, grim and pale;*
> *I'll toll the bell, I must go in*
> *I never passed a hail.*
> *Stop her! Let her come in slow;*
> *There, that will do—no more;*
> *The lines are fast and angels wait*
> *To welcome me ashore.*
> *Say, Pilot, I am going with them*
> *Up yonder through the gate;*
> *I'll not come back—you ring the bell*
> *And back her out—don't wait.*
> *For I have made the trip of life*
> *And found my landing place;*
> *I'll take my soul and anchor that*
> *Fast to the throne of Grace.*

CHAPTER 11 ≈ EULOGIES

Two captains return to port: The author's father, left, Capt. Edward Heckmann, 1884-1974, and Capt. W. L. "Steamboat Bill" Heckmann, 1869-1957.

≈ STEAMBOAT TREASURES ≈

Big Muddy Rolls Through 60 Years of Capt. Bill Heckman's Memories

From the Jefferson City Sunday News and Tribune
March 30, 1941

By Capt. Bill Heckman, as told to Leo Hirtl

Every mile of the Missouri river has a story—some tragic, some humorous, many long since forgotten.

In writing these stories for every mile on Big Muddy, I am going to tell only of those things that occurred during my 60 years on the stream. My story begins at the point where the muddy water of the mighty Missouri mingles with the clear Mississippi.

One could write a book of river disaster here. The mouth of the Missouri river is perhaps the hardest stretch of water to navigate at night on western rivers.

Here, in 1879, the big sidewheel steamer, David R. Powell, sank a barge loaded with 9,000 sacks of wheat. The Powell, one of the last of the sidewheelers on the Missouri, was coming out of Big Muddy with over 18,000 sacks of wheat on board and two big wooden barges. That cargo would have set a record if part of it had not been fed to the fish.

Fifty years ago, the sternwheeler, Dora, burned to the water's edge here. She was running in the St. Louis-Black Walnut trade in charge of Billie Hoelscher. Soon after the disaster, Hoelscher went to the Yukon River as a master pilot and became a noted character on those waters.

There are hundreds of stories about pilots' difficulties in navigating the mouth at night.

One prominent pilot tried for a whole night to get a boat into the Missouri. When daylight came, he was near Alton, 4 miles above the mouth, looking for the hole that would take him to Kansas City.

(The hole is a riverman's term for the channel used for navigation.)

Capt. Bob Bailey once hired to an Ohio River boat owner at a fancy salary to take his boat to Omaha, Nebraska. They hit the Missouri about dark. The mouth was in bad shape; the river swift and shallow. The old boat kept bumping and hitting the bottom and was going nowhere. The owner stood this so long as he could, then went to the pilothouse and said, "Capt. Bailey, how often have you been up this river?" Bailey replied:

'Once a-foot and twice on horseback."

Mile 1—Here the steamer Nadine sank in what later was called Nadine Bend, which now is shut off by dikes. The incident serves to demonstrate the inaccuracy of much of our river history.

The Nadine sank coming out of the river while loaded flat with shelled corn in the late '70s. Capt. LeRoy Coulter moved to Exeter, California, and soon after he arrived there, one of his neighbors told the captain all about the disaster, adding that his father lost 5,000 sacks of corn.

Coulter did not correct him, but later he told me what I already knew—the Nadine could not carry more than 2,000 sacks.

That man's story is about as nearly right as are many of the other tales about our rivers.

(Loaded flat means to burden a boat with all she can carry. Boats, when running light, have a sheer or curve, which tends to flatten out when the craft is heavily loaded. This sheer is maintained by the use of "hog chains" running the length of the boat.)

Mile 2—During the days of Prohibition, one of the largest stills in the state was operated on Missouri Point here.

Mile 3—Here, at the foot of Columbia Bottom, the historic Bald Eagle of the Eagle Packet Company ended her days as a quarter boat.

(A quarter boat is used to house men working on the river.)

Mile 4—Cora Island, named after the sunken steamer, Cora, the only boat ever sunk by Capt. E.M. Baldwin, a veteran mountain pilot.

Mile 5—As late as 1937, this was the crookedest crossing between St. Louis and Kansas City.

(A crossing is a place where the river's channel crosses from one bank to the other.)

Mile 6—Head of Cora Island. This island has shifted from one side of the Cora's hulk to the other more than a half dozen times in the last 60 years.

Mile 7—Crewmen of the fast steamer Kennedy noticed that a fat lady—weighing about 300 pounds—always was asleep in the recess of a shantyboat that lay near the channel of the river. The Kennedy was a tremendously fast boat and threw a mighty swell behind her sternwheel. Coming down stream one day in 1904, the pilot on watch said, "Say, Capt., that old lady is asleep again. Let's give her a ride."

He signaled for full speed ahead. The boat began to snort, and when opposite the shanty, the pilot pulled her big wheel hard over towards Big Mama's home.

When the first swell disturbed her beauty sleep, she made a leap for the bank some five feet away. She hit the water 'kersmack' about halfway to the shore.

As far back as we could see, both she and the shantyboat were bobbing up and down like a cork in the Atlantic during a storm. After that episode none of the pilots wanted to run Cora Bend until Madame, Her Boat, and Her Man had floated out into the Mississippi, where we could see them no more.

Mile 8—Bellefontaine railroad and highway bridges span the river here.

Mile 9—Little's Island, named after an old-time captain.

Mile 10—Head of Brick House Bend, an old-time river graveyard. One time when Capt. Joe Kinney was coming down river on one of his fine, big boats loaded flat to the water, he hit the bend as night came on. Capt. Kinney went to the pilothouse and asked the pilot if it was safe to run the bend at night. The pilot said it was. He claimed he could show Kinney every obstruction in this place.

About that time, the boat's head popped up, and a hard, grating, nerve-racking noise told them they had hit something mightily hard. They pushed her down over it, and the pilot said: "There's one of them snags now, Capt. Put her to the bank for the night—I do not want to show you any more obstructions."

They managed to get the boat into St. Louis with a damaged cargo. They put her on dock and replaced 100 broken timbers.

Mile 11—Foot of Commerce Bend, the most beautiful place of river between St. Louis and Kansas City.

Mile 12—Foot of Pelican Bend, where the steamer Judith sank while coming downstream with a load of wheat 60 years ago. Boss Brandt

APPENDIX ≈ MILE BY MILE

was the pilot on watch. Some 35 years later the General Meade sank right near here while Pilot Bob McGarrah was on watch.

Mile 13—Here jug-fishing Turner Coonce and Rodney Heckman caught a 60-pound catfish.

Mile 14—Pelican Bend, the first large sandbar. Until 1905, every spring and fall this bar would be covered by thousands of pelicans. After they would leave for the North or South, this bar would be white as snow from the feathers. Why these birds left is a mystery, which can be classed with the story of our wild pigeons.

Mile 15—Here was once the largest crow rookery we ever had on our river.

Mile 16—During Prohibition a large still was operated here. Some 2,000 sacks of sugar came here by boat many a night.

Mile 17—Head of Commerce Chute, first large concrete dike put in the Missouri. Steamer Alert sank here about 1928 with Pilot Louis Moehle on watch. No lives were lost. Yellow Dog Landing on left bank of the river was named after an unusual occurrence, the details of which are not fit for publication.

(A chute is the stretch of water between an island and the mainland.)

Mile 18—Halls Ferry, one of the first steam ferries on the river and home of Bill Clayton, one-time American champion wingshot.

Mile 19—Little wood yard. One of the last on the river, it was abandoned in 1909.

Mile 20—Keokouk power line crosses the river here. In 1937, a big crane or blue heron hung himself on a loop hanging down from the wires.

Mile 21—Here, in 1882, the steamer Far West sank while coming downstream with a heavy cargo. This disaster sent Capt. Hal Dodd and Vic Bonnot of Bonnot's Mill home as poor men. The steamer Fannie Lewis, one of the last big sidewheelers on the river, came up from St. Louis and salvaged most of the cargo. The boat was a total loss. The historic Far West and Capt. Grant Marsh were made famous by books written by Miles Hanson.

Mile 22—Capt. Sam Heckman once caught a 106-pound catfish on a jump line here to show Joe and Dina Wyss of St. Charles that it could be done.

Mile 23—Another of the Heckmans, Capt. J. Fred Heckman, once killed three geese out of one flock off the boiler deck of the steamer W.H. Grapevine, and then, just to show off, killed another lone goose on the sand over a thousand yards away. He was using a high-powered rifle.

(River craft have several decks. The lowest is the main deck, then comes the boiler deck, hurricane deck, Texas, and perched on top of all is the pilothouse.)

Mile 24—La Barges Landing, No. 1.

Mile 25—Crazy Point—so named because of the big swirling eddy below the point, now partly cut out by dikes.

Mile 26—Cul de Sac Landing, a big shipping point in steamboat days.

Mile 27—Where the steamer Kennedy cut the telegraph wires and went over the M.K.T. railroad tracks to rescue victims of the 1903 flood, one of the most costly we ever had on the Missouri. Capt. William Heckman Sr. did some of his last steamboating in the flood. He never removed his clothes in two weeks.

Mile 28—In 1915 there occurred an incident here, which illustrates the feeling between inland folk and river people. That year a girl had been waving and flirting with the crew of the steamer Advance in the St. Louis and Kansas City trade. That fall, Turner Coonce, his wife and myself landed the boat and went out to get better acquainted. We found the house locked.

The girl peeked out of an upstairs window and said, "My folks do not allow me to associate with rivermen and women."

Mile 29—$3,000,000 Wabash railroad bridge. Abutment on St. Charles side of the river at Bull Wheel Landing is part of the first river improvements to be put in. Constructed about 1875.

Mile 30—St. Charles. The old Wabash railroad bridge has been taken out of the river and junked. It always had been a menace to navigation. The sternwheeler Montana sank here while coming upstream on the bridge with a 68-ton cargo. William R. Massie was on watch when the boat went down. It was the only craft to be sunk by the greatest pilot on western rivers during his 60 years as a steamboater. The St. Charles electric highway bridge crosses the river here. Under the cinder point below this bridge lie the hulks of three sunken ferryboats, the stern-wheeler Fawn, the sidewheeler Gage and a third, which sank before my time.

APPENDIX ≈ MILE BY MILE

Mile 31—Capt. Hal Dodd was in charge when the steamer Ella Kimbrough sank on the right bank across from the St. Charles water works in 1884.

Mile 32—As late as 1937, this was a very bad, crooked and shallow stretch of river.

Mile 33—Here contractor Farney stood on the M.K.T. Railroad and issued his order out of a good pair of lungs to his boys working on pile drivers and boats clear across the river.

Mile 34—Wreck of the John Bell, Spring Hose Bend on the left, Howards Bend on the right side of the river. This does not happen often, a bend on each side of the river.

Mile 35—Foot of Catfish Bend, in my boyhood days the shallowest place on the river. Here the old boats had plenty of trouble hurdling the shallow spots. Capt. Archie Bryan jumped one of his sternwheelers over this bar. In so doing, her big sternwheel fell overboard and lay in the river for months. Hall Dodd, the pilot, said the old tub was so slow they had almost reached St. Louis before finding out the wheel had been lost.

Mile 36—Stickney Bank Head at the foot of upper Howards Bend. Major Stickney came on the river in the early '90s and proposed to save the long bends from cutting by putting what he called a "bank head" at the extreme foot of the bend. He claimed the river would cut back until it formed a half-moon bend and then would quit cutting without any further protection for the bend.

This old river fooled Stickney like it has nearly every other engineer since, with the exception of Capt. S. Waters Fox. Stickney had a lot of these contraptions put into the river without any success. There is not a pilot on the Missouri River today that can locate all these so-called bank heads.

Mile 37—Another Stickney bank head.

Mile 38—New St. Louis waterworks, a fine structure.

Mile 39—Here the crew of the steamer Eugenia Woods put out two trot lines one evening. Knowing our reputation, Louis Bickel went to Chesterfield that night and sold $5.95 worth of fish, which we delivered without fail the next morning.

Mile 40—Bon Homme Island and Green's Chute, now entirely shut off by dikes.

In the latter '80s, Capt. Archie Bryan and Pilot Ed Anderson were bringing the steamer downriver. At the foot of this chute, there was a big snag. Bryan wanted to go down one side; Anderson wanted to go down the other. While they discussed the virtues of their particular routes, the boat went through the middle and over the snag. Boat and cargo were almost a total loss. The big roof bell of this boat tolled in the steeple of a Negro church at Washington for many years after.

Mile 41—The U.S. towboat Alert burst a steam pipe here in Green's Chute in the latter '90s. Chief Engineer Al Emerson was badly scalded, and the mate, blown overboard, swam to a sandbar in midriver. Silent Bill Lingo was in charge of the boat. Buck Tilden and Bill Heckman were pilots. Many in Jefferson City remember Tilden as master of the U.S. towboat Hour when Ewing's boatyard was in bloom.

Mile 42—Here lies the wreck of the sternwheeler towboat Fearless No. 2 and of the first barge-line venture on our river. The latter was a colossal failure. The best boatmen we had at that time said the Missouri River was not a barge-line stream, and I am still of that opinion. The only solution, which will lead to success on this river, is big freighters in one unit. Bob Wilson had about a million feet of fine walnut lumber on the Fearless' barges, and her tow was an immense cargo. Her three barges finally got to St. Louis, but the Fearless is still at the bottom of Big Muddy.

(Some rivermen dispute Capt. Heckman's view on the barge lines. The federal barge line has been operating for some time. Last Sunday the "Tom Sawyer" and three barges passed Jefferson City on the first run of the year. Capt. Heckman's theory about single-unit craft, however, has considerable support. The channel of the Missouri is contrary and particularly hard to maintain during low-water stage. The Helena and three barges were stranded in Jefferson City for several months by low water last summer.)

APPENDIX ≈ MILE BY MILE

Boatmen Fought Each Other, But All Fell Before Onrush of Railroads

From the Jefferson City Sunday News and Tribune
April 1941

By Capt. Bill Heckman, as told to Leo Hirtl

Capt. Bill Heckman of Hermann resumes his stories of Big Muddy during the days of steamboating's glory.

Mile 43—Twenty-five years ago, Ed Heckman turned the towboat Leavenworth on her side during a storm. He later salvaged the boat and took her to Leavenworth, Kansas, for repairs. The crew of the Eugenia Woods once caught 114 sturgeon on three trot lines here.

Mile 44—Howell's Landing, a large shipping point that tops the Big Gumbo Bottoms. Here the old boatmen fought, prayed and pleaded for freight.

In the middle-'70s, my father put the steamer R.W. Dugan in the St. Louis and Rocheport trade against Star Line, a large company that had seven big boats running between St. Louis and Kansas City. In fighting this line and the oncoming railroads, my father, the Dutch captain, took up the most bitter task in his long life on the river.

The Star Line put their crack captain, Ralph Withledge, and one of their fast boats, Mattie Bell, against my father and the Dugan. For two years a cutthroat rate war flourished in the lower-river trade. My father and the Dugan finally were pushed to the wall, but the Star Line knew it had been in a battle. The line in turn succumbed to the surge of the railroads in 1880.

Typical of the tricks on which the rival captains relied to disturb each other's schedules is one that occurred at this landing.

The Mattie Bell was coming down river with every pound of freight she could carry when a girl hailed the boat at Howell's Landing. Pilot E.M. Baldwin argued with Withledge that it was useless to land the boat because she was carrying a full load already. Withledge replied that he would go ashore to be sure the Dutch captain did not get any of the freight that might be waiting there.

They landed, and the dapper captain went ashore where the girl handed him a bouquet of flowers. There was no freight.

Withledge went back to his boat smiling, apparently undisturbed by the serious blow to his fast schedule, and, when Baldwin asked him where the freight was, replied there was none.

"But," he added, "I made the girl promise to hail the Dutch captain ashore when he gets here this afternoon."

Mile 45—Foot of Howell's Island. Once this island was full of wild cattle—the bulls would make one climb trees. It also was the best mushroom island on the river.

Mile 46—Here the crew of the Eugenia Woods found three wolf cubs. But they grew up to be gray foxes.

Mile 47—Capt. Tom Craig sank the Barbara Hunt here. The boat later was raised. On the other side of the island lies the wreck of the Lilly, a sidewheeler lighthouse tender, that sank with Pilot Campbell Hunt at the wheel.

Mile 48—Where big yellow catfish lie in a big deep hole under the bluff.

Mile 49—More pretty girls. (The captain declines to make further comment.)

Mile 50—Dozier's Bend lies on the right. Many famous steamboat men came from this neck of the woods.

Mile 51—Happy Jack Hollow—named after a noted character whom few ever knew or saw—lies on the left.

Mile 52—Tavern Rock, where Lewis and Clark were held up by a heavy wind and rain for several days.

Mile 53—Where James Murdoch lost a two-story house and a large farm in the 1903 flood.

Mile 54—The Browns and Mrs. Johnson had a big lawsuit as to who owned Brown's Island. Mrs. Johnson won.

Mile 55—Mrs. Johnson's palatial home near St. Alban's.

Mile 56—Where a colony of blue heron, our common crane, had about 15 nests on a large cotton tree. The bank cut this tree into the river just as 60 cranes were ready to leave their nests. Calamity, sorrow and disaster.

APPENDIX ≈ MILE BY MILE

Mile 57—Where Louis Bickel and Bill Heckman got lost one hot summer night while going poaching and looking for the railroad reservoir near Matsons. Dipped two buckets of river shiners out in a wheat field and got back to the boat at midnight after walking around lost for two hours almost within sight of the pond.

Mile 58—A big cave in Augusta bluff here was a hangout for hoboes.

Mile 59—The crew of the steamer Kennedy once killed 40 coots, or mudhens, in one flock here. They did not stop to pick them up. I have been on the river during many a duck season since then but have never seen that many coots again.

Mile 60—Klondike Silica Sand Works. When this company moved in here some 40 years ago, they reportedly offered the owner $1 for every car of sand they took out. He said that was not enough and sold out for $680. The company has taken out more sand than that every year.

Mile 61—Sanders Landing and a big wine cellar below Augusta.

Mile 62—Augusta, a busy town in steamboat days, now almost two miles from the river. Here the boats picked up flour, wines and fruit to St. Louis. This town used to ship more by river in one month than it now does by railroad in a year.

Mile 63—Foot of Hinkles Bend.

Mile 64—Hinkles Bend, where some of the first concrete bank in the Missouri river was constructed.

Mile 65—Here Capt. Bill Heckman Jr. took his wife on a famous ride in a Model A Ford from the river to Labadie and back.

Mile 66—I first saw the laughing red face of Irish W.O. Wymore here. Now farming in Arkansas, he was one of the grandest characters I ever met on the river. An iconoclast, a socialist and hard as nails.

Mile 67—Ming's Landing.

Mile 68—Someone in the brick house on the hill always had a friendly wave for a steamboat.

Mile 69—Mouth of a creek. Here, too, is South Point, the point furthest south on the Missouri River. A large saw mill and box factory was here after the Civil War. The home of Capt. E.M. Baldwin was here. All boats salute the captain's widow, who is still living and is an authority on old-time steamboating.

Mile 70—Washington highway toll bridge.

Mile 71—Washington, home of many prominent boatmen. The first corncob pipes were manufactured here. Here lived Capt. Archie Bryan, Capt. Frank Hoelscher and son, Billie, of Yukon river fame, Capt. Bob Rohrig—all three of his sons went on the river—Agent Wellenkamp and his family of pretty daughters. Ferryboat May Bryan sank in front of this city 40 years ago. Her boiler was taken out of the river in 1937 by the dredge Mitchell Boyd. The Steamer Osage sank here in 1936.

Mile 72—Foot of St. Chute's Chute and of Hellbush Bend. Both are now shut off by dikes.

Mile 73—Watkins Island, home of a large flock of turkeys 25 years ago.

Mile 74—Miller's Island. One squatter killed another during an argument over the ownership of this island and buried him in a rack heap.

Mile 75—The steamer Dora was sunk by ice at the mouth of Charette creek 48 years ago. She was raised and taken to St. Louis for repairs.

Mile 76—Tieman's Point. Right below here, the government made what I consider one of its first costly mistakes. The river was turned away from a rock bluff shore re-vetted by nature for all time to come. Since then the river between Chitwoods Bluff and Washington has been put in three different places at the cost of millions. It is still in bad shape.

Mile 77—Here the crew of the Eugenia Wood established beyond all doubt its reputation as fishermen.

Mile 78—Bocklages' Landing, a big shipping point until 1890.

Mile 79—Chitwoods Bluff, one of the highest points on the lower Missouri. Mr. Chitwood is buried in solid rock on top of this bluff overlooking the river.

Mile 80—Foot of Emily Bend.

Mile 81—Dundee, home of one of the best trot-line fishermen on the river.

Mile 82—Here is the grave of the great Indian scout Coulter, who paddled from Fort Benton, Montana, to St. Louis—a distance of 2,300 miles, in 30 days.

Mile 83—Dundee Reach, where the water was 2-feet-deep—or less—during two years of construction.

APPENDIX ≈ MILE BY MILE

Mile 84—Mouth of Boeuf Creek.

Mile 85—Here Capt. Ben Winters sank the Jefferson City Sand Company's boat, H.J.W., while en route to Blaske's drydock at Alton, Ill.

Mile 86—I have passed a big farmhouse here over 500 times but have never seen a living being. It is the most unfriendly place on the river.

Mile 87—Park's Landing, home of old Bill Parks, champion fiddler in Missouri. Across the river, below the landing, the Mill Boy was sunk by ice in 1910.

Mile 88—New Haven, the best town on the river. It was patronized by steamboaters to the end. The steamer Commodore was built here 50 years ago. About the same time, the steamer Vienna sank coming out of Emily Bend with a full load of flour and wheat. The city's main street to the river is now cut off by dikes.

Why our government should shut off a town from the river when they are improving the stream for navigation and cheaper freight rates is more than I can understand. I think dikes are on the wrong side of the river anyhow.

Mile 89—The old rivermen were diplomats. Here at the foot of Pinkney Bend 60 years ago the Dutch captain, my father, landed the R.W. Dugan. He had 1,000 sacks of wheat to take on but had worked his darkies for some 36 hours and did not want to ask them to load the wheat before morning.

The stevedores were sitting on a pile of wheat in front of the warehouse when the captain called to the landing keeper:

"Say, Jim, when did you say that ghost comes around here?"

The keeper responded. "Midnight," and continued with a dissertation on the spectre's awe-inspiring habits. The captain allowed he would go to bed for the night.

He had hardly reached his room when one of the head darkies knocked on his door. If the captain didn't care, he said, they would load the boat in a hurry provided they could leave before midnight.

Mile 90—Here the W.H. Grapevine went down into Pinkney Bottom through tree tops, stumps and wire fences to rescue victims of the 1903 flood. We worked three days and nights. When night came, we would take the boat's yawl and pick the chickens off trees. We had been feeding our Negroes chickens for about two weeks when Rabbit, their spokesman, told us:

"Captain, I have been appointed by a committee to come up here and talk about eating all these chickens.

"Personally, I never thought that I could eat enough chicken, and I can stand it a little longer—but if you do not give the rest of the gang some bacon and pork chops, they're going to strike."

Steamboat Bill Conjures Up Old Memories of Jefferson City's Port

From the Jefferson City Sunday News and Tribune
April 13, 1941

By Capt. Bill Heckman as told to Leo Hirtl

Capt. William 'Steamboat Bill" Heckman resumes his memories of his 60 years on the Missouri River, a story for every mile between St. Louis and Kansas City.

Mile 91—The steamer George Woods lost most of her paddle wheel on a snag here while going up river towards Sioux City in 1934.

Mile 92—Here one of our most faithful darkies drowned while loading a cow on the steamer Kennedy in 1907. In 1909, Mate Ben Winters shot a roustabout off the Linda Givens in the leg. On that trip, we left St. Louis with 27 roustabouts. We returned with seven. Some deserted, some we ran away, and some just naturally quit. It was the meanest crew I ever saw.

Mile 93—Klausmeyer Landing, a big shipping point for hams, shoulder and side meat when the farmers were curing their own meat. In 1881, when the Knights of Labor staged their big strike against the railroad, my father went to Klausmeyer's Landing with the Dora and loaded her flat with hams, shoulder and side meat—200 pounds of eating going to the Mound City. While this strike was raging, the steamboats strutted their stuff for the last time on the Big Muddy.

Mile 94—Once a vicious bull killed a man here.

Mile 95—Wehmeyer's Landing, the best deer stand on the river. The sidewheeler Clara sank here in the early '70s. My father bought the wreck, took off the cabin and moved it to Bluffton, where he built a two-story house and started to raise a tribe of 14 children.

Mile 96—Thieves robbed a freight car here and threw a lot of silk on the bank. Some fell into the river and floated down to a small town where a resident salvaged it and bedecked his home with silk curtains.

Mile 97—Henry Zibelin had trouble with a half-grown calf here. While he was untying the creature from a sapling, the calf began running around the tree until Henry was bound tight. The crew of the Grapevine laughed themselves sick until the owner, a big, buxom woman, came down and unloosed a choice and inclusive vocabulary of "cuss" words. Henry was cut loose in a hurry.

Mile 98—Lost Creek, where what was then the last deer in Warren and Montgomery counties was killed.

Mile 99—Bates or Rush Island, where a fellow named Bates made a fortune selling cordwood to steamers.

Mile 100—Head of Bates Island. Fine bottom land, big crops and big floods.

Mile 101—Boyhood home of John and Bill Massie, noted river masters. Bill Massie held a pilot's license from Fort Benton, Montana, to New Orleans. He knew more noted men of his time than any other pilot on the river.

Mile 102—Gonsolis landing, home of the Gonsolis boys, almost as noted on the river as the Massies.

Mile 103—Hermann, Missouri, where some 20 riverboats have been constructed. The wreck of the John Heckman lies at the lower end of the town. She was the last packet boat on the river and was retired in 1929. In this city's cemetery lie Capts. Henry, August and Gustave Wohlt, Henry L. Heckman, Junior and Senior, William Heckman Sr., John Heckman and Henry German, all fine pilots in their day.

When the sidewheeler Washington burned here 50 years ago, two girls—weighing over 200 pounds—jumped overboard, but their hooped skirts caught enough air so that they floated like corks.

A slim woman jumped with them but was drowned.

The Hermann Ferry and Packet Company operated from this city for 50 years and never lost a boat, a record unequaled on any river, although the Missouri and the Gasconade are the most treacherous of them all.

I made my first big money on the river right here. When 8 years old, I ferried a man across, and he paid me a dollar. Once during flood stage, I swam across the river and back. I was 9 then.

Mile 104—When 10 years old, I and Jimmie Smith elected to swim two-thirds across the river and rest on a snag before coming back. But we missed the snag, and the current carried us until we landed far below the town, exhausted and naked as jay birds. Our clothes were a mile upriver.

Mile 105—The Chester, the last big passenger boat, grounded here in 1912.

Mile 106—A silica plant started operation in 1937.

Mile 107—McGirks, Grafs or Heckmans Landing, which was owned by my father. He had nine houses on this island and 600 acres in cultivation. In 1903 the flood covered the island and left him with one house and 40 acres of land. The house was lying on its side. By 1938 the river had restored the land it had taken.

Mile 108—The $300,000 dredge Cappa sank on the wreck of the old snagboat Missouri here. The same pilot was in charge of both boats when they went under.

Mile 109—Where the boys and girls crossed the river to go to a famous dancing place.

Mile 110—Mouth of the picturesque Gasconade River, the river of clear waters. Here a government boatyard has been operating since 1890. The steamer R.H. Durfee sank here. When I went to see the wreck with my father, tobacco, cattle, hogs and all sorts of rubbish were floating in the river.

The craft had been overloaded, and when it struck a snag, the "hog chains"—which run the length of the boat to preserve its sheer—broke and the craft snapped in two.

Mile 111—Keith's Rock, a large, round crag, 100 feet high. The towboat Lancaster sank on this rock. Capt. George Keith—after whom the crag is named—always said he wanted to live until he could run his boat between the shore and the rock. He proved he knew the ways of the river because he did it before he died.

Mile 112—A prominent farmer buried his savings along the shore here. The river washed it away, and he lost his mind grieving over the loss.

APPENDIX ≈ MILE BY MILE

Mile 113—Henry Schnell of Glasgow caught a channel cat weighing 187 pounds here. A man named Big Bill—who was one of the finest specimens of manhood I have ever seen—fell off the U.S. towboat Alert about 47 years ago. He swam to within 10 feet of the bank before his enormous strength failed, and he drowned within sight of the entire crew.

Mile 114—Capt. Ed Heckman killed Mrs. Tod Hampton's tame turkey here during the World War.

Mile 115—Bluffton's Chute, where the government rebuilt a dike 12 times in an effort to shut off the chute. This was started 48 years ago, but the contrary, headstrong Missouri still runs through this chute.

Mile 116—My father built a large frame house here at Holstenberg's landing 60 years ago. It still stands.

Mile 117—Melius's Point. Capt. Henry Zibelin proposed to Annie Melius up on a big, flat ledge of rock, was accepted and lived to celebrate his golden wedding. One mile from the river here was the home of the Day boys, desperadoes in their day, second only to the James.

Mile 118—A big catfish lay in the eddies of the Missouri here for 20 years, a menace to fishermen and smaller fish. He tore up much tackle, stole over 50 jugs and was seen to swallow a 20-pound fish. When the railroad blasted off the face of a bluff here, the fish disappeared.

Mile 119—Sixty-six years ago a 15-year-old boy named Henry Struttman caught a 315-pound fish here.

Mile 120—Portland, a great little town. A river mate was killed by a roustabout 44 years ago. The old boats used to take on as many as 400 hogsheads of tobacco at one time. The Fearless No. 2 loaded 1,000,000 feet of lumber at one time; thousands upon thousands of railroad ties were burned by the boats coming here. Bob Tooms, the raft pilot still lives here. He had lived long enough to call my father "Old Bill," and now he is calling me by the same name.

Mile 121—Mouth of Logan Creek.

Mile 122—Another Stickney bank head, far out from the shore, which it originally was intended to protect.

Mile 123—The government-named Dozier's Chute, which was called Berry's Chute long before the Millie Dozier sank here in 1879. Since the Dozier sank, the George Spangler sank on top of the wreck with a full load of railroad ties.

Mile 124—Chamois, or Fisher's Landing, which is now about one-fourth mile from the river. It once was over two miles from the stream. Mostly a railroad town with little boat history.

Mile 125—Where Henry Fleeman fell off the towboat Arethusa and drowned in the middle-'90s.

Mile 126—Head of Chamois Bend where the river once washed away bottom land almost as fast as you could walk away from the bank.

Mile 127—Mouth of the Auxvasse River, where the steamer Gasconade once took on 1,000 cords of wood for the penitentiary in Jefferson City. She also took about six boat and barge loads of lumber to the same place and about 100,000 railroad ties to Cedar City. This all was done after the spring rise, when boats supposedly were unable to go up the Auxvasse, which is really just a big creek.

Mile 128—Benson's Island on the right and Geising's Island on the left.

Mile 129—Mokane, used to be on the river bank and was known as St. Aubert's Landing. A river mate was killed here by a roustabout. The mates did not do all the killing on the river, and sometimes I think the roustabouts did not do enough.

Mile 130—Mouth of Middle River, once a good lumber and grain point.

Mile 131—Where St. Aubert's Chute was shut off by Woods Brothers Construction Company.

Mile 132—The steamer Chester ran aground here. The river is still crooked and shallow here.

Mile 133—Mouth of Loose or Bear Creek. Just below here, the A.M. Scott, with William Young as master, grounded with a barge loaded with cargo for Kansas City. The ice caught the barge before it was refloated, and the cargo was taken off and over the ice to Isbell Station. The empty barge stayed in the river and was sunk during the ice break up during the spring of 1913.

Mile 134—Isbell Station.

Mile 135—Hoard's Landing, a busy point in its day.

Mile 136—This is now the permanent mouth of the Osage River, the little Hudson of Missouri. The Osage is one of Missouri's most historic and picturesque rivers. From here to Jefferson City the river has been the scene of many colorful incidents.

Mile 138—We are now opposite Bonnot's Mill, home of the Thompsons, Bill, Hal and Arthur, who were among the best pilots on the river.

Mile 139—Dodd's Island, largest on the lower Missouri, named after a famous steamboat family. The father of this family moved here and operated boats before the Civil War. Here, too, is the foot of Cote Sans Dessein—hills without valleys—where, according to Capt. Joe Dearing, was built the first railroad in Missouri. It was a small line that ran to a coal mine near Fulton and brought coal to the river for the boats. Capt. Dearing said a giant of a man lived here. He could lift the engine and the cars back on the track if they left the right of way. We will leave Capt. Dearing's story here.

Mile 140—Head of Cote Hill Bluff.

Mile 141—Head of Dodd's Island and old mouth of Osage Chute, many wrecks here, but all before my time.

Mile 142—Barkesville Landing. Just below here, the old Missouri boats used to transfer their loads to lighter craft for traffic on the Osage River. Before the Civil War, this was one of the busiest spots on the river. I moved the entire landing by steamboat to Dry Creek despite a short-lived mutiny by my Negro roustabouts who objected to working on Sunday.

Mile 143—Rising Creek, where I saw about the last wild turkey along the Missouri. Here the historic Osage river packet Emma ended her days. This boat belongs to Governor McClurg.

Mile 144—The old Ewing home, later part of the penitentiary's holdings. They dumped some 3,000 tin cans over the bluff here, a ghastly sight.

Mile 145—Moreau River where Robert Vivion—one of the most efficient overseers on the river—lost a daughter by drowning.

Mile 146—The hapless Chester went aground here, too.

Mile 147—Bogg's creek, where the government used to lay up its fleet while it was operating the now abandoned Rising Creek Boatyard.

Mile 148—Big channel cats are caught here on trot lines made of cable.

Mile 149—Jefferson City, a river city of note during steamboating's peak. Here lived Mr. Lohman, warehouse keeper, steamboat agent and boat owners Capt. Perren, Bill and Fred Kay, and famous Capt. Alex

Stewart. Capt. Fred Heckman and his wife are buried in Riverview cemetery here. Cy Turner, famous as an engineer, lived here for a time, and Skinny Walker, old-time river mate, ended his days in darkness here after he went blind. The St. Louis and Hermann Packett Company had the last river warehouse here but abandoned it in 1910.

The capital city was the home of Jim Ramsey, part owner and clerk of the General Meade. Capt. Phil Chappel, whose history of the Missouri is among the most valuable books on the river, lived here. Capt. Ed Herndon began his river career on a skiff here.

Here the Wallau family operated the Jefferson City Sand and Gravel Company. No one was more popular on the river than Capt. Hank Wallau. The Struttman family, first to operate gas boats successfully, lived and boated out of this port. Capt. George Young, who often was my partner pilot, lived here. He once helped get the steamer Chester over the river, and anybody that could do that was all right.

Steamboat Bill Turns Memory River Craft From Jefferson City

By Capt. Bill Heckman as told to Leo Hirtl

Capt. William Heckman, having stopped at Jefferson City, continues his memory trip up the Missouri River.

Mile 152—Much sand for commercial use has been taken out of Turkey Creek here.

Mile 153—Grays Creek. The seemingly ever-grounded steamer does it again.

Mile 154—This stretch was very bad river in the old days. It still is very close and has never been fully improved.

Mile 155—Murry's Bend and the big penitentiary farm.

Mile 156—Cedar Creek, where an obliging agent helped the farmers ship and sell their wheat but neglected to return with the money.

Mile 157—Boone Point, where the pretty twin sisters lived before the railroad arrived.

APPENDIX ≈ MILE BY MILE

Mile 158—This stretch once had some of the worst obstructions in the Missouri before the government improved the river.

Mile 159—Haunted Rock House, a fine big home uninhabited for many years. I won't attempt to explain why—but the shade of somebody dragged chains around the place for many years.

Mile 160—Foot of Stanley Island and an ample demonstration that well-constructed river projects do some good. The chute formed by the island has been shut off by a dike and is now so dry that a farm has been established in it. It was once the main channel.

Mile 161—Where I shot five wild geese with two shots.

Mile 162—Here Jonnie Holloway, Bill Heckman and Red Wymore went hunting when the temperature was 15 below.

Fable With a Moral

Mile 163—A man built a very large steamboat hull on the bank in Stanley Chute here when I was a boy. The hull, made of native oak lumber, was made extra strong—he thought—and was constructed upside down.

When came time to put on the decks, he found out that he couldn't turn the hull over, and it rotted on the riverbank. The hull finally caved into the river. He should have named it "Shebrokeus."

Mile 164—Sugar Loaf or Ceasar's Rock, a peculiar river landmark.

Mile 165—Rock Creek, where Porter and Turner Coonce caught some large catfish.

Mile 166—A deck hand fell off the steamer A.M. Scott in Mudd Creek and drowned in 1915.

Mile 167—Marion. Pilots Turner Coonce and Tommie Taggart hail and sail from this port.

Mile 168—Eureka Bend, one of the places where thousands of acres of fine bottom land has been washed into the Missouri.

Mile 169—Wilton. It is said of this town that once a group of women set fire to the town's lone saloon. A brisk wind came up and set some of their homes afire. When the women asked the men to help fight the blaze, they answered:

"No. What use are our homes when we have no saloon?"

The steamer Columbia sank part of her load of wheat here at a country cemetery landing.

Mile 170—Sandy Hook, where the Pin Oak sank out of sight after having floated down river for several miles.

Mile 171—The steamer Julius F. Silber moved the entire Coonce family out of the lowlands during a flood here.

Bull and the River

Mile 172—The steamer W.H. Grapevine tried on three trips to take a big bull to St. Louis. Each time the animal jumped overboard. The fourth time we tied all four feet to the deck and put a ring in his nose. His majesty was delivered without further incident.

Here an old Negro roustabout butted Capt. Fred Heckman amidships and knocked him out for an hour. The darky drew his pay and left in a hurry. He got to Jefferson City before the captain recovered his senses.

Mile 173—Cook's Landing.

Mile 174—Historic Providence Bend. It was deep river before the government made it shallow.

Mile 175—Big Bon Femme Creek where the Chester went aground in 1913.

Mile 176—Easley Station sprang up here with the coming of the railroad.

Mile 177—Little Bon Femme Creek, Pecan Landing and foot of Plow Boy Bend where the Emily La Barge sank.

Mile 178—Perche Creek leads towards Columbia. The Buck Elk broke loose in the ice one winter and floated from Rocheport to a spot behind an island near here. The owners gave the craft up as lost until they received a letter from some people who had found the grounded boat. They said they had a steamboat and please, what could they do with it.

Mile 179—Providence, once a busy port, now almost deserted and two miles from the river.

Mile 180—Head of Providence Bend where Red Wymore, Jonnie Holloway and Bill Heckman took the steamer Eugenia Woods out of an ice gorge in 1932 and got her over into a chute to save her from being crushed.

Mile 181—Here a little girl hunting wild flowers fell to her death off the bluffs.

Mile 182—Lupus, once called Wolf's Point, a busy landing before the railroads. When river work was in full blast, most of the men from the town were on the river.

Mile 183—Mt. Vernon, a big shipping point in its day.

Mile 184—Petit Saline Creek, just halfway between St. Louis and Kansas City.

Mile 185—Big McBaine Bottom, fine bottom land. At Gile Landing, on the left, the W.H. Grapevine turned back on her weekly trips from St. Louis from 1900 to 1903. Doug Giles ran this landing during the last days of the packets.

Mile 186—Huntsdale Landing, home of Charles and Roy Clay, two of the best present-day pilots. A party of excursioners came here from Columbia on three occasions to catch the Chester. Each time this super-deluxe tunnel boat was either so far behind time or aground they went back home.

Mile 187—Terrapin Creek and foot of Rocheport Bluff, finest scenery between Kansas City and St. Louis.

Mile 188—Mill Rock, where the old water mill, now long silent, used to operate.

Mile 189—There is a big cave in the bluff here, where Big Cave Creek empties. Jessie James and his gang used to hang out here. One winter during the Civil War, Ed Anderson and his cohorts used this cave at times. They fired at passing steamboats for their entertainment.

Mile 190—Some 25 years ago, a big cyclone crossed the river here, taking everything in its path. It cut a swath 300-feet-wide, and standing to one side of this freak, one could hardly tell if the wind was blowing. The gale blew the sand right out of the river and over the railroad tracks. Section men said they could see the bottom of the river almost all the way across.

Frightened Fireman

Mile 191—Once the W.H. Grapevine was coming up along the Rocheport bluffs one dark night. Just as the boat pulled out from under the point of a bluff, the pilot turned on the big searchlight. The fireman on the train coming towards the spot thought the light was on another train and jumped for his life. The engineer was about to pull stakes, too, when he realized the mistake.

Mile 192—Where the tame pigeons went wild and raised their young high up in the Rocheport bluffs. People began to kill them, and now they are few, if any survive at all. Every bluff from Tavern Rock to the head of the Rocheport bluffs had from one to three pairs of wandering falcons or duck hawks until 1915.

≈ STEAMBOAT TREASURES ≈

Best Looking Girls on Missouri River Lived at Historic Rocheport

By Capt. Bill Heckman as told to Leo Hirtl

Capt. William Heckman, veteran Missouri River pilot, recalls the time everything went "boom" in Boonville as he continues his mile-by-mile description of Big Muddy.

Mile 193—Historic old Rocheport, where the best looking girls on the Missouri River lived.

Mile 194—Diana Bend and a big dry bar. The Chester always found plenty of trouble here.

Mile 195—Capt. Roy Miller and Bill Heckman wreaked havoc in a crow rookery one moonlight night in 1913.

Mile 196—The Floyd sank on one of the dikes above Diana Bend here.

Mile 197—Bell's Mill where the Commander sank on rocks in 1930.

Mile 198—Bonne Femme Creek, a hard piece of river to navigate in the old days.

Mile 199—The Chester pulled a new one here. She ran her sharp nose between two rocks and had a hard time getting away.

Kinney Mansion

Mile 200—On the Franklin side of the river is the $50,000 Kinney mansion built in 1869. The most historic place on the river, this house was built by Capt. Joe Kinney who went down swinging before the railroads.

Mile 201—Boonville, home of many boatmen, where the Bright Light sank on the bridge 55 years ago. The new bridge is safe for boats.

A little gas boat was leaving this port in 1901 towing a barge loaded with dynamite and blasting powder. The boat caught fire.

Everything went boom, and Boonville shook from stem to stern. When its captain saw the boat could not be saved, he left and was halfway home before the fireworks exploded.

Mile 202—The old Haas brewery. A fine, beautiful elm tree was cut

APPENDIX ≈ MILE BY MILE

down to make way for the railroad here. Nature has no chance with capitalism.

Mile 203—Candle coal of the finest quality was mined in the Fiddler coal banks on the Boonville side.

Mile 204—The river left the bluffs here without any help from Uncle Sam.

Mile 205—Howard's Rock. No one seems to know how the place got its name.

Mile 206—Mouth of the Lamine River.

Mile 207—Fine bottom land.

Mile 208—Slaughter House Chute, a familiar piece of river.

Mile 209—Robinson's Bend, where Jonnie McCoy was once a large merchant.

Mile 210—Salt Creek Bend, where the Chester went out of commission in 1912.

River Tricks

Mile 211—Kit Carson Chute, where the Julius Silber got a hole punched in her side while loading lumber in 1906. Instead of unloading her, they kept putting lumber aboard and patching up cracks. She left there fully loaded but low in the water.

Mile 212—Capt. Don Kuhn caught a lot of catfish here.

Mile 213—The farm of Capt. Zeits of Boonville.

Mile 214—Head of Salt Creek Bend.

Mile 215—Carl Mosely sold $11,000 worth of rock to the government out of a river quarry in a single season.

Mile 216—Arrow Rock bluffs where the Benton sank 50 years ago. She later was floated only to sink again, this time for good, on the Sioux City, Iowa, bridge. The original Sante Fe Trail crossed the river here.

Mile 217—A foot cutoff was made in 1915 at the foot of Saline City Bend.

Mile 218—Nigger Bend, bottom of the river here is full of fish and snags. So many snags, the fish can't be caught.

Mile 219—The head of Nigger Bend.

Mile 220—When Capt. Gerald Friemonth found the young crows in a nest here, he discovered that it is a poor bird, which fouls its own nest.

Mile 221—Where two cub pilots, Clarence Friemonth and Roy Miller, played ghost to entertain themselves and frighten passengers on the Chester.

Mile 222—When a native came aboard and sold 12 gray squirrels and one old fox squirrel, the crew asked him how he had killed so many. He replied, "With rocks. I had to throw twice at the old one."

Mile 223—The snagboat, Missouri, and the towboat, Monitor, got caught in an early freeze-up here.

River Graveyard

Mile 224—Many old steamboat wrecks are in this vicinity. The Chester lost a bunch of passengers here when she was held up by sandbars and low water.

Mile 225—Near the Fish Creek dikes, the Keith turned turtle some 20 years ago. Capt. Edgar Friemonth, his wife and small child lost their lives. Friemonth, Hank Wallau and Jonnie Heckman all lost their lives on the river.

Mile 226—Where the government first revetted Fish Creek Bend on the right side of the river, then shut the bend off with dikes, then diked off the left side. They finally got a good channel here.

Mile 227—Here the old boats used to turn in toward Saline City.

Mile 228—The same old boats used to turn down the left bank below Bluffport to run the left-hand shore past the mouth of Richland Creek.

Mile 229—Now a very fine piece of river.

Mile 230—The DeWitt and Shobe rock quarry.

Mile 231—Hurricane Creek, the C. and A. railroad bridge and the railroad bridge.

Mile 232—Glasgow, the home of Capt. S. Waters Fox, the greatest of all river engineers, who lost his life in the sinking of the Norman below Memphis, Tennessee. When going upstream, Glasgow is considered the halfway point between Kansas City and St. Louis. Downstream travel has Boonville as the middle point, although it is 32 miles downstream. The halfway points are judged by the time it takes to travel the upper and lower Missouri. The upper Missouri is swifter, closer and harder to navigate, and boats run slower up stream.

Engineers Outwit River

Mile 233—Here the river tried to make Glasgow an inland town and would have left the bridge hanging on an island if it had not been for the government's river improvements.

Mile 234—Away over yonder, up on Chariton River, stood Lewis Mill, a town before Glasgow was founded.

Mile 235—Rotten river here. Never did respond to treatment.

Mile 236—Horseshoe Lake, made by the 1903 flood.

Mile 237—Pecan Grove, where the Chester lost her wheel. The C. and A. has to climb here to get to Slater.

Mile 238—Foot of Wilhoit's Bend. There are three of the Stickney bank heads in the bend, one of them still visible.

Mile 239—Bear Creek. Above this creek lies Cambridge, once a busy river town. The fastest boats made this their turning point in their weekly trips from St. Louis. The Martha Jewett made weekly trips to this point, very fast time for a river boat.

Mile 240—Rock shore and swift river.

Mile 241—Little Missouri Bend. There is a lost Stickney bank head in the river here somewhere. Do not believe there is anyone on the river now that could find it.

Mile 242—A captain once won a hat full of money in a crap game here while the Arethasa was tied up in a fog in 1895.

Mile 250—A bootlegger here and an old hog weighing about 300 pounds fell in and drowned. A riverman talking to the darky about the disaster said that he must have suffered quite a loss.

"Nassaw," he replied, "we et the hawg, made whiskey outen de mash and sold it all to boys working for the Kansas City Bridge Company."

Steam Boat Bill Brings Memory Trip Up Mighty Missouri River to an End

By Capt. Bill Heckman as told to Leo Hirtl

Capt. William Heckman abandoned his mile-by-mile description of the Missouri river and completes his journey from St. Louis to Kansas City with a story typical of the Big Muddy's boisterous ways.

≈ STEAMBOAT TREASURES ≈

Most of the following story is laid near Big Wolff Island. The year was 1915. The country, beautiful, even for the Missouri, was once haunted by the James boys and their lesser brethren, the Youngers. In the early '80s, bushwackers boarded a steamer here and questioned the captain concerning certain monies missing from his safe. The questioning included hanging the old gentleman by the neck, which very seriously hindered his breathing and almost terminated his career.

When the Advance, pushing a 600-ton steel barge ahead of her arrived at Napoleon Bend, the Missouri had begun to cut through the bend, forming a new channel. The river aborning was wild, full of shallow spots, and so swift the water churned as if in rapids.

At midnight, Pilot Bill Heckman was relieved and went below to sleep. As day began to break, I heard the indicator ringing for full speed ahead and, looking out of my stateroom window, I saw a wall of water that appeared to be a waterfall.

I am not a young man and am unused to sudden action, but my frightened feet carried the rest of my carcass to the pilothouse while I almost unconsciously yelled for the engineer to back her up.

The younger pilot who had relieved me was trying to force the Advance through the new river, where I knew it was impossible for a boat to go.

The warning came too late. Coming up in the big eddy, the Advance was stepping along at a terrific rate, and both boat and the huge barge went into the whirlpools at the head of the rapids.

Out of control, the head of the barge hit the upper side of the bank and tore loose from the boat, its steel bulk crazily swinging in the river like a giant battering ram.

After several wild swings, it finally got past the boat without crashing into her side and started down the new river just in the making.

By careful maneuvering—all of the crew was on deck by this time—we managed to keep the Advance from overturning or following the barge down the rapids.

Three of the deckhands, Porter Coonce, Heinie Maushund and Silk Hat Harry were on the lost barge. When it hit a small "tow head"—a miniature island not yet washed away by the new river—Silk Hat Harry grabbed the end of a 2-inch hawser and jumped, thinking to tie one end to a big sycamore tree that was left on the tow head.

So swift was the river, however, that the barge broke loose and 1,200 feet of the hawser slid overboard before two hands left on the craft could make the end fast to the big bits. Harry was marooned.

Meanwhile, the Advance was maneuvered out into the main river, and Chief Engineer George E. Berry, now retired, turned on full steam in an effort to catch the barge when it left the rapids eight miles below.

When we came abreast Wellington, about 200 persons were on the banks, and they told us the barge had floated past. Just as we caught it entering a mean, snaggy chute where no boat had been in 40 years, our laboring engines stopped.

The ice plant's ammonia tank below decks had burst flooding the boat with noxious fumes.

All the crew came on deck, and boat and barge drifted idly down the Missouri while we tried to rid the craft of the ammonia. Finally we got her tied to some trees near Lexington.

The ice plant was given first aid and an airing, and then we looked the old boat over.

Our monkey rudders and one balance rudder had been knocked off when the Advance was backed up to let the runaway barge past. It took us three days to get back the miles we lost in a half-hour.

When we got back, the river was so shallow we just got through.

Silk Hat Harry had been forced to stay on his fast-vanishing island for a day and a night before some fishermen ventured out to rescue him.

Meanwhile, all the rabbits, snakes, raccoons and assorted animals that had been trapped on the island had crowded around him. The big sycamore had been washed away. Within a few hours the whole island was washed away.

Silk Hat swore he would never again be seen on the river. I guess he kept his oath, for we never saw him again.

Just above this spot is Napoleon, Missouri, where the river is very deep. The towboat Leavenworth sank out of sight here, not leaving so much as a riffle. This boat had a famous whistle. With 225 pounds of steam up on a still day, this whistle could be heard for some 30 miles, which I think is a record.

Like the whistle on the Joe Wheeler, the captain thought more of his whistle than he did of the boat.

≈ STEAMBOAT TREASURES ≈

I had sold the whistle to the captain of the Leavenworth for $25. Later I thought I was going to buy a passenger craft and thought I would have to use the big horn again and offered $60 to get it back. The Leavenworth's master refused. Shortly after, his boat sank, whistle and all.

Missouri River Moral—Sell anything you got when you can get a good price for same.

Farther up the river at Cement City, two of the cub pilots once moored the Chester to a very necessary little building at the rear of a shack.

When the Chester backed out the next morning, it pulled down the little building, the platform on which it stood and part of the house to which it was connected. These cub pilots were very reluctant to do any more steamboating in these parts thereafter.

When the Woods Brothers Construction company was working on the river here, there was a Beau Brummell among the gang. This fellow had a fine diamond ring, which he presented to some girl every time his gang started work. When their job was finished, he always managed to get the ring back so he could give it to a girl at the next stop.

This little idea worked to perfection until he hit Rudolph, Missouri, where the girl was put wise and kept the ring.

Three hundred and ninety one miles up river from St. Louis is the Kansas City wharf, and a mile farther is the mouth of the Kaw and the Missouri-Kansas border.

Kansas City was the home port of four tremendous packets, all of which came to unhappy ends. The Decotah sank in Providence Bend; the Wyoming hit the rocks below the mouth of the Moreau river near Jefferson City; the Montana hit the Wabash bridge with 680 tons of freight aboard; the David Powell fell prey to the railroads.

Several companies made half-hearted attempts to revive river boating. The largest is the Federal Barge Line, which is still operating.

Although in my opinion the Federal line has not been too successful, it has done much good in the way of securing river improvements. The line's big terminal is just below the mouth of the Kaw. Above it is the $3,000,000 grain elevator.

Kansas City is one of the largest cities on the Missouri, but it gave very few great rivermen to the Missouri. Strangely, all of the famous pilots, engineers and captains came from the smaller towns.

So ends my tale of the mighty Missouri, Big Muddy.

About the Author

Dorothy Heckmann Shrader was born December 3, 1913, in Hermann, Missouri, at the home of her maternal grandparents. She attended school in Hermann and spent her summers living and working with her parents aboard the Steamer John Heckmann.

Shrader received two degrees from the University of Missouri-Columbia—one in journalism in 1935 and one in education in 1947. Graduate

Dorothy Heckmann Shrader accepts an award from Mark Cedeck of the Mercantile Library for Steamboat Legacy, the first book of her Missouri River trilogy.

study in Iowa led to work in special education. She was principal of Wilson School for the Educably Retarded and founder of the Beloit Campus School for the Emotionally Disturbed in Ames. At the same time, she ran her own small publishing business, editing and publishing *The Bulletin Board: A Guide to Ames* for 25 years and serving as the city's public relationist. In retirement, she has devoted her time to researching Missouri River history.

Dr. William D. Shrader, her husband of 62 years, is an Iowa State University emeritus professor of agronomy. The Shraders have three children, John Shrader, who is in engineering management at Aerospace Boeing in Seattle; Dr. David L. Shrader, dean of the School of Music at North Texas University in Denton; and Maggie Shrader Ford, an administrator at the School of Music at Virginia Commonwealth University at Richmond. They have six grandchildren and two great-grandchildren.

Steamboat Legacy, Shrader's first book, has won numerous honors since its publication in 1993, including the Literary Award from the Missouri Library Association, the Walter Williams Award from the Missouri Writers Guild and the Donald B. Wright Award, a national prize for maritime journalism, from the Mercantile Library.